The Ties That Buy

Early American Studies

Series Editors: Daniel K. Richter, Kathleen M. Brown, David Waldstreicher

Exploring neglected aspects of our colonial, revolutionary, and early national history and culture, Early American Studies reinterprets familiar themes and events in fresh ways. Interdisciplinary in character, and with a special emphasis on the period from about 1600 to 1850, the series is published in partnership with the McNeil Center for Early American Studies.

A complete list of books in the series is available from the publisher.

The Ties That Buy

Women and Commerce in Revolutionary America

ELLEN HARTIGAN-O'CONNOR

PENN

University of Pennsylvania Press

Philadelphia

Published by
University of Pennsylvania Press
Philadelphia, Pennsylvania 19104-4112

Printed in the United States of America on acid-free paper
10 9 8 7 6 5 4 3 2 1

Library of Congress Cataloging-in-Publication Data
Hartigan-O'Connor, Ellen.
  The ties that buy : women and commerce in revolutionary America / Ellen Hartigan-O'Connor.
      p. cm. — (Early American studies)
  Includes bibliographical references and index.
  ISBN 978-0-8122-4144-0 (alk. paper)
1. Households—Economic aspects—United States—History—18th century.
2. Women—Economic conditions. 3. United States—Commerce—History—18th century.
I. Title.
  HC104.H37 2009
  381.082'0973—dc22   2008040925

Contents

Introduction

In her civil case against Benjamin Wickham, Jr., Abigail Stoneman presented an unusual form of evidence to the court: the nine of clubs. By the time of its court appearance, this playing card had traveled across the landscape of the late eighteenth-century economy. It had also transformed repeatedly in meaning and purpose. Created in an English print shop as part of a full deck, the card was loaded onto a ship for export to Newport, Rhode Island, where it came to rest alongside towcloth, limes, stone mugs, and linen on the shelves of Thomas Brenton's shop. Selected by Stoneman's slave and carried through the streets of the northern seaport, the nine of clubs, still in its deck, was finally unwrapped by Stoneman, a widow who had recently taken over her dead husband's tavern business, and deposited onto the table of her club. On its journey, the card had been repeatedly exchanged on credit by interconnected merchants, retailers, and patrons. As it was passed along, the nine of clubs shifted from profitable export to desirable import to token in a game of chance. Then, on March 20, 1769, Benjamin Wickham reached for the card from a pile of discards, split it open, and on the blank surface exposed, wrote a promise to pay Stoneman £13, plus interest, in one year.[1] When he failed to deliver, the playing-card promissory note concluded its journey in a court file, removed from circulation at the same time that thousands of other promissory notes entered local economies as investments, cash, and loans.

Plucked from its creased folder in the twenty-first century, Stoneman's playing card is transformed once again, from court evidence into historical evidence of a commercial urban economy during the revolutionary era, fueled by imported drinks, service work, a spirit of risk, bonds of credit, and regular business transactions between men and women. Stoneman's place in that economy, like that of most people, was a mixture of old and new. As a widow with young sons, Abigail Stoneman supported her family through traditional "women's work": feeding, cleaning, and serving alcohol. It is easy to look at her life and see continuities with past generations of free women. But her playing-card note embodied a new kind of mobile, transferable credit that few women of her grandmother's generation knew. The nine of clubs with the £13 promise underscored the urban tavern keeper's connections to an expansive, commercial society. Stoneman was in many ways an exceptional widow, particularly in her taste for litigation, but the connections of credit, commerce, and culture embodied in her promissory note were central to the lives of thousands of unexceptional women in the years surrounding the American Revolution.

This book is about those connections. It investigates everyday economic networks in revolutionary America with women at their center. Economic life for women has often been portrayed as a story of deviance from domestic norms—of runaway slaves, of prostitutes, of desperate widows. Certainly, many of these women found themselves at the mercy of an economic and legal system that favored male property-holding and sanctioned the ownership of human beings. But urban life was commercial in ways that touched every facet of city dwellers' lives, from the rooms they lived in to the buttons they bought to the way they understood personal relationships. Women were quintessential market participants in this context, with fluid occupational identities, a firm investment in cash and commercial goods for power and meaning, and cross-class social and economic ties.

Economic ties were essential for urban Americans because mediated access to the marketplace was the rule. Chains of credit bound customers, retailers, shopkeepers, and merchants. Families and associates circulated goods, found jobs for one another, settled estates, and loaned money. Since corporations, banks, and insurance companies were still in their early stages, the business ties of elites stretched to perform new financial functions, channeling the flow of goods and information around the Atlantic world in a burst of expanding trade. The success of these business partnerships rested on trust built on the kept promises between individuals. Business failure was therefore personal failure; a disrupted friendship was financial ruin. In other words, the late eighteenth-century port economy was an "embedded" one in which financial relationships were social and vice versa.[2]

Gender, race, and rank all shaped the kinds of connections a person could make, but being female, being black, or being poor did not preclude participation. Revolutionary-era networks demanded the involvement of intermediaries, and these go-betweens were often employees and subordinates. Wealthy southerners placed their rice in the hands of "commission merchants," who not only arranged for sale in Europe but also purchased appropriate tools, groceries, and dry goods with the proceeds. Scottish merchant houses installed "factors" in the Virginia countryside to sell imported fabrics to the local farmers and remit the profits. Every day in port cities, servants who wanted to buy tea or shoes

Slaves as intermediaries

shopped at stores that let them charge the goods against future wages. Slaves earned cash bonuses for carrying messages and money between plantation and city markets. In each case, intermediaries provided the labor, the information, or the money that made transactions possible.

Intermediaries have not always received much attention, perhaps in part because our ideas about market activity have been shaped by abstract concepts that were emerging in the late eighteenth century. Markets at the time were still specific places where goods were exchanged under legally controlled conditions. Formal marketplaces, housed in galleries built specifically for them, were even on the rise in late colonial America. But Revolution-era Americans were embracing a newer meaning of "the market," one familiar today. This market was more abstract, an imagined force that set prices and controlled the distribution of goods based on individual choices separated by hundreds of miles. Through this market, a group of new writers, such as Adam Smith, believed thousands of individuals acting in self-interest naturally produced rational results that served the larger community.[3] A fair government stayed out of the way to let the market operate freely rather than step in to impose restraints in the name of its own agenda.

Given the reality of commercial practice in Atlantic cities, self-interest could be hard to calculate, much less act upon. Information traveled slowly and was often unreliable, forcing economic actors to make decisions in the face of great uncertainty. Intermediaries, agents, and proxies helped fill the void and in the process created an interconnected world of exchange.[4] But the independent, self-interested man who had been invented for the new economy—motivated by what Smith called "the uniform, constant, and uninterrupted effort of every man to better his condition"—had a powerful grip on the minds of writers and lawmakers.[5] Free married and enslaved women, like enslaved men and children, were legal dependents chained to the identities of others and so fit uneasily into the new formulas.

The late eighteenth- and early nineteenth-century world of exchange was a paradoxical place for women. Women had long been an active presence in urban marketplaces, but at the end of the eighteenth century a new understanding of "domesticity" began to posit a world divided into "public" masculine and "private" feminine spheres.[6] According to this ideology, men controlled matters related to the world of business and politics, while women were responsible for the domestic world of childrearing and housework.

In this world of divided lives, the market, in its abstract sense, was part of the public world; whatever women continued to do in actual market stalls was portrayed in popular literature as a household matter explicitly disconnected from larger economic and political trends. Smith's ideas about political economy fit these new cultural codes of expected behavior: the public arena was a place for competition and contract, the private was for compassion and feeling. Numerous historians have dem- onstrated that the ideal was far from the reality—in fact, the home and the market were not mutually exclusive for most women, who crossed boundaries regularly. Farm women in rural Pennsylvania, for example, transformed their butter making from domestic art to market product to meet the demands of a changing economy, thereby helping to create a new system of commercial farming.[7] Poor and enslaved women labor- ing in New York "made their lives . . . on the streets as much as by their hearthsides," by bargaining, scavenging, and performing waged work abroad and piecework at home.[8] Still, there remains a persistent sense that free women as a group lost out in this ideological shift, tied to what historian Cynthia Kierner has summarized as "a narrowing of women's economic roles, a decline in their public economic activities, and a cor- responding expansion of their domestic labor."[9]

Women's commercial exchange networks were more than exceptions to the rule that men exclusively dominated the market. Their activities suggest that the idea of a boundary separating market from domestic worlds obscures more than it reveals. Free women combined their own labor, credits from neighbors at local shops, and cash to mobilize spend- ing power in the marketplace. Enslaved women made and received gifts, took clothing from mistresses, and sold it to support themselves. All kinds of women produced some goods in order to consume others, or struck financial deals to meet social and emotional obligations. With such actions, women were as responsible for the spread of commercial goods as the merchants who placed advertisements in urban gazettes. Women's prominence in these activities indicates that commercial ex- change itself existed at what Margot Finn calls "the fluid interface of the public and private spheres."[10] With this in mind, the relationship be- tween economic ideology and economic experience for women likewise needs rethinking.

Pioneering work on the flourishing of the eighteenth-century "con- sumer revolution" has shown how imported goods, newly within eco- nomic reach of a wide segment of the seaport population, provided fresh sources of pleasure, creativity, sociability, envy, competition, and disguise.[11] As shoppers and provisioners, urban women were ideally po- sitioned to reap the benefits of an expanded material life. The status competition, dressing up, and interior decorating that resulted from this wave of goods are typically credited to consumer "choice," and it was this opportunity to choose from a world of goods that seemed to hold out new possibilities for middling and elite women's influence in the market.

The possibilities that consumer culture afforded to nonelites are less obvious. We are just beginning to understand the dynamics of "involuntary consumption" by people who could not choose what they used.[12] Renters did not choose their own furnishings, slaves did not choose their uniforms, and yet both were participating in an imported consumer culture. Tracing the ways that people obtained goods, promissory notes, or money reveals a commercial culture that was far less liberating than Adam Smith would have envisioned. The fact that most consumers obtained goods on credit in this period, for example, meant that commercial exchanges resembled gift exchanges, in which obligation adhered to objects. Urban women had to shop where their connections permitted, and if they wanted to continue to charge items to third parties, they had to be sure to cultivate those ties. More people—like renters and slaves—could participate in the consumer revolution, but their participation was defined by dependence and obligation.[13] The consumer economy grew from these dependent connections as much as from independent self-interest, a fact that recasts the meaning of choice for all.

Throughout this book, I focus on everyday practices of economic life that would have made sense to Revolution-era women: finding living arrangements, working, obtaining credit, handling cash, and using material goods. Rather than examine more static forms of wealth, such as landed property or inheritance, I try to catch money and goods as they passed through the hands of women to see how ideas about exchange, value, and subjectivity shaped economic practices. Wealth based on property-holding was unevenly distributed in the urban population, with a broad base of the poor and propertyless, middling ranks with shifting proportions of urban wealth, and a narrow peak of the very rich, who held a disproportionately large percentage of the community's wealth.[14] Legal restrictions gave free white men control over most of these resources. Describing the economy in terms of a wealth pyramid, therefore, relegates most women to a secondary relationship to money. The story of women and money becomes a story of their relationships to free white men rather than a story of how they experienced and understood economic life. By locating women in the shops, streets, yards, alleys, and parlors rather than in the probate records drawn up after death, I restore them as active members of urban economic life. The result is necessarily a partial picture—women pop up for a few transactions, then disappear—but it captures the dailiness and dynamism of economic life otherwise lost to us under the veil of law and ideology.

In an age of commercial and political revolution, the ideological stakes of women's everyday transactions were high. From the imperial crises of the 1760s through the experimental struggles of the early republic period, the politics of the marketplace attained national significance, with consumer choice holding out the hope of independence with one hand and threatening the impotence of debt dependency with the other. The playing cards in Abigail Stoneman's tavern were among the items slated for taxation under the despised Stamp Act of 1765. Stoneman's fellow Newporters joined the unprecedented demonstrations of outrage that greeted the Stamp Act and led to the first nonimportation agreements. They took to the streets over "internal" taxes that threatened their rights as Englishmen to govern local affairs and signed petitions vowing to give up intoxicating and enchanting consumer goods in order to preserve the purity and incorruptibility of their communities. From Charleston, South Carolina, to Newport, Rhode Island, and beyond, neighbors exhorted one another to make more and buy less.[15]

Patriots endowed the daily economic lives of men and women with political import, and historians have followed their lead. Buying, lending, and borrowing at the local and international levels are recognized historical forces that shaped American politics and character. But while we have learned much about the meaning of independence and republican virtue by linking economic life to these revolutionary themes, historical work has tended to reinforce the centrality of independence to economic motivation rather than question the scope of its influence. Political and economic independence were unrealistic aspirations for most enslaved and free women, as well as for many men. More important for many were the financial and social uses of material culture, or the power of credit as a familial strategy. This does not mean that women were more "traditional" or that they were isolated from the possibilities of commerce, but that politics was only one register in which economic life took shape.[16]

As a political event, the Revolution brought few lasting transformations in women's lives. Free women did not win the right to vote; married women still labored under coverture, a legal principle that denied them autonomy and identity; enslaved women continued to suffer under slavery. Over the longer span of the revolutionary era (from the 1750s to about 1820), however, many women across the social spectrum encountered expanding opportunities for economic ties. Urban growth, international trade, and population mobility provided women and men with new prospects for work, new connections to a wider world, and greater exposure to commercial life. Although the economic and political upheavals severed some business links, they forged others. Changes in business cycles had different effects on different segments of the working community. The varied story of change that emerges resists a single narrative of decline or uplift.

Sometimes, women's economic transactions crystallized moments of status reversal. "The market house, like the grave," eighteenth-century

poet Philip Freneau gloomily reflected, "is a place of perfect equality."[17]
His overstatement spoke to the social anxieties produced by economic
change in the years surrounding the Revolution. The wages enslaved
women earned by "hiring out" their time, for example, presented a challenge to their status as objects to be traded by the market, since financial
remuneration acknowledged the value of their work. While these wages
still belonged to their masters and mistresses, depending on the arrangement, slaves might keep some cash of their own. It was an exploitative
system, but these women had some measure of self-direction in negotiating the terms of their paid work. This kind of work also created different
social relationships between worker and employer than those between
slave and mistress.

Other economic exchanges reinforced hierarchy and dependence.
Poor women, who could not obtain credit in local stores on their own
merit, had few choices when they wanted to purchase a pound of sugar.
They could scrape together enough cash through scrimping and service
work to pay the merchant on the spot, or they could arrange for a neighbor with an account at the store to extend them a loan. In either case,
their subordinate status in the community was reinforced in the arrangements they made locally and was inscribed on the very coin they used to
make their purchases.

Goods themselves transformed in meaning according to the particulars of each exchange. An enslaved woman, a poor white woman, and a
wealthy woman might all agree on the aesthetic and economic value of a
fan. Each was capable of selecting it from among a group of similar fans,
justifying her choice with shared criteria, and bargaining with the shopkeeper for a good price. All might use the fan as a model for constructing
similar ones for sale or trade. But what for the wealthy woman could be
one of many articles designed to present a genteel social persona might
represent for a poor woman a single emblem of cosmopolitan culture.
For both the poor and the enslaved woman, the fan might be more valuable for its potential resale value if she needed cash. A middling neighbor might have envied the wealthy woman's fan or disapproved of the
poor woman's, but she could do little about either. She could, however,
walk up to the enslaved woman, seize her fan, and accuse her of theft.
Power was a part of every transaction and shaped women's access to and
appropriation of goods, money, and knowledge of both.

To allow for some measure of depth and detail, *The Ties That Buy* focuses
on women's economic networks in two port cities: Newport, Rhode Island, and Charleston, South Carolina. In 1750, Charleston and Newport
were roughly the same size, and by the Revolution were the fourth and
fifth most populous cities in British North America. They were home

to wealthy merchants who conducted international trade; skilled artisans and shopkeepers who made and sold an increasing variety of goods;
and white and black laborers who worked the docks, cleaned the homes,
cooked the food, and provided muscle power and expertise that made
the commercial economy possible. In these features they resembled all Atlantic port cities, focused on trade more than industry and services more
than production. Both Newport and Charleston were also central hubs of
the African slave trade that moved people, money, and goods around the
Atlantic world.[18] The labor patterns and living arrangements in these two
cities highlight another truth of all the North American ports—that slavery was pervasive in the transactions and economic decisions of urban life
and commerce.[19] The trade of port cities supplied plantations around the
Atlantic and in the North American interior; the ships clearing their docks
held enslaved bodies and the money won from selling them.

Although Newport and Charleston were secondary in terms of size
to the centers of Boston, New York, and Philadelphia, they had a pivotal role in supplying these larger ports with labor and money through
coastal exchanges and are therefore of primary importance in investigating how economic information flowed within and between Revolution-
era ports. Residents, too, viewed port cities as a single interconnected
marketplace. Philadelphian Mary Morton visited shops filled with beautiful imported lawn, poplin, camblet, and other fabrics that were the
envy of her friends in Newport, but she did not like the candles, wool
yarn, or potential servants. While she shopped for friends' fabric in one
port, they vetted maids for her in another. Her mother wrote from Newport of these negotiations: "I have been some time treating with a Negro
woman and in order to Judge the better of her hired her in the house a
week, but she has not had the Small Pox and those with whome she had
lived and wanted her again frighten'd her from going I offerd her a dollar and a quarter pr week. . . . I have also thought of [a] white woman.
Hannah Shearman of Portsmouth her mother is a first cousin of Becky
Biddles a very capable cleanly woman. . . . when I know thy mind I will
see her."[20] The themes of mutual dependence, intermediation, and information exchange were so central to urban experience that they reso-
nate at multiple levels in this book, illuminating both the transactions
between neighbors and the relationship of individual ports to the larger
Atlantic system.

Drawn together by ties of commerce, business, and friendship,
Newport and Charleston exemplify the urban consumer culture of
the late eighteenth and early nineteenth centuries. At the same time,
geographic difference and the vagaries of war produced two different
expressions of that culture. Newport was established in the late 1630s
on southwestern Aquidneck Island by religious and social rebels from

Massachusetts who fled the older colony in search of religious freedom and economic opportunity. By 1750, the city was a major center of international trade. Merchants imported goods from England and molasses from the Caribbean; bought, sold, and transported slaves around the Atlantic; and exported locally produced rum and whale oil candles. The city also had a reputation as home to privateers who preyed upon French ships during the numerous imperial wars and carried the spoils home. Charleston, originally a walled, fortified town, was constructed by settlers and enslaved workers from England and the English Caribbean in the late 1670s on a strip of land between the Ashley and Cooper rivers. The city began as an export center for the hide trade with local Native American tribes, but in the eighteenth century devoted the bulk of its business to exporting rice and indigo and importing and transporting slaves. This slave-driven trade created some of the largest fortunes in colonial North America and tied the southern capital tightly to Great Britain.

Trading connections linked the two communities in prosperous times. Newporters William Vernon and Caleb Godfrey sold African slaves to prominent Charlestonians Henry Laurens and Gabriel Manigault as well as to many smaller slaveowners who attended the auctions in Charleston. In return, Newport merchants bought South Carolina rice to provision slave ships.[21] Coastal trade generated frequent voyages between the two cities and a regular stream of business correspondence peppered with comparisons between the two cities. In 1764, Newport's Moses Lopez traveled to Charleston with a shipload of New England cargo that his brother Aaron had sent to the southern capital. As he crossed the city looking for the most profitable sales for his merchandise, he was struck by the wealth and the potential for quick profits in Charleston. To succeed in Newport was a sign of "superior intelligence and keen insight"; in Charleston the "goodness of the earth" so guaranteed success that no mortal could claim credit for it.[22]

Though the "earth" in Charleston may have been good, the "air" was not. Newporters with Charleston connections constantly fretted about the health dangers posed by the southern climate; to relocate children to such a city seemed "like taking the dear little lambs from a peaceful enclosure, where they are guarded, & instructed with tender & judicious care, & exposing them to the ravages of the destroyer."[23] Given the opportunity, however, few could resist. Kin who had established businesses in Charleston provided access to superior natural and manufactured products. Frightening though the climate might be, sweltering Charleston offered valuable connections to those urban families seeking information about the relative prices and availability of imported goods and local produce in ports along the eastern seaboard.

While Newporters ventured south for business, Charlestonians sailed north for pleasure. Wealthy families like the Manigaults, Middletons, and Izards sought in Newport a healthy and relaxing retreat from their steamy Charleston homes. Whole families together with their servants arrived in the late spring, planning to stay until well into the fall. A welcome haven from the malaria and yellow fever of the South Carolina low country, Newport earned the name "Carolina hospital" for lodging and nursing the well-to-do of the South. Travel to Newport offered financial as well as climate relief. In 1787, Catherine Read advised her sister to vacation in Rhode Island rather than in New York, both for its healthy climate and because "it is also a very cheap place which is another very material advantage[.] I dare say you could board there cheaper than in Long Island & Carriage hire is very cheap there."[24]

Together, transplanted Carolina "families of fortune" and native New-porters created what the governor of Granada, Robert Melville, called "the refined and polished Society of Newport."[25] The resulting urbane culture partook of assemblies and concerts, created demand for French teachers and dancing masters, and required the labor of a widening service sector. Although small by British standards, American port cities were eager to adopt the practices (and, eventually, architecture) that had transformed city life in western Europe's shopping galleries, theaters, and parks.[26] Each year, Newport newspapers announced ship listings of arriving Charlestonians in what amounted to an early social column. In fact, the presence of so many familiar faces became an additional draw for elites, who resumed the traditional vacationing patterns after the Revolution. In 1801, John Ball wrote from Charleston to his son, who was attending Harvard, recommending that he might spend "his summer vacation pleasantly at Newport as there will be so many Carolina family's there."[27] Newport's summer season offered an appealing mix of the familiar and the novel. After they returned home, Charlestonians who had developed a taste for local specialties requested that their traveling kin seek out items like salted fish and country-made cheese.[28]

These ties between the two cities promoted a shared cosmopolitan culture that was not confined to the elites educated within the walls of the dancing schools. Scholars who study networks note that although strong ties, like those of kinship, are crucial to the trust-dependent activities of raising money and risky business ventures, weaker ties of acquaintance and employment can act as important bridges for transferring knowledge.[29] Applied to the economic life of North American port cities, this insight yields a dynamic story of women's central place in commerce. Knowledge about goods, about credit-worthiness, about value, was produced through circulation and verification among visiting elites, resident service workers, and their contacts. Commercial language, as well, filtered through the community long before most owned bank accounts or worked in a factory. Connection and circulation created this culture; they are also the lenses through which to understand it.

Exchanges of goods and labor drew distant communities together. On wharves and in city marketplaces, women and men met in public to form economic links that crossed wider distances than those between neighbors. Through connections of family and friends, women sent goods to distant communities, creating a shared material life stocked by urban shops and markets. In the letters that accompanied these goods, well-to-do women articulated a shared appreciation of style and value that became the language of consumption in the late eighteenth and early nineteenth centuries. Forged in the urban culture of commerce, this language and these goods were exported to the countryside. As populations after the Revolution became more mobile, these cultural ties helped spread cosmopolitan culture deeper into the American interior.

Economic life is typically seen as dividing people, and for good reasons. Money, or the lack of money, dictated sharp contrasts in the ways city residents spent their days. I have found it important to stress, however, the connections between participants in urban culture. While differing access to cash, credit, and goods exacerbated distinctions of rank in Newport and Charleston, commerce created shared experiences and a mutually intelligible language that bridged geographical, racial, and social distance as well. There were stark power differences between an enslaved woman and her owner, but they shared a knowledge about money and price and needed to agree, at some level, on what made chintz good quality. Likewise, a poor market peddler and her customers often had material lives that dramatically diverged, but they came together in a public place to bargain over the value of goods and the appropriate form of payment.

Instead of isolation and unbridgeable status differences, the urban setting fostered shared lives. Economic collaboration began in the fluid membership of urban homes, where women struck deals with family members or strangers-turned-housemates. Work, credit, and money forged connections within the city and allowed women to shop for imported goods and incorporate new forms of material culture into their lives. Their ties formed an expanding web of Atlantic connections and attained a larger importance that was never visible in the terms of any single rental agreement or purchase of a pound of flour and yet underlay both.

The chapters that follow reconstruct this net of interconnected economic life. White women and women of color, married and single, enslaved and free of all sorts appear together, just as they did on the city streets, illuminating the contours of gender and power in the marketplace.

Each chapter discusses a particular aspect of commercial culture as lived by women in Newport and Charleston across the late eighteenth and early nineteenth centuries, pulling out important distinctions of time, space, or rank as they emerged. The "ties" of my title are constructed along the way. Women started with what they had—strong backs, sewing abilities, extra space on the floor—to establish commercial connections. They used these connections to tap into chains of credit and to transform one form of money into another. Shopping and consumerism in the larger sense gave purpose and meaning to their transactions. All of these processes came together in the full texture of women's lives. Commercial connections pervaded city economies and societies in these years. Women were not exempt from these aspects of urban life; they were central to them.

Chapter 1
Urban Housefuls

Census-takers, like historians, understood early American society in terms of households. The smallest building block of society was also the organizing principle of the population count. As they made their tallies, census-takers grouped residents together under a single name, called "head of family," defined as the "master, mistress, steward, overseer or other principal person" in each household.[1] The identity of that "principal person" might differ, but his powers, under law and by cultural agreement, were broad. The household, which included kin, servants, and slaves, was supposed to govern individual behavior, channel productive and reproductive energies, and serve as the foundation of the social and political order. It sustained itself through the collective contributions of its members, joined together in what scholars have called a "family economy."[2] Economic cooperation mirrored spatial cohabitation.

What worked on a farm foundered on the demographic and social reality of the city, where households were smaller and more varied, and increasingly, home and workplace were not the same. These realities meant that the economic powers of the urban household head were restricted in practice, if not in law, because the household itself was porous and variable. In fact, some argue that it is better to think of urban households as "joint ventures" rather than centrally directed enterprises.[3] Economic communication became more complex and economic cooperation more tenuous.

If census-takers grouped individuals by kin ties and ownership, people in early port cities more often grouped themselves according to economic and social needs. When the census-taker for 1790 recorded Charleston shopkeeper Mary Kemmel, he described her as the head of a small household that included herself and two slaves. On another page, he noted Thomas Abernethie's more substantial and conventional household as two adult white men, a boy, a white woman, and six slaves. He said nothing of the fact that Kemmel's household and Abernethie's household in fact shared the same location, 42 Queen Street, where they crowded together along with baker John Smith and his free black servant.[4] It was a common arrangement among the highly mobile residents of early port cities, and one that disrupted typical eighteenth-century conceptions of household authority and order. Even the idea of a family venture fails to capture this basic unit of urban life.

What did the Kemmels, Abernethies, and Smiths know that the census-taker ignored? Family historians sometimes use the term "houseful" to describe coresidence of households that might or might not be related by family ties.[5] Such collectivities have existed in a range of settings, from rural Pennsylvania farms to densely urban London. Applied to the living and working conditions of Atlantic port residents, the term "houseful" shifts from useful descriptive to powerful analytical tool for understanding urban women's lives. The houseful at 42 Queen Street, for example, challenges the notion of an urban "family economy" and raises questions about female economic activity in particular. Many homes contained multiple businesses; many residents rented rooms in one building and worked someplace else. Schoolmistresses, shopkeepers, and boardinghouse keepers shared living space with unrelated merchants and craftsmen. Mixed-race groups of free and enslaved people defied easy categorization into "families" as well. A significant number of black and white residents lived in households headed by women. All of these combinations had to find new models of economic self-support, and the age and gender hierarchies of the rural household loosened to accommodate them. The new entities were not lonely, failed households but rather distinct social and economic forms that pervaded urban life. Even Thomas Abernethie's conventional, male-headed "household" was subsumed within a houseful.

The houseful was the smallest knot in a web of economic ties that reached into the city, up and down the coast, and out to the larger Atlantic world. It organized space and constituted relationships marked by contention rather than obedience. It was forged from the most personal, local circumstances and yet also functioned as a pivotal actor in global commerce. Housefuls were not the only arrangements that combined economic and social functions, of course. Neighborhoods organized social networks that paid economic dividends. Extended kin bonds supplied business partners and sympathetic words. But the urban houseful provided women—who were more likely to raise children, launch small businesses, trade, and work close to home—an economic link to life in the city and beyond.

Most studies of urban economic life have focused on established spaces such as the exchange building, merchant's warehouse, and coffeehouse and have explored the relationships forged in those institutions. The economic connections between merchants and planters, importers and craftsmen, traders and investors depended on these public locations that choreographed the social interactions of free white men within. Scholars of "informal" slave economies, in turn, have pointed to the rivers and back roads of the early South and mapped a complex, multiracial world of exchange onto these informal routes. In each case, networks of exchange had overlapping spatial, metaphoric, and economic dimensions. For the women of Charleston and Newport, the houseful, and the economic relationships forged within it, is the place to start.   *add the female 'houseful' to the array of literature that focuses on merchant spaces, etc. in port cities*

The Geography and Demography of City Life

The path of a girl walking through Newport, Rhode Island, in 1750 was directed by the sea (Figure 1). Newport's streets and buildings stretched out along the southwestern part of Aquidneck Island around a series of wharves that filled the coastline. She could walk from "the point," a growing area around the cove at the north end of town, down one of two parallel streets, Thames Street along the docks or Spring Street to the east, for about a mile before reaching the city's southern edge. The residences, warehouses, and public buildings she passed were mainly frame structures made of wood, and houses sat beside shops, storehouses, stables, and distilleries. The city was home to several churches, a Quaker meeting house, the brick Colony House, and a new library. Some of the main streets, such as Thames and Queen streets, were even paved so that carts, carriages, and horses could proceed through the city without becoming trapped in mud.[6]

Had the same girl time, money, and connections to take the ten days' coastal journey to Charleston, South Carolina, she would have found a city of similar size and prospect (Figure 2). Oriented around a series of wharves on the Cooper River where it spilled into the Atlantic Ocean, Charleston had spread to fill the tip of the peninsula formed by the Ashley and Cooper rivers. Traversing the city from East Bay Street along the docks across to the work house on the other shore or from the tip of the peninsula back to Boundary Street, the girl's path would have followed the grid that organized Charleston's streets. Commerce was oriented on the east-west axis of this grid, with merchants and artisans choosing to make more intensive use of the space rather than spread very far up the "neck" of the peninsula as the city developed. Although many of the houses, particularly the smaller and poorer dwellings, were framed in wood, buildings of brick and stone were also under construction, encouraged by regulations instituted in the wake of a devastating fire in 1740. Houses popped up in a wide variety of styles, frequently incorporating commercial and domestic space in the same building.[7]

The pedestrian's eye would focus on the external spaces of city life; in these, the commercial focus of eighteenth-century ports was manifest.

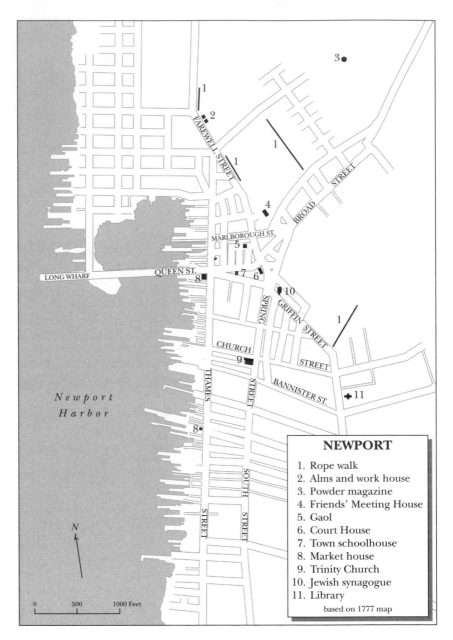

Figure 1. Newport, Rhode Island.

NEWPORT

1. Rope walk
2. Alms and work house
3. Powder magazine
4. Friends' Meeting House
5. Gaol
6. Court House
7. Town schoolhouse
8. Market house
9. Trinity Church
10. Jewish synagogue
11. Library

based on 1777 map

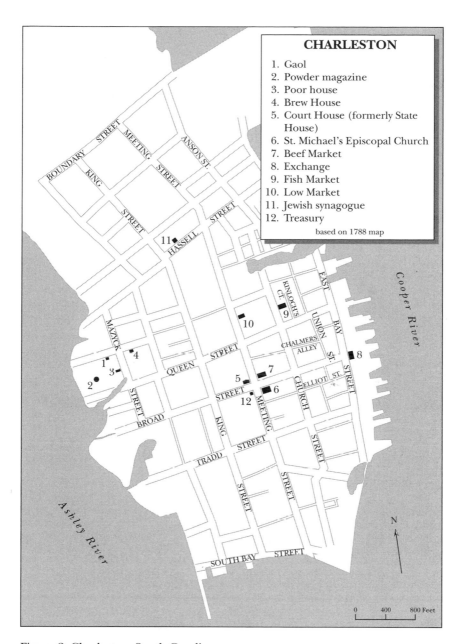

Figure 2. Charleston, South Carolina.

She would see marketplaces with blacks and whites haggling over prices; she could watch cargo unloaded on the wharves; she could observe men and women weighed down with barrels, bushels, and packages disappear into houses and alleyways. Spatially, both cities were oriented around the docks that connected them to an Atlantic world of trade, but whereas Charleston residents expanded their city in orderly city blocks away from the water, Newporters followed the curve of the coast, creating new wharves as they progressed. These divergent geographies were shaped in part by the land, in part by divergences in each city's economy. While Charleston had a close connection, via river travel, to a rice- and indigo-producing hinterland, Newport's dominant rum industry turned the sugar brought up the Atlantic coast from the Caribbean into a valuable liquid export. Thus local geography spoke to each city's place in Atlantic trade. Charleston's shipping was to and from Great Britain: prior to the Revolution, 50 percent of export tonnage was bound for Britain and 53 percent had come from the same. [8] For Newport, coastal and African trade were more important than direct voyages to Europe; in the decade prior to the Revolution, as much as 70 percent of the North American African trade was cleared on Newport ships.[9]

The space the pedestrian entered when she opened her own door served equally commercial purposes, since inside she might encounter a sailor renting a room or a shopkeeper selling goods in a corner. The houseful to which she belonged, like all such combinations, witnessed economic negotiation right at the hearthside, from the agreements that brought transient city dwellers together to the hard-nosed calculations that forced them to move on. Its dynamics were directed by the setting and the players just as those in the counting-house were.

An urban houseful was usually made up of several small households, typically one person smaller than nearby rural ones. In 1790, the year of the first federal census, Charleston had an average of 4.5 free people per household, or 8.5 people when slaves were included. Mean household size in Newport in the same year was 5.4.[10] Contained within these averages were a striking number of extremely small "households" of one or two people that were possible only in an urban setting, where single individuals could ply a trade, work as wage laborers, or piece together several kinds of paid work and charity in the absence of a safety net of mutually supporting kin. The fact that they could live apart did not mean that they lived well, since urban poverty was entrenched by the late eighteenth century, but they did live different kinds of lives than their rural counterparts.

City women were far more likely to head their own households than rural women, who lived under male authority in greater proportions. In Newport, the phenomenon of female heads of household was linked to the fact that women outnumbered men overall. As was true in other

New England seaport cities, particularly Boston, male deaths in mid-eighteenth-century wars, the absences and losses of men who worked as sailors, and the opportunities urban society offered to unmarried women all led to a preponderance of women in Newport by the late colonial period that continued past the Revolution.[11] Charleston suffered its fair measure of demographic disasters, but none of the epidemics, fires, or wars resulted in a glut of women. In fact, there was a glut of men in the southern city for the entire revolutionary period. The prevalence of female-headed households, however, was a marked characteristic of both ports, reaching 21 percent of heads of families in Newport and 17 percent in Charleston in 1790, proportions mirrored in other eighteenth-century cities.[12] A substantial number of city folk lived under the legal authority of a woman, especially if they were part of the free black community in Charleston, where 58 percent of household heads were women.[13]

Poverty and the prevalence of slavery shaped female householding in port cities, as a sample of female heads of household from 1790 reveals. In Newport, female-headed households were even smaller, by about one person, than the average small urban household. Their circumstances appear pinched and their resources limited. In Charleston, however, female-headed households were similar in size to the overall average.[14] Widespread slaveholding by free women made for much of the difference: fewer than 10 percent of Newport households included slaves, compared with 70 percent of the Charleston households.[15] Whether she was black or white, a woman in Charleston had more workers at her disposal to send out to earn income, making it possible for her to live independently. To put these trends in specific context, compare a typical Newport female-headed household like that of Nancy Forster, which was composed of three white women and one white boy, with a typical female-headed household in Charleston, like that of Elizabeth Mitchell, who presided over two white boys, two other women or girls, and three slaves. To be a free household head in Newport often meant a life of poverty and scarce resources for a woman; a Charlestonian need not expect the same.

Slave-owning was widespread in both cities prior to the Revolution, due to the ventures of Newport and Charleston merchants.[16] Imported human beings regularly stood up to be sold on city wharves, and while free customers from the surrounding countryside clustered around for the chance to make a bid, hometown masters and mistresses also purchased people to work in their homes and workshops. As a result, Newport and Charleston, like most American ports, had multiracial populations that included free and enslaved people of color—about half the population in the southern city, and a smaller proportion of the northern port, declining from 18 percent in 1755 to just under 10 percent of the population by the turn of the nineteenth century.[17]

The fact that blacks were 50 percent of the Charleston population meant that they were actually a less-dominant presence than in many of the plantation-based parishes surrounding the city, where slaves could amount to 90 percent of the population.[18] In Rhode Island, too, Newport was flanked to the south and west by the counties of the Narragansett planters, who employed enslaved field and dairy workers. In these New England plantation regions, enslaved people made up a third of the population—far more than in the urban centers.[19] Enslaved people in the countryside were part of a large agricultural labor force, living and working together. In the cities, enslaved people were dispersed to help staff trade and service industries. They lived, worked, and socialized in a multiracial world.

The presence of enslaved workers did not "cause" female householding, of course. Free urban women actually had fewer slaves than their rural counterparts, and yet they were more likely to head up their own families. It was the intersection of slave labor, a market for service work, and the practice of "hiring out" enslaved people that sustained female-headed households of many stripes. In cities, masters and mistresses regularly rented out the surplus time of their slaves to others in need of extra workers. As long as a basic wage was paid to the owner, some slaves were even allowed to negotiate for and keep additional payments. This waged, market solution to the labor problems that faced early cities had particular significance for free women, since it created a pool of mobile workers for short-term contracts. In Charleston, women who lived off the income generated by hired-out slaves even came to constitute a separate class of "rentiers."[20]

A male household head's death created a crisis that often pushed free widows and daughters to rent out the labor of their slaves in order to bring in income. One Charleston family seeking employment for their female slave, an accomplished cook, washer, ironer, and general house worker, explained, "The Master of the Family's dying, where she lived six Years, is the Reason of her being to be hired out."[21] Widows and other free single women not only provided but also rented labor for their smaller households. Newport widow Elizabeth Almy hired her female slave's labor to widow Mary Searing for seventy-five days in 1765, forty-four days in 1766, and ten days in 1767, all at the rate of thirty-five shillings (old tenor) per day. Each day that the woman worked earned Almy the credit to purchase two and a half quarts of milk, small amounts of tea, or even a cash payment from Searing that she could use in Newport's shops.[22] The two free women supported themselves by exchanging the body and the labor of the enslaved woman.

Renting out the labor of household dependents was a common practice in the eighteenth century and made young people mobile and often temporary residents of rural households. In the countryside, free fathers would send sons out to work on a nearby farm during lulls at home; daughters helped neighbors with spinning and eventually weaving. These traditions of exchanging workers, while certainly social in part, were always economic transactions as well, entailing careful accountings and wage negotiations.[23] In rural areas, they were also linked to life cycle, since families that needed help with young children one year might have more than enough laborers five years later, and exchanges ended when dependents came of age. Enslaved people never outgrew this kind of work; households were always open to renting out or accepting in enslaved labor.

In the city, where free and enslaved people lived side-by-side and room-by-room, those same elements of pay negotiation and instability were therefore permanent parts of an enslaved person's life. Their lives and labor patterns contributed to the pervasive urban phenomenon of people on the move. City dwellers moved into and out from the cities as finances and opportunities dictated; immigrants regularly arrived from other continents. In Newport, as much as half the population died or moved away from the city in a typical ten-year period, making the census-taker's job a challenge each time out.[24] The urban population was a transient one, and urban economic culture sprang from the constant circulation of people and the regular appearance of strangers.

Even those residents who remained within the city often moved from house to house. Hard times forced relocation, as renters, boardinghouse lodgers, and the poor found themselves seeking better arrangements or cheaper prices on a regular basis. Optimistic calculations also prompted moves. The Downs sisters announced their new coffeehouse, located on busy Thames Street in Newport, in the same advertisement that they inquired, "Any person who hath a commodious house to let, in some public part of the town, may, by application to the said Mehitable and Abigail, receive a good rent therefor."[25] They planned to live and work in different locations in Newport, but even in their private quarters, they sought a "public" location that afforded them constant contact with potential customers and suppliers.

Cities like Newport and Charleston were demographically distinct from the communities surrounding them in ways that made them appear dangerously unstable to their critics. They had large, concentrated populations with substantial numbers of blacks and whites gathered in smaller-than-average households. Because of the work opportunities available in the city, each had fewer enslaved people and more female household heads than the nearby plantation districts. As eighteenth-century observers commented on these demographic trends, they also identified a calculating, duplicitous quality to city life, sparked by men and women on the make and freed from traditional constraints. Cities were places where fashions gripped a public eager to partake in them; where new codes of behavior loosened old mores; and where exciting (or dangerous) intellectual currents flowed through institutions such as libraries, theaters, and private societies.

Two poems written in the late 1760s, one about Charleston and one about Newport, focused not on the cities' central dependence on slavery, the transient nature of the population, or the access to transatlantic and coastal supplies of goods and information but on the culture created by these influences. After cataloguing the perils of the southern climate, the author of the Charleston poem turned to the population:

Everything at a high price
But rum, hominy and rice
Many a widow not unwilling
Many a beau not worth a shilling
Many a bargain, if you strike it
This is Charles-town, how do you like it.[26]

John Maylem's 1768 poem about Newport began on a positive note with a complimentary tour of the city's urban infrastructure but quickly adopted a more caustic tone:

A Dancing School and Town House hie!
A synagogue of Satan—fie!
A Castle too, a building—where?
G-d d-m you Sir! Why in the air.
A Gallows too without the City
To hang all rogues but theirs, O pity![27]

Coastal and international trade supported great wealth and poverty, calculating social relationships and castles in the air, proceeding from uncertainty bred of instability. The theater (Maylem's "synagogue of Satan") was in many ways the ideal metaphor for city life: actors, like city dwellers, had shifting, unstable identities; foreign plays and players dominated the culture; and even social rank was open for a price—depending upon where on the sliding scale you made your ticket purchase.[28]

For the average woman, however, the houseful—a residential and economic creation of individuals, families, and households—was a more relevant metaphor and reality. Port cities, while different from one another in important ways, created a unique urban context for women. Small families and female-headed households needed to devise economic strategies that did not rely on home farm production. Small families had fewer children, which meant that free women within them devoted less time to child care and more to paid work in the marketplace. The close proximity of rich and poor, native and immigrant meant that no woman remained isolated, socially or economically, by her domestic responsibilities. Instead, she had to navigate the shifting social terrain, not as performance but through a series of practical alliances and, as the poem put it, "many a bargain."

Making and Remaking Housefuls

Most of the one- and two-person "households" noted in census records did not live alone, clattering around a half-empty building. Instead, they rented rooms above stores, contracted with boarders, or shared a roof with others.[29] The resulting housefuls were a product of urban demographics and architecture that fostered temporary, extensive economic ties rather than permanent, intensive ones.

Charleston city records from 1790 offer a snapshot of the women who combined with others to form housefuls as well as some clues about how these combinations worked. That year, 15 percent of the two hundred female heads of household listed in the census can be clearly identified as sharing space with another head of household, though the actual numbers of women who did so are undoubtedly higher. Relative poverty, crudely measured by slaveholding patterns, prompted many to share living and working space. For example, while female householders in general in that year had five slaves; those who shared had 3.5. Put another way, among the women who identified themselves as schoolmistresses in the pages of the city directory that year, only those with one or no slaves shared living space. Free women who owned several slaves were more likely to be wealthy and less likely to live with other households.[30]

Poverty measured in slaveholding alone cannot explain housing arrangements. Of the women with listed occupations in 1790, for example, shopkeepers were least likely to have slaves and also least likely to share space with another head of household. Women weighed several factors when making economic decisions about where to live, and some kinds of work demanded certain kinds of space. Shopkeepers—men and women—clustered on wharves because that was where their goods were. To make a profit, shopkeepers needed to invest in stock and be located near customers; they were less likely to have investments in enslaved people. Boardinghouse keepers needed workers, whether free or enslaved, to wash dishes and make food; their most important investment was in labor.

Female-headed households typically shared living space with male-headed households. No community of enterprising women emerges from these records. And yet it was not a quest for a man in the house per se that motivated living arrangements. Female householders who chose to share space were no more likely to lack adult men in their families than those who lived alone. What they sought were qualities that their own men lacked. In some cases, co-residents may have hoped for commercial synergy, as when merchants and shopkeepers lived together. Economic strategies could even trump family ties. Peter Sudor was a cigar maker who ran a shop at 28 Union Street with a journeyman, three apprentices and six slaves. Elizabeth Sudor, surely a relative and also a cigar maker, decided to forgo the family connection in favor of her own arrangements. She rolled leaves at 35 Meeting Street with the help of just one other white woman and two slaves. Rather than join forces with other Sudors, Elizabeth created a houseful with Alexander McNabb, watchman, Robert Pierce, a bricklayer, and their wives.[31]

Although female householders did not always seek out other women to share housing, they did form pockets of similar households in port cities. Before and after the Revolution, white women with their own households clustered together on certain streets, such that sometimes several houses in a row were headed by women.[32] These neighborhood groupings strengthened local economic networks and may have contributed to a unique cultural character in these spaces common to port cities. In colonial Philadelphia's North Ward, for example, female kin ties and neighbors' financial support nurtured a group of shops all run by pairs of spinster sisters. Interconnected neighbors provided the basic support services of daily life by witnessing legal documents, cooperating on public works projects, and pitching in for charity.[33]

Some combination of choice and necessity created similar residential clusters of urban black women. In Charleston, these groupings tended to be more heterogeneous because the households that constituted them were a mixture of free and enslaved people. Lidia Watson and Clarisa Cross, both designated as "free" on the Charleston census-taker's tally, lived in neighboring households of eleven and five people, divided evenly between slaves and free people of color. In Newport, these clusters were exclusively of free blacks. Isabel Gould, for example, lived in 1790 near three other small free black households, none including slaves.[34] Free black women in Newport did not have the resources to support enslaved people; free blacks in Charleston did own and live with slaves. Enslaved women, too, faced different choices in each city: Charlestonians sought out jobs and apartments in the larger city; Newport slaves lived separately from their owners much less often.

Census records privilege household and neighborhood. Their vagaries tend to obscure the importance of the houseful as an economic strategy for urban women. Although census-takers faithfully preserved the general locations of free blacks, most of those who compiled city directories were uninterested in their precise living arrangements. Black women who were heads of household existed as numbers in city records—a general phenomenon—rather than as living people with strategies and support systems. In those rare cases of an exceptionally thorough city directory, however, some "neighborhood groupings" emerge as clusters of housefuls. Along the short span of Charleston's Anson Street in 1819, a neighborhood group of fourteen free black female househeads was concentrated in seven housefuls.[35] The tantalizing glimpses these recorders left behind suggest the presence of intertwined housefuls that served as economic units as well as cultural ones. A shared neighborhood might embody a defiant, independent culture, but shared houses meant tight (even grimly tight) interdependence.

Free black communities in New York, Boston, and Philadelphia, which boomed in the postrevolutionary period, all formed clusters of housefuls. Faced with the difficulty of making a living and perhaps new to the city, newly freed people found the mixed houseful a practical intermediate step between living in the mistress's house and establishing an independent single household.[36] White residents used similar strategies, not to escape the residue of slavery but to make urban life economically feasible. A free couple—black or white—might one day achieve the independence of separate living space, but for unmarried women, the houseful was a solution with staying power.

The most common way for a houseful to come together was through renting, which was widespread in revolutionary-era cities. Newspapers were filled with advertisements for homes, rooms, and shops for rent. As many as 70 percent of the real estate advertisements in the *South Carolina Gazette* in the pre-Revolution years offered property for rent rather than purchase.[37] By necessity or choice, all sectors of society could be found in temporary residences, a pattern that continued into the nineteenth century. Artisans and service workers moved frequently, advertising each relocation to alert customers. Charleston slaves who hired out their services sometimes rented houses together to serve as a base for their specialized occupations.[38] Renting was common even among the wealthy. The Manigault family in the first decade of the nineteenth century hunted for rentable homes in Charleston for relatives and friends planning long-term visits, sent copies of newspaper rental notices, and visited prospective houses on behalf of friends and kin. Competition for space could be fierce: Margaret Manigault's brother, Henry Izard, warned her in 1808 that "several applications had been made" for a certain unfurnished house, "though it is not yet engaged. I felt strongly tempted to secure it for you."[39] Furnished and unfurnished, large town home or cramped garret, space was urgently needed and used to capacity.

A typical rental agreement established the rate for a year and asked for quarterly payments, but tenants did not feel bound to remain for the full term if a better option arose. Mary Brown, a Newporter whose husband was away at sea, lived in the garret of Bathsheba Loveland, paying a rent of £8.15 New England currency per quarter. A mariner's wife had to scrimp and plan, however, and when she decided "she could get a rume Cheper in another place," she sublet her space in Loveland's house to carpenter Timothy Witherel in 1749.[40] All parties seemed satisfied with the arrangement until Witherel overstepped his rights as a sub-letter by digging up more than his share of the yard.[41] Loveland had legal rights by the rental agreement and it was Loveland who brought all the parties together (plus an eyewitness neighbor) at the houseful's dissolution in court. She had not, however, controlled the sublet or even vetted Witherel's presence. Authority, as experienced on a day-to-day basis, was therefore highly negotiable; the very creation of a houseful happened often by chance and circumstance rather than any kind of long-term planning.

Renters such as Brown and Witherel relied on informal connections and secondary markets to gain shelter. The process of renting a house involved information gathering and negotiation, activities that helped integrate newcomers into the existing community. When Charlestonian John Rutledge left his vacationing family in Newport to attend Congress in Philadelphia, his wife, Sarah, made all the arrangements in town, settling local accounts and looking for lodgings for the following year: "I went yesterday to speak to the Man who has the charge of the house Mrs. Tousard staid the summer in, on the point, & as the house and situation, is a very good one. . . . I wanted to take it for the ensuing summer, & get him to put it in a little repair—he says he wishes you would speak to Mr. Redwood, the owner of it who lives in Philadelphia, on the subject."[42] Sarah Rutledge's description of her labors traced the flow of information within and between the urban ports of the East Coast. She heard about a house for rent from a fellow Charlestonian, and then walked herself over to the caretaker of the Newport home. He advised her to contact the owner in Philadelphia regarding the condition of the building and terms of the rental, which she, in turn, directed her traveling husband to do. She then discussed the particulars of the house's interior and its rent with her local contact, passing along the information to her husband so that he could close the deal. In the process of integrating herself into the networks of information about the Newport housing market, Sarah Rutledge allegedly got to know the residents of Newport a bit too well. The resulting sex scandal played out down in Charleston and its surroundings, with an enraged John Rutledge pursuing his rival, Dr. Horace Senter, through the southern city, to his own plantation, and finally to

Savannah, where Rutledge delivered a fatal shot to Senter's leg. Connecting personal, printed, and professional networks in its coverage of the affair, the *Newport Mercury* reflected sadly that the "cruel business" was "the means of destroying Mr. R's peace of mind and ruining his wife's character forever."[43] Sarah Rutledge might find it difficult to set up a vacation rental again.

Once ensconced in their new surroundings, renters and those who "rented beds" (boarders) made new, useful connections that only occasionally ended in adulterous affairs. A stream of wealthy southerners, fleeing the sweltering heat for lengthy therapeutic visits up north, began their stays in Newport at Mrs. Rogers's establishment and conducted business from there, using her address as their contact.[44] Returning families sometimes maintained long-term relationships with their Newport hosts. Writing from Charleston, John Ball instructed his son to arrange for the boarding and education of two boys from the household of their Newport landlady, Mrs. Cottrell. John Ball Sr. had observed the two boys the previous year "kept confined like prisoners over the kitchen" and recommended farm life for them.[45] In imposing his charity on his distant landlady's children, Ball materialized connections he and his family had made with local Newporters. While Mrs. Cottrell surely never planned for it, and may not have been terribly enthusiastic about it, living in close daily proximity with wealthy newcomers had created a new economic resource for her family—with strings attached.

Elite renters mobilized whole service industries around themselves; their temporary homes generated new economic ties across the city. Newport servants who assisted the Balls on one of their frequent summer visits could expect extra money in the form of tips from a wealthy family accustomed to comfort and well versed in elite codes of liberality.[46] Settling the Rutledge family in Newport in 1798 (before things went bad), in "a charming House, in a very airy part of the Town, with two large gardens," required the services of two landlords, two schoolteachers, and numerous other retailers and laborers. John Rutledge was happy with the results. He commented favorably on the house, "which our Landlord keeps in good order for us, for thirty dollars a month—the House is well furnished with every article we want—even linens."[47] His sons studied with Mr. Rogers but boarded across the street, with "a very worthy woman, who has children about their ages," and received additional instruction from her son. Charleston visitors, who sometimes extended their stays for months, enmeshed themselves in their temporary communities by hiring nurses and washerwomen, purchasing clothing and food for the convalescent and their slaves, and contributing directly to the poor of the town.[48]

Most newly constructed housefuls did not depend upon an army of servants, but the patterns of elite ties are recognizable on a smaller scale with regular folk. Middling and poor people found housing though personal contacts; they also met new customers, clients, and fellow conspirators in their temporary homes. The Hall family of Newport and their tenant Sarah Fitzgerald were getting hungry in the late winter of 1776 when Fitzgerald hit upon the plan of sneaking into her former mistress's house to steal provisions. She remembered just where the barrel of pork was kept in Sarah Weeden's closet, and would have feasted with her new houseful that evening had not two vigilant watchmen appeared at the door and forced Mrs. Hall to turn over the contraband.[49] The charity Fitzgerald had to extend to her landlords was not as bountiful as Rutledge's (nor was it really hers to extend), but the mixture of social and economic impulses grew from similar foundations.

Housefuls dispersed when families or individuals found new arrangements and moved away. This everyday phenomenon accelerated during the Revolutionary War, when the destruction and occupation of urban houses broke up housefuls permanently, and at the end of the war, when families loyal to Great Britain fled into exile. In Newport, renting still had not recovered in the nineteenth century. Destruction of many residences left families with nowhere to live and single landladies with no means to make a living. In Charleston, the opposite was true. The reconstruction of the city led to more living space and more opportunities for women to earn rental income.

In between major reshufflings was the constant ebb and flow of houseful composition brought about by the shifting presence of servants and slaves. By the late eighteenth century, paid work by live-in and part-time servants replaced indentured servitude in urban centers. Short-handed urban families hired a mixture of short-term workers to help with cooking, washing, sewing, and other maintenance work, resulting in what could seem like a revolving door for local labor. Slave owners willingly broke apart their own housefuls and gave up direct authority over their slaves in search of profits. New England minister Abiel Abbot, visiting Charleston in 1818, commented that black slaves "make so large a part of every domestic establishment" that owners "are obliged to exercise their wits to devise a sufficient variety to keep them employed"; renting them out to neighbors was the common solution.[50] Labor calculations within individual families rippled through the houseful with the arrival or departure of an extra set of hands.

Each houseful had its own logic and personalities undoubtedly shaped the fate of many combinations of families and individuals. But the restless circulation of people through city residences followed common patterns and moved along familiar trajectories. Following up on leads shared across local and distant ties, they pursued low rents and convenient locations. Sent by opportunistic mistresses, they moved their beds to new settings where they would work for employers with money to spare. The new connections they made could be quickly dissolved, but they also might endure to provide much-needed economic or social support.

Economic Ties in Shared Spaces

Economic factors motivated decisions about space use; in turn, those living situations fostered new economic relationships. Whether two families rented from the same landlord or one boarded with one another, possession and ownership were contingent and authority over the whole was fleeting. A sizable portion of the population lived not as members of "Mr. Smith's household" but as boarders "at Mrs. Smith's." These people not only ate at her table, but also plied their independent trades in her rooms. The following year, some would alert their customers that they now resided at "Mrs. Jones's," signaling the negligible control Smith had over them.

It is tempting to portray these arrangements as contracts and leave it at that. But for city folk, these ties created social instability and highlighted the ambiguities of houseful authority. Consider the experiences of Newporter Mary Viall. In 1760, Viall rented one of the rooms in Jonathan Chandler's house while her own husband was away at sea. One day in late summer, Viall was at home with Chandler's wife Hannah and daughter Catherine when two carpenters came to make some repairs to the floor. While one of the workmen, Christopher Lyndsey, relaxed and smoked, the mistress of the house went about supervising the efforts of the other. Viall went out to the well and was returning with two buckets of water when Lyndsey jumped up and teasingly tried to bar her reentry. Irritated, she told him "that she had more business there then Lyndsey had for she Did not hire sd house of him." The standoff ended in a nasty water fight and a lawsuit.[51]

As a lone renter, Viall was in a difficult position. On the one hand, Viall made an important contribution to the houseful in the form of rent; on the other, her lack of a permanent dwelling signaled inferior status. Mary Viall "lived in one of the chambers of the house"; Hannah Chandler was its mistress. Hannah, therefore, oversaw the work of the carpenters on her own cellar floor and cautioned Lyndsey that "he had better leave her alone" when he announced his plan to "make friends" with Viall "and kiss her." Standing in the doorway, Lyndsey was a man amusing himself at the expense of a woman whose husband was far away. Viall's sharp response to him countered on the grounds of their relative authority in the social world of the port city. She had more "business" being in the Chandlers' home as a renter than he did as a hired worker.

Nor was she without defenders—Catherine Chandler provided the testimony for Mary's lawsuit. Alliances between female members of the same houseful appear in the court records of other port cities, as well. Poor Mary Wallace, who rented a small room in Joseph Yeates's home in Philadelphia, had only Nan, Yeates's slave, to assist her in the minutes after the secret birth of her illegitimate child.[52]

Urban housefuls organized diverse individuals not for the convenience of census enumerators but for daily economic life, however temporarily. In some cases, this meant cooperation—individual members exchanged money and labor. In other cases, families worked to maintain distinct households in spite of shared residence by dividing rooms and cooking spaces within the building.[53] The houseful form did not dictate warm friendships and it did not guarantee profitable alliances. Proximity of individuals and the multipurpose nature of urban structures did lead, though, to certain kinds of social and economic interdependence. Hannah Chandler needed Mary Viall's rent money; Mary needed Hannah's room and protection against assaults. They both needed Jonathan Chandler's income from the distillery to keep the house; he needed his wife and daughter's domestic management.

Mutual dependencies within the houseful could be as changeable as the use of the building that held them. All kinds of city houses had multiple personalities, and a houseful's members did not need an interior designer to enact transformation.[54] Many buildings included both residential and retail space, designations that could change in the blink of an enterprising would-be shopkeeper's eye (Figure 3). To the Charleston community, Mrs. Wood's house on Church Street was a respectable and central location. Thanks to Samuel Gordon's negotiations with Wood, it came to include a corner from which he could sell imported linens to a discriminating public.[55] Homes that took in boarders often doubled as schools, particularly if the female proprietor could make arrangements with a local traveling master. James Oliver taught writing and arithmetic "at Mrs. Simpson's boarding school, every forenoon, and at Mrs. Girardeau's every afternoon, Saturdays excepted." He offered private tutoring in bookkeeping "either at his own lodgings, at Mrs. Peronneau's . . . or at Mrs. Girardeau's."[56] Oliver's appearance at the door with his books and quills turned an ordinary lodging into a place of learning, a feminine space filled with girls practicing fine sewing into a masculine place of business for future clerks. The circulation of people defined space at the same time that the availability of space motivated their movements.

The multiple personalities of urban architecture took their particular character from contests between elites, middling folk, and the poor and enslaved to control city space. The single-house style, which dominated

Figure 3. This eighteenth-century residence has adjoining retail space. Christopher Townsend House, 74 Bridge Street. Courtesy of The Preservation Society of Newport County.

late colonial and early national Charleston, was designed to ensure elite surveillance of the enslaved and serving population (Figure 4). Strategically built perpendicular to the road so that access was tightly controlled, these houses compelled both visitors on business and slaves on errands to pass by the discriminating eyes of the master class in order to reach the interior or any of the outbuildings that circled the property. In spite of the elite's best efforts to control the population by controlling architecture, however, the reality of a constantly circulating public, close quarters, and the economy's dependence upon poor and enslaved intermediaries meant that informal and unauthorized uses of seemingly rigidly controlled space were common.[57] Outbuildings, found at the back of city lots, separated the messy and sometimes dangerous business of food preparation from increasingly refined interiors, yet they also created corners for decidedly nonpolite conversation.

Enslaved people took advantage of these conditions to create their own commercial spaces in the cities, initiating enterprises as washerwomen, marketeers, craftsmen, and cooks. Charleston slaveowners tried to counter the latitude granted other people's slaves by legislating restrictions on their movements and formalizing hiring-out practices. Masters in the *South Carolina City Gazette* began to name monthly wages for the slaves they planned to hire out. One offered the services of a young female

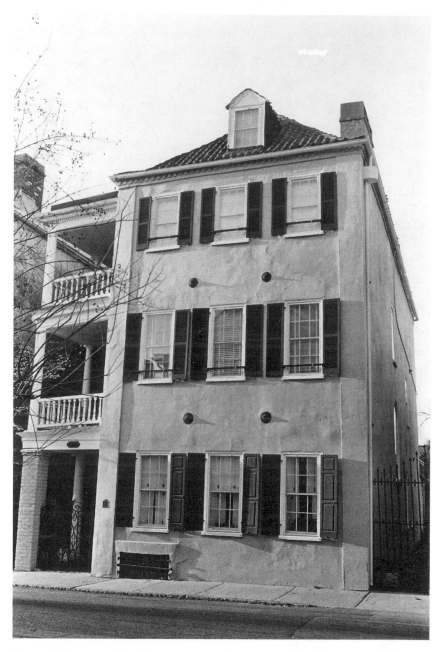

Figure 4. Access to the living quarters of this single house is at the left. In the revolutionary era, there was a door on the front at ground level to allow street access to the print shop inside. Cleland-Wells House, 58 Tradd Street. Historic Charleston Foundation.

slave who specialized in the care of children with the blunt warning: "To save unnecessary application, the prices is six dollars and a half per month."[58] Such owners hoped to leave less to the negotiations between hired slave and employer, which took place in other homes and back lots, far from a mistress's oversight.

If there were economic opportunities to be found in sharing space, there were also economic dangers; a blending of the personal and the contractual could work to women's detriment. In 1779, Freelove Boss went to live with Timothy Peckham's family in Newport, agreeing in exchange for her board and a pair of shoes to "keep school" for his children for a three-week trial period. She stayed on for eighteen weeks, teaching his children, eating in his home, and expecting to receive wages as well. Peckham, however, presumed that as long as he provided the board, Boss could be expected to teach his children as a matter of course. When he commented as much to Boss, she later reported to the court that "she thought he was only Joking." She still was not laughing when the court awarded her only a small proportion of back wages.[59] City dwellers had conflicting understandings of the obligations and perquisites of living together. While some boarders, in their words and actions, proclaimed themselves free agents, others were held captive by unspoken assumptions or their inability to make better arrangements.

The houseful, therefore, was a place of economic negotiation, particularly for the women who presided over it or sought service work within it. Although women were usually hired as general maidservants, some were able to establish limits on what kinds of chores they would perform, and others promoted themselves as specialists. The lure of the market drove other bargains between servants and employers, whether a maid was borrowing money against wages or loaning cash to strapped employers. Mistresses were supposed to guide the behavior of their servants, but advice books for new well-to-do brides acknowledged that a young mistress might learn much from experienced servants by "*unobserved attention.*"[60] The results of these negotiations were widely varying experiences among female servants, even those who worked in the same house. Hannah Robinson and Dorcas Jack, for example, both worked in the household of Thomas Robinson in the 1790s. Hannah worked a day or two each week, filling in when daughter Abigail Robinson was away from home or some other event left the household short-handed. Dorcas, in contrast, worked solidly three to six days per week in the Robinson household for four months in 1794. Abigail Robinson, who was in charge of the wages and workloads of these women, paid them as they worked: Hannah occasionally (in cash or potatoes), Dorcas weekly (in cash and shoes for herself and her child). Abigail Robinson's watchful eye and diligent pen took note of every day of work and every pair of shoes handed out as partial payment, ensuring that although the servants' time in the Robinson house was variable, it was not casual.

More even than the transient male workers familiar to all port industries, women moved from house to house, as paid and unpaid obligations pulled them. Wealthy Newporter William Ellery hired a succession of white and black women to serve and live in his home in the last decades of the eighteenth century. Like Robinson, William Ellery employed both regular servants and temporary help. Female servants worked for a lower weekly rate than male servants and received irregular payments, to boot, when compared with the single large sum that Ellery doled out to his male servants and the end of each month. From Ellery's point of view, conceptualizing female service in short-term installments acknowledged the competing claims for a female servant's time. Betsy Fry left Ellery's house to care for her sick mother before returning, sick herself, and in need of a cash advance several weeks later.[61] The needs of multiple households made these women permanent members of none. As the next chapter will explore in more detail, urban women performed similar domestic work for free for their families to what they did for pay in the larger service economy of Atlantic port cities. These responsibilities, combined with low, irregular wages, necessitated and even dictated lives as service nomads.

The close quarters of urban housefuls brought the characteristics of the urban trading economy right to the heart of domestic life. Urban merchants, for example, struggled with problems of obtaining market information and finding the right partners, often looking to members of the same religious group or a family connection for help. For their part, city dwellers drew on their own informal networks to chase down favorable rental rates and reliable tenants. Merchants looked for ways to add to their businesses by trying out smaller private "ventures" along with their main trade. Within homes and boardinghouses, too, servants and landlords struck deals that capitalized on existing economic relationships, whether agreeing to sew a pair of breeches for a tenant or asking a servant for a cash loan. As in the world of merchants, commercial relationships within the houseful had a social quality that was as essential as it was at times difficult to navigate.[62]

The Changing Cityscape

If we imagine the girl who walked through the early paragraphs of this chapter making her way through Newport and Charleston as an old woman in 1820, we see in her progress a tour of two transformed landscapes. Charleston had fallen to the rank of sixth most populous city in the United States by 1820, and its population and economic growth were slowing, but it was still a commercial center and thriving port.

Charleston's newspapers advertised plentiful imported goods and specialty services, land for sale, and the arrival and departure of ships carrying freight around the Atlantic. Multiple churches, a neoclassical city hall, brick exchange building, theaters, and other imposing public and private buildings increased the scale of the city and impressed upon residents and visitors a sense of developed urban culture. Paved streets and garbage collection would have improved an old woman's safety and comfort as she crossed the city toward the new tree-lined city square that had replaced a dense tangle of poor homes. She would have to walk farther, too, to view the entire city, since commercial activity and dwelling spaces had spread to new streets. As Charleston's King Street developed from an outlying residential area to a busy retail center many of the newly constructed buildings had space for street-level window displays, shop rooms, living quarters, and outbuildings.[63] While admiring the various monuments of civic culture, a sharp-eyed old woman could not overlook that urban architecture also testified to the chronic problem of urban poverty in the large, brick orphan house on Boundary Street.[64]

Newport had not weathered the turn of the new century so well. While the number of Charleston residents had more than doubled since 1750, Newport's fluctuating population had settled back down to close to its 1750 level. Physically devastated by the Revolution and cut off, finally, from its lucrative slave trade, Newport in 1820 had become a much smaller satellite of larger New England commercial centers such as Boston, New York, and Providence, and it ranked somewhere between fifteenth and twentieth among most populous United States cities. Its relative isolation from productive hinterlands and overland transportation, combined with the loss of most of the risk-taking merchant community of the prewar years, left it a much quieter town, unable to take advantage of new developments in manufacturing. Happily, it was no longer the ghost town of the postoccupation years, when "miserably stocked" shops were haunted by "emaciated children and the pale, thin men, whose sunken eyes and shifty looks put the observer ill at ease."[65] By 1820, lard, iron, and ships' masts were available for sale on the wharves, and the shops of Thames Street offered imported goods for sale again. Trade with southern ports had resumed, and a few Newport firms had started ventures in the China trade. Rather than dodge crowded wharves and densely packed neighborhoods, an old woman could stroll along the new town square, enclosed by a picket fence and shaded by formal rows of trees, which had been constructed between the courthouse and the market building.[66] She would note that although the town was not expanding, churches, a bank, and new homes had replaced those lost in the war years and the Touro Synagogue remained undamaged. Even vacationers had returned to take advantage of the weather and low prices. Charlestonian Charles Fraser commented to his mother, Mary, "Although I was disgusted at first with the appearance of New Port yet when I came to know the society there I thought of leaving it with great reluctance."[67]

The reconstruction required after the Revolutionary War reshaped much of the familiar cityscape, but upheavals in those years tended to accentuate many of the influences that had created urban housefuls. Populations experienced transforming fluctuations as large numbers sought to escape the fighting, as slaves escaped with the British Army, and as loyalists fled in the wake of British defeat. Former residents abandoned their homes, new immigrants filled in and sought rentals. Individual manumissions of slaves in the North and South, as well as gradual emancipation laws in Rhode Island, created a rising population of free blacks, and port cities continued to be destinations for the newly freed in search of work, family stability, and community. As they grew larger, free black communities organized, forming separate schools, churches, and benevolent societies that competed for space with white institutions. The 1808 constitution of Newport's African Benevolent Society stated that its objects were "the establishment and continuance of a free school for any person of Colour in this Town," and "to receive and faithfully to appropriate all monies given for the benefit of the coloured poor in this town"; similar subscription societies were formed in Charleston.[68]

In the early decades of the nineteenth century, many port cities witnessed new levels of spatial segregation between living and working spaces and between rich and poor residences.[69] In Newport and Charleston, however, elites kept their homes in bustling urban centers, retreating to plantations and country houses when the crush of polyglot ports became too much. For urban merchants, retailers, and craftspeople, living above the store remained common, and these cities continued to be economically mixed in the years of the early republic. Urban elites were successful in claiming more public space for classically inspired buildings, stately promenades, and fenced-in parks that reinforced order, and these monuments to order and enlightenment claimed the eyes of contemporaries. But it is important to remember what the old pedestrian saw when she returned to her own doorway. Newport and Charleston were still, in 1820, driven by service economies and the presence and needs of transients, from sailors to traders to vacationers to people in search of work. Neither became the manufacturing center that city fathers had hoped, and both suffered due to the shift in transportation from sailing vessels to steamships and turnpikes.[70] Heterogeneous living and working spaces, filled with motley housefuls, however, endured.

In the 1757 *South Carolina Gazette*, Eliza White advertised her new school with a firm announcement that though it would be located "in a convenient room in the house where Mrs. Cranmer lives in Broad Street, . . . the said room is free from, and independent of any transactions of the house."[71] White's emphatic declaration of economic independence calls attention to the uneasy cultural identity of housefuls in the local economies of port cities. Female economic activity took its shape from networks that extended beyond the household to the houseful, the broader city, and the Atlantic world. Paying rent, hiring slaves, or serving with another family required women to mobilize these networks. Yet the fact that renters and boarders like Eliza White felt compelled to shore up their status with verbal confrontations and newspaper announcements suggests that urban societies were not completely comfortable with the social implications of mobile and changeable housefuls. They reached for familiar forms, such as advertisements, account books, and census lists to impose order on negotiations that threatened to fall apart under challenge or confusion. Neither a receipt for used candles nor a promissory note for rent could completely capture the expectations or potential obligations involved in living with other people.

Historian Carole Shammas has argued that the rise of modern American society came from the decline in the powers of the household head in favor of the government and government-supported specialized institutions like asylums, poor houses, and schools. A legal assault on the broad powers of the head of household did take place in state after state in the middle of the nineteenth century, as his authority over his children's labor, his wife's earnings, and his slave's bodies faced political challenges, but this political timetable does not map as well onto the social and economic experiences of city-dwellers.[72] Late eighteenth-century demographic realities and diverse living configurations suggest that there were already many competing sites of authority in urban people's lives, and that the patriarchal household model was only one, and not necessarily the most widespread or salient. Eighteenth-century law maintained that a free man owned his wife's wages and his slaves' time, but wives and slaves regularly struck their own deals with borders and employers and spent the profits. The constitution and breakup of housefuls dispersed and fragmented authority, not always to the advantage of urban women, who could profit from the greater fluidity of authority or suffer from the absence of kin and supporters.

The unified household has served as the explanatory key to early American women's lives. Since in theory it bound together legal, economic, and cultural power, it can be linked to the segmentation of the labor market, the ideal of separate male and female spheres of influence, and persistent female legal subordination. The fact that these familiar hallmarks of the nineteenth century emerged also in cities where such households were rare and fleeting suggests that the household per se is not to blame, however. City housefuls did not have the architecture or membership to be inhabited by idealized domesticity. At best, the secure, private home watched over by a domestic angel became an unattainable dream for urban Americans whose lives were relentlessly commercial; at worst, it was a cynical construction used to shore up the status of white middle-class families. The houseful was neither ideal nor idealized, it was a contingent choice—a product of its members' circumstances, calculated year by year, house by house.

The relationships that bound housemates together were an often frustrating mixture of calculation and cooperation. Dependent on others for information and business, city dwellers nevertheless looked for opportunities to strike a better deal when possible. Urban women, by their roles and through demographic accident, were at the center of these calculations. As landladies and boardinghouse keepers, they struggled to maintain a profitable mix of tenants. As laborers, they entered housefuls to work side-by-side with existing residents, injecting new kinds of negotiations. As household heads, they relocated frequently in search of amenable neighborhoods and reliable partners. For most women, links at the level of houseful formed the first essential connections of economic life. The rest of this book follows those relationships as they moved between homes, marketplaces, shops, workrooms, warehouses, and back again, bearing the money and goods of international commerce.

Chapter 2

Work in the Atlantic Service Economy

Most of the women who moved through the streets of Newport and Charleston were hard at work—carrying goods, pumping water, attending the market, and visiting stores. In some ways, these tasks echoed what generations of African, European, and American women had done on behalf of themselves and their families. But international commerce, in the form of goods and people, left its stamp on every kind of work that women did in the revolutionary era and transformed what it meant to them. In particular, commerce widened the possibilities for women to earn money for their labors. Their small, often self-employed businesses in port cities depended on outsiders. Through this work of providing services for pay, women became vital agents of connection not only within their communities but also between local urban economies and Atlantic ones.[1]

Cooking and cleaning for others, trading and selling, sewing and educating—these activities formed the core repertoire for white and black urban women. As they labored in these tasks, women forged ties across many of the seeming divides in the eighteenth-century economy. They linked home and market, as many of the skills of women's work were to some degree associated with the home and frequently acquired from mothers and aunts. They bridged paid and unpaid labor, when they performed the same kinds of services to earn money and credit that they did, for no pay, in support of themselves and their relatives.[2] They also connected production and consumption, by bringing the products of their needles and poultry yards to shopkeepers or market hawkers willing to accept these items as payment for consumer goods. This adaptability of female market participation proved crucial in the national shift to a capitalist economy, given the importance of flexible, intermittent labor to families facing new sources of competition.[3]

Through all of these connections, women's work lives linked local transactions to international transformations. Urban women who worked for money, either as servants with wages or self-employed small businesswomen, staffed an Atlantic service economy that intersected with the developing port functions of the revolutionary era. The expansion of the British empire in the eighteenth century created new customers, new suppliers, and new goods for enterprising merchants. To manage these interlocking opportunities, businesspeople had to mobilize cooperative partners and tap into transatlantic information networks. They had to balance long-range planning with an acceptance of risk and competition. New activities demanded new support structures—shipping services, work crews, credit instruments—and generated more dirty clothes, hungry stomachs, homeless sailors, and unclad bodies.[4] These last, unglamorous features of the trading economy may have worried city fathers, but they simultaneously provided a broad base of customers for self-employed city women (Figure 5).

In turn, interaction with the Atlantic economy fundamentally altered the scale and meaning of women's domestic labors. Pursuit of profit in the larger urban marketplace required a greater investment of time, a marshaling of resources from outside of the household, and a qualitatively different relationship with other actors in the urban economy. Seasonal workers, transient residents, and other city dwellers were more likely to pay for the services of prepared meals, laundry, and clothes-making. By placing a monetary value on women's domestic work, the exchange of cash or credit for "female" skills changed how these skills were perceived and how they fit into people's economic lives. For example, women and men recognized skill and specialization within "women's work" and expected to pay more for superior abilities. Married free women's work also earned valuable credit for family members with local shopkeepers, which enabled them to purchase desirable imported goods. Imported goods then became the raw materials for new female business ventures, from well-stocked taverns down to hastily pawned jackets.

The Atlantic service economy was a paradoxical place for working women. Enslaved women bought themselves a measure of autonomy and material sustenance with paid work. Free daughters earmarked small sums for purchases meant to satisfy themselves alone. But by opening women's lives to potential allies and an expansive worldview, commercial connections forged by work also exposed them to unfamiliar competitors and unforeseen market shifts. These, too, rippled across the economy and into daily life, as goods and people circulating in the Atlantic community met in the work of port-city women.

Serving Atlantic People

"Boarding," the cornerstone of the service economy catering to a fluid urban population, ranged from informal arrangements with family members to advertised, well-established businesses geared toward a particular clientele. Women, who dominated this industry, could find themselves

years from that time, they may expect to gather the fruit of their care, and what a pleasant reflection it must afford, we leave for them to try, and wish our young farmers all success.

BAKED PEARS.

"*Bake Pears.*"

A little black girl, with pears in an earthen dish, under one arm, cries "bake pears." They sell one, sometimes two or three for a cent. This too is an honest way to procure a living. It is much to be lamented, that any person, white or black, should be willing to live by any means that are not honourable and honest.

Figure 5. Female hucksters were a common sight and sound on urban streets in all Atlantic port cities. "The Cries of Philadelphia ornamented with elegant wood cuts" (Philadelphia: Johnson and Warner, 1810). The Historical Society of Pennsylvania.

providing for boarders in many ways.[5] Some made room for relatives, like widow Alice Lillibridge, who had to sue her kinsman Captain Robert Lillibridge for the costs (twelve shillings per week) associated with board-ing his wife for almost forty weeks in 1790.[6] Others were pressed into service by a town council, who paid individuals to board and sometimes nurse the poor and infirm in their own houses.[7] Finally, some women advertised that they would take in boarders, either as an extension of an existing business (such as a tavern) or as a separate enterprise.

Fluctuations in the seaboard population increased the numbers of all kinds of boarders. The rigors of life as a sailor, ropemaker, or slave con-tributed to physical disabilities that thrust individuals on the charitable institutions of the city.[8] Imperial warfare swelled the ranks of the dislo-cated and abandoned. Families of men at sea needed to find temporary lodgings that would accommodate them. Relatives might take up the slack, but as with Alice Lillibridge, this work was not performed for free nor purely out of a sense of community.[9] Providing for the maritime population formed a significant opportunity for the working women of Newport in particular. About a quarter of all the cases that brought New-port women to the civil courts between 1750 and 1820 involved mari-ners, most frequently for unpaid costs associated with providing lodging for the mariner himself or for his family. This meant that one of the most common ways for women to earn money depended directly on the vagaries of the Atlantic world.

At first glance, boarding seems like a "natural" fit with free women's activities, a matter of sweeping a few more crumbs and stretching the food a bit further. But few arrangements were as casual or as easy as this; board-ing, in fact, provides some of the clearest testimony about how women's work was segmented and valued. In Charleston, the law and custom had an inclusive attitude toward the obligations associated with boarding. The formulaic language of the courts in cases of unpaid boarding tabs referred to "meat, drink, washing and lodging and other necessaries," tak-ing a broad view of what should be included. In Newport, however, no set language described the services to be provided. Instead, individuals sub-mitted bills that took separate account of the services Charleston courts considered as a whole. Katharine Sheffield, who from late 1767 boarded Captain Andrew Christie, broke down her charges as follows:

67 weeks board at 18 shillings lawful money per week	£60.6.0
67 weeks washing and ironing	£5.6.0
67 weeks mending stockings, including supplies	£0.15.0
For fire and candles when sick[10]	£0.18.0

Certain services were always accounted for separately. Nursing, mak-ing new clothes, supplying expensive liquor, and lending money were classified as "extraordinary" services, not included in the general agreement. On the one hand, these charges stemmed from the domestic context of boarding; if a boarder living in a woman's home fell ill, she would be on hand with the knowledge and the obligation to nurse him back to health. On the other hand, such charges suggest the commercial potential of having a boarder in the house. In late 1803, George Dougherty boarded with Charlestonian Sarah Brown for eleven weeks, which included his washing and mending, at the charge of eighteen shillings and eight pence per week. Brown also made three jackets, five pairs of pantaloons, a waistcoat, coat, suspenders, and stockings for Dougherty and his journeyman, each itemized and billed separately.[11] The presence of a boarder therefore created opportunities for extra earnings, though for most women, these remained supplemental to the primary source of income. Making individual items was more lucrative than boarding, washing, and mending for someone—it took two days of performing these tasks to earn the same as from constructing a single pair of blue velvet pantaloons. But the boarding was regular, and for women unwilling or unable to establish themselves as seamstresses, boarding added up to more over the long term.

There was, therefore, a hybrid kind of entrepreneurship that emerged from the houseful arrangements of port cities. Sarah Brown did not set up a separate shop or advertise her new venture. She did, however, cultivate and develop a new business in clothes-making that she, her customer, and the courts saw as distinct from the "mending" included in the boarding charges. By intensifying existing customer relationships under her own roof rather than seeking out new ones, she was able to expand her enterprise despite the familiar limitations of capital and mobility that revolutionary-era women faced. She exhibited the kind of self-employment that was possible at the nexus of consumer imports (the blue velvet), flexible non-kin living arrangements (Dougherty), and a service economy based on money for housework.[12]

The boardinghouse keeper's operating costs included rent and food. When Mary Rose charged Daniel Whyte $5 per week for board and lodging in 1808, she was buying about seventy-five cents' worth of meat daily, presumably for her whole establishment. There is no record of whether she owned her house or rented, but typical house rents in Charleston at the time ranged from $120 to $300 per year, or somewhere between thirty and eighty cents per day. In other words, her meat and rent bills alone could have cost more than she was earning from Whyte, and she surely needed other customers to come close to making a profit. In fact, she boarded his "two Negros" as well, at a reduced rate (and fewer services) of 87½ cents per week each.[13] Boarders helped cover costs, but for many women who served them, they probably failed to bring in large sums. No opportunity to earn a little extra money sewing in the evenings could be easily turned down, especially since a boarder also had the potential to incur sudden and unexpected costs. Mary Nichols was boarding the wife and children of Herbert Nichols in 1769 when they fell ill and required "necessaries," presumably including medicine and doctor's fees. Mary Nichols was forced to "hire" ten dollars to cover these costs, a sum she did not recover until three years and a lawsuit had passed.[14]

Undoubtedly many women who provided boarding lived close to the margins and were driven into business more by urgent necessity than entrepreneurial zest. Evidence from city directories suggests that most women who operated boardinghouses had smaller-than-average house-holds and were not blessed with large numbers of female helpers on hand. Ten of the fourteen female boardinghouse keepers in the 1790 Charleston directory had three or fewer slaves, which meant they had fewer slaves than the average female-headed household.[15] The presence of household slaves, even in small numbers, however, profoundly shaped seaport life and the meaning of "women's work." As historians of New England have noted, "the work of slaves undergirded entrepreneurship and increasing market participation" by their owners.[16] By performing nonmarket household work alongside free women, enslaved women and men increased opportunities for making money. Rosanna Theus may have owned only three slaves, but their labors enabled her to run a boardinghouse to support herself and the only other free adult in the family.[17]

Sufficient space was crucial to the provision of boarding, lodging, and entertainment; property ownership was not. The providers of temporary lodging themselves moved frequently. Newporter Mary Doubleday of-fered a bed, food, and washing for temporary residents. Though more rooted than her customers, Doubleday had no fixed location herself, moving from "the House of Mr. Walter Easton, near the Brick-Market, to the House belonging to Mr. Augustus Newman, on the North Side of Bannister's Wharf" in 1795.[18] The same was true in Charleston, where mo-bility was the rule for all kinds of businesswomen, including those listed as keeping a boardinghouse. In 1790, Hannah Turpin, who presided over a household of seven, ran a boardinghouse at 53 Church Street. In 1794 she was based in Berresford's Alley; by 1801 she had moved to 26 Elliott Street; and two years later she had moved next door to 28 Elliott Street.[19] What might seem like home-based operations, therefore, were part of the very public, temporary meaning of home familiar to most city dwellers.

In the years before the Revolutionary War, female advertisers in both cities frequently added boarding to other services they promised to pro-vide. Tavern keepers regularly offered boarding, as did schoolteachers with country pupils. Increasingly, these arrangements became more formal and predictable. By the first decades of the nineteenth century, full-time boardinghouses came into their own. Newspaper notices offering boarding as an "extra" in both cities were crowded out by businesses dedicated to providing "boarding and lodging" together. Legal language in Newport kept pace with the institutionalization of boarding, replacing the earlier task-based approach. By 1820, Sarah Wise's attorney briskly cited the "meat, drink, washing and lodging and other necessaries" she had provided, all together worth $87.75.[20]

The emergence of boardinghouses in the northern port, by formalizing and institutionalizing the kinds of services that women had provided piecemeal in the prewar years, influenced the ways that all women conceptualized their work in the nineteenth century. For Sarah Wise and the other Newport women who took in boarders, washing, for example, was transformed from a special service to one provided as a matter of course, as one of an undifferentiated group of domestic services. Institutionalization in New England, while charging cash rates for housework services and therefore acknowledging the value of work traditionally provided by female kin, also had the effect of reinforcing the division between "productive" branches of housework (such as making clothing) and "nonproductive" ones (such as washing it) by charging differently for them.[21] Producing clothing earned a separate fee; cleaning it was an expected part of women's boarding work.

But not in every case. Over the same period, "clothes washer" became an occupation and a working identity for black women in Charleston, moving out of an undifferentiated category of "housework" and into the category of separate paid service. "Washers" of any kind were almost never listed in city directories in the eighteenth century, but by the early nineteenth century, this intimate chore had been publicly outsourced to free black women: of the sixty-five "colored" women listed with occupations in the 1819 directory, eighteen were "washers"; more strikingly, only one of the nineteen washers included was not identified as a woman of color.[22] Urban slavery and a tradition of black self-employment shifted the profile of paid housework in the South in a different direction.

The availability of washing as an occupation for free blacks had its roots in the mid-eighteenth century when masters who were "renting" out the time of their slaves frequently highlighted women's washing skills. In advertisements, slave owners touted the particular abilities of their female workers and charged extra for the special skills of a woman described as a "blond lace cleaner" or "good clear starcher." Because they were trying to sell it in the marketplace, slave owners identified expertise within the "women's work" of their slaves in a way that they would not for their sisters and mothers. Owners therefore singled out enslaved women as noted "plain cooks," "bakers," and "dairymaids." Enticements could be very specific; one Charleston slave was billed as an expert seamstress, "particularly for boys clothes."[23]

Enslaved women's own initiative in hiring out their time and establishing themselves as clothes washers for sailors further helped create a close identification of black women and laundry services. The master who complained that his slave, Sarai, was "well known at Sullivan's Island and Fort Johnson, having been in the habit of washing for the soldiers there" was acknowledging that this woman had essentially established her own business (Figure 6).[24] In doing so, Sarai achieved a degree of autonomy in daily life. There were many enslaved entrepreneurs in cities like Charleston, given the long history of allowing slaves to make their own hiring-out arrangements. Enslaved male artisans have attracted the most attention for the relative independence they achieved with their specialized skills and mobility. But female slaves were also prominent in this group because they did the kind of service work that the transient urban population demanded. While the majority of enslaved urban women worked in households under the eyes of masters and mistresses,

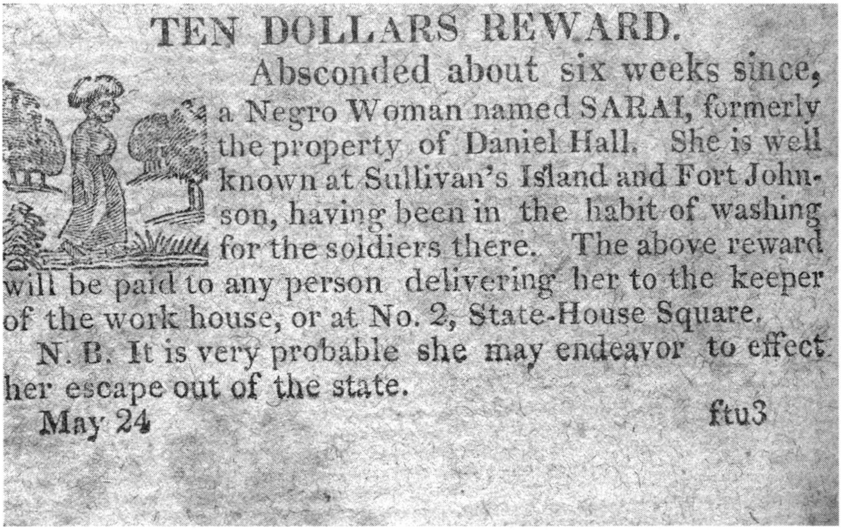

TEN DOLLARS REWARD.

Absconded about six weeks since, a Negro Woman named SARAI, formerly the property of Daniel Hall. She is well known at Sullivan's Island and Fort Johnson, having been in the habit of washing for the soldiers there. The above reward will be paid to any person delivering her to the keeper of the work house, or at No. 2, State-House Square.

N. B. It is very probable she may endeavor to effect her escape out of the state.

May 24   ftu3

Figure 6. Sarai, the woman named in this runaway slave advertisement, operated her own laundry business. *South Carolina Gazette and Commercial Daily Advertiser,* May 30, 1816. From the collections of the Charleston Library Society.

those with claims of specialization found a ready market for more independent service entrepreneurs.

After the Revolution, a swelling free black population took advantage of the market niches created by slaves, and by the nineteenth century, clothes washing was a bona fide occupation dominated by free black female entrepreneurs. This niche of self-employment was never secure, however, given white interest in exploiting the service economy for their own profits. For example, whites established "Negro washing houses" in Charleston to turn entrepreneurs into paid laborers. Runaway Kate found refuge in the city for years at a time because she could easily "get into some of the negro washing-houses or kitchens, to be employ'd in them."[25] The contrast between Sarai's and Kate's experiences mirrored those of many women providing "housework" services for the marketplace. Institutionalization provided a haven for women without capital or tools, but they paid in foregoing the precarious autonomy of self-employment.

As they struggled to forge public identities as skilled entrepreneurs, free black women drew on personal relationships, not only with potential customers and patrons but perhaps with one another, as well. Free black women with businesses in the early nineteenth century convinced the men who compiled city directories to list them by occupation, rather than with the default designation of "colored." From their efforts, we can see that they created residential communities for themselves within the larger city. Charleston's Anson Street, mentioned in Chapter 1 as an example of intertwined free black female-headed housefuls, was home to washers, seamstresses, and nurses.[26] In forming these residential clusters, women shaped the geography of the service economy and the personal terrain of entrepreneurship.

Clothes washing, whether done in the back yards of urban free blacks or in the shadow of a military fort, was grueling, wet "women's work" that defied categorization as "domestic." Its performance outside of the family and its status as a job for black women marked it as a part of the service economy, where it became a proving ground for debates about work and skill. In some ways, this process paralleled the changes in the craft sector of the revolutionary-era economy. Marla Miller, a historian of free women's needlework, has called "artisanal skill" a "process shaped by local relationships" more than "something codified by contract."[27] The identity of a "good clothes-washer" was also relational. The mobile Atlantic community had to see clean laundry as a service worth paying extra for. Together, self-serving masters and black women themselves created the racialized category of "good clothes-washer." Free black women mobilized this new category for their own support by developing reputations as skilled workers.

The unstable nature of a skilled working identity in this period of "relational" identities was most dramatically realized in the use of enslaved women's labor. In 1815 Henrietta Campbell apprenticed her slave Barbara as a seamstress and mantuamaker in Charleston with Hannah Humphries. Hoping to profit from Barbara's skills and willing to wait three years for her to acquire them, Campbell paid Humphries $50 and a barrel of rice. Humphries accepted the money, the rice, and Barbara into her home but did not train her in needle arts. When Campbell discovered the trick, she took Humphries to court to recover not only her original investment but also the wages of $6 per month that Barbara would have earned her, had Humphries not monopolized her time for free. Campbell saw Barbara as a potential specialist because she hoped to benefit from the increased value of her labor. Humphries saw Barbara as a source of free labor. Without training or access to capital, Barbara saw her worth reduced to the monthly wage of a general laborer.[28]

Given the uncertainties of skill being rewarded in the service economy, the presence of potential customers alone was not enough to create niches of autonomy for the poor and enslaved. In Charleston, enslaved women were encouraged to apply their talents to make extra money; in fact, white Charlestonians periodically worried that the presence of industrious slaves sapped the will and ability of poor whites to get by.[29] Enslaved women in Newport, who lived in smaller households under more intense oversight from white owners, were not able to use the prerogatives of the market in the same manner. The lack of clamor surrounding their commercial activities suggests either that Newport whites were unconcerned with expressions of physical and economic autonomy on the part of slaves or that those expressions were too few to raise objections.[30]

Domestic services were mundane, but the intersection of the market and the household at the cash nexus had economic and social ramifications that echoed into the nineteenth century. Someone who paid a specific fee for housekeeping might more freely complain about the level of service. In return, a woman serving non-kin might be more inclined to set limits on what she would do. These tensions occasionally boiled over in public disputes between the providers and the consumers of women's work, as boarders protested the quality of housekeeping and diners demanded the right to eat and drink as much as they desired. While the particulars varied, all combatants shared a common assumption that women's work had economic value, whether the disgruntled diner paid the woman who cooked, cleaned, and served directly or paid her husband, father, or master. Financial gain, rather than affectionate care, motivated the female worker, a fact that would become increasingly disturbing for observers in the nineteenth century, with the emergence of the middle-class home as a highly sentimentalized ideal. As Wendy

Gamber observes, boarders in the mid-nineteenth century complained about boardinghouse keepers' parsimony "in part because they feared they were getting less than their money's worth, in part because assiduous frugality exposed the economic underpinnings of the relationships in which they were enmeshed."[31] If, in the minds of some white women, working at home and reading the sentimental words of ladies' magazines and domestic manuals, "the labor and economic value of housework ceased to exist," for many others, mistresses and servants, the precise economic value of that work was a matter of daily calculation.[32]

People on the move in revolutionary-era port cities did not demand an angel of domesticity in a boardinghouse or a selfless laundress. The Atlantic service economy was commercial and the terms by which women worked commercial, as well. Within that context, providers and consumers of women's work tested each other over prices and quality. As they jostled for good customers or good deals, urban residents probed the limits of "skill" and the meaning of specialization in defining service work.

Atlantic Goods and the Raw Materials of Work

Newport and Charleston developed into commercial centers through a mixture of favorable geography, entrepreneurial zeal, supportive laws, and historical accident. Both found a combination of products and markets that enabled them to thrive in the years leading up to the American Revolution primarily as trading communities. For Charleston, this was the staple agriculture of rice and indigo, made possible by the work of slaves cultivating and processing on large plantations surrounding the city, and the slave trade itself. Charleston was the collection point for staples preparing for export as well as the tons of goods and thousands of people arriving from ports around the Atlantic.[33] Newport's industry depended on the sea—to bring in headmatter (the valuable oil in the head cavity of sperm whales) from whaling voyages and molasses from the West Indies, to carry rum back out to the ports of the Atlantic, and to transport enslaved Africans. Of all the British North American colonies, tiny Rhode Island exported the most goods per person, depending upon coastal trade and the African trade for its livelihood.[34]

This trading economy brought a wave of lower-priced goods to urban lives that changed how people ate, dressed, amused themselves, reckoned with one another, and supported their families. The increased volume of goods and their use in new rituals of socializing among a mobile population has earned the title of "consumer revolution"; cities such as Newport and Charleston were among the first to experience the transformation in the American colonies. As we will see in Chapter 6, women's access to the new goods caused a firestorm of controversy among critics who saw female consumers as driven purely by status competition and frivolity.

A significant number of women, however, bought imported goods not for what they could say about the shopper, but for how they could be translated into money. In fact, in seeking ways to make money, women became key nodes in the distribution of these goods through the economy. Female shopkeepers stocked dry goods and millinery, offering customers a diverse range of finished goods imported from Europe.[35] Tavern keepers depended increasingly on hard liquors, distilled from imported sugar or imported whole, as well as foreign wines like Madeira.[36] Poor servants and slaves ran away from their employers with clothing made from imported fabrics that found a profitable second life in underground and secondhand economies. All of these small glass-by-glass or shoe-by-shoe transactions, when taken together, amounted to a major force in the circulation of imports.

The business strategies of women working in the Atlantic service community depended on the integration of imported goods with "domestic" services. Tavern keepers, for example, served imported beverages and provided a complement of services that many poor women offered separately. They supplied food and space for entertainment, housed and fed boarders, and sold items to make extra money. Ann Little Norcliffe Cross, who operated a tavern in Charleston from 1769 to the late 1780s, even made a pair of stockings and did the washing for William Huggins for a time in 1775.[37] Proprietors of larger taverns also took on expenses and reaped the benefits of enterprises that went beyond an extension of household duties, managing financial matters independently and pursuing innovations in order to attract customers. Abigail Stoneman, who ran several popular taverns and coffeehouses in Newport in the years before the Revolution, advertised amenities like billiard tables and space for dancing to interest her patrons and highlighted the imported delights that could be had within, calling her establishment variously a "coffeehouse" or "tea-house, etc." In 1769, she advised the public that "she has been at the Expence of enlarging her House, and making an elegant ROOM 35 Feet in Length, with many other suitable Advantages, for their better Reception."[38] Her ability to make capital improvements like this set Stoneman apart as a particularly wealthy and successful businesswoman.

Stocking the libations that customers demanded required frequent purchases. In January 1769, for example, Stoneman shopped at Samuel Brenton's store on eleven separate occasions. Six times that month she purchased limes and rum, five times she purchased loaf sugar, and four times she bought playing cards.[39] Women who kept smaller establishments followed the same practices. Newport merchant Nathaniel

Coggeshall sold rum, Madeira, claret, and cards to seven regular female customers in the 1760s, each of whom received a replenishment of their rum supply about every three days.[40] The practice of buying a few shillings' worth at a time was a regular feature of the alcohol business. More than forty years later, Sarah Wakefield purchased sherry, Madeira, and raspberry cordial in addition to sugar, coffee, and candles to serve guests at her Charleston establishment in small, weekly increments.[41]

Women who sold alcoholic drinks thus interacted with merchants, distillers, shopkeepers, or auctioneers every week. In the course of these transactions, they arranged credit, reported on customer preferences, and gathered information about upcoming shipments. Their interactions in turn shaped the businesses of their more widely connected suppliers. While merchants imported alcohol and groceries in large quantities, they doled them out in smaller, regular increments to their most familiar customers, the tavern keepers. Leading merchants depended on these women and their sometimes frustratingly intermittent payments to sustain their own businesses.

Female shopkeepers had an even stronger connection with Atlantic commerce, since the shopkeeper's livelihood depended on the relationship between the urban consumers and the international suppliers (Figure 7).[42] Smaller shopkeepers kept close tabs on international trade through business contracts with merchants or at the regular auctions of overstock and damaged goods. Wealthier shopkeepers had direct access to European credit and selection, a connection they emphasized in their advertisements with the words "just imported!" or "a fresh supply." Prominent milliners and shopkeepers even named the ship captains who had ferried their supplies, confidently promoting their business connections as part of their value. In September 1760, Susannah Crokatt, Eleanor Dryden, and Mary Cooper all advertised goods recently brought to Charleston by Captain Strachan.[43]

Free women were concentrated at the level of smaller retailers who operated between the local and the Atlantic economies. Most obtained their stocks of imported fabric and notions—horn buttons, thread, scissors, felt hats—from city merchants and relied on their generous and lenient credit. Margaret Nichols stocked her dry goods shop with purchases from Newport merchant Jabez Carpenter, weighing the quality and utility of goods from "linnin chex" to "black chaimber pots" to "alspise." Sometimes she paid in cash on the same day that she made new purchases; other times, she brought cash to Carpenter after the fact. Anticipating her customers' various needs and varying incomes, Nichols would, in the same trip, stock up on cheap and fine handkerchiefs, small and large platters and plates, and narrow and wide tape.[44] Her attention to price points, combined with her extension of consumer credit to the

Mary Maylem,

At the Sign of the FAN, in Thames-Street, hath juſt imported a compleat and genteel Aſſortment of SILKS and other Goods, conſiſting of

Corded and ſpotted Luteſtrings, figur'd ditto, ¾ and ¼ ell changeable Luteſtring, blue, green-brown and changeable Mantuas, pink and brown Ducapes, black Paduſoy, Perſian and Taffeta's, black, white, green, blue, pink and crimſon Sattin, and Pe, longs, cloth colour'd ditto, Perſian and Sarſnets of all colours, Lawns and Cambricks, undreſt ſtrip'd and dreſt figur'd Gauzes, white and black ſilk Nettings, blond and trólly Laces of all ſorts, a great variety of new faſhion'd Ribbons, ebony, bone Paddle-Stick, bamboo and ſilver plated Fans, of the neateſt kind, kid, lamb, ſilk and cotton Gloves and Mits of all ſorts, both women's and children's, men's ſilk Stockings and Gloves, black and white Cat-gut, figur'd Modes, white Taffeta Handkerchiefs, black ditto, wax Necklaces and Ear-rings, Garnets, black and white Feathers for Hats, ſtrip'd cotton Hollands, white Callico, fine book Muſlin, purple Chintzes, dark ground and fancy ditto, blue and white Peneaſcos and Bengals, of the beſt ſort, Ginghams, ſilk Shoes, ſilver Turbans and Tippets, cotton ditto, ſummer Cloaks and Hats ready made. Gauze Handkerchiefs, calcutta's, brolios and Pruſſian Mantuas, cap and hat Wires, breaſt and head Flowers, women's and children's Bonnets, boy's Jockeys, Iriſh Linens, Dowlaſs, Checks and Sheetings, Tammies and Shalloons, chip Hats and Bonnets, men's Cravats, children's Morocco Shoes, women's black Calimanco and Everlaſting ditto, Stays and wove Stays, ſilk and linen handkerchiefs, boy's worſted Stockings, ſtone, ſhoe and knee Buckles, Broaches, ſtone Necklaces & Ear-rings, fine Dandriff Combs, white Swanſkin, women's and miſſes Umbrellas, excellent Bohea and Hyſon Tea, Loaf Sugar by the Quantity, Flour by the Barrel, Tilloch's Snuff by the Dozen, all which will be ſold at the cheapeſt Rate. Likewiſe a Number of good Trunks.

All Perſons who will pleaſe to favour her with their Cuſtom may depend on being uſed in the moſt honourable Manner, and treated with the greateſt Civility; as the moſt unexperienced in the different Qualities of Goods, ſhall be charged not a Farthing more than the moſt knowing.

Figure 7. Mary Maylem's advertisement is designed to impress potential buyers with the variety and volume of imported goods. A note at the bottom reassures timid shoppers. *Newport Mercury*, May 2–9, 1768. Courtesy the Rhode Island Historical Society (RHi X3 7896).

middling and poor, enabled a wide range of the population to participate in and support international commerce.

Shopkeeping women drew on extensive business ties rather than
single sources of imported goods, just as their male counterparts did.
In 1798, shopkeeper Martha Stukes Surtell visited B. Booth and Company several times each month for replenishments of her stock of dim-
ity, gingham, humhum, and other fabrics. When John Lowe received a
shipment of leather slippers, she purchased thirty-five pairs in various
styles. In October, Annely & Lewis's appealing selection of cloth, bobbins, padlocks, mustard, and perfume prompted her to make a large £83
purchase. Purchasing on credit as she made her way through the city, she
placated her suppliers with regular cash payments in small increments
toward the balance of her accounts.[45] Surtell and women like her were
able to serve an urban clientele because the merchants who imported
the goods sought out an expanding network of retailers to market the
goods to different members of the community. Together, the goods and
the credit system that ushered them onto American shores provided the
resources for female businesses.

Goods brought enslaved women in search of economic opportunities
into the streets, where cash rather than credit ruled. In spite of constant
complaints over the years and desultory attempts to enforce the provisions of the 1740 Negro Act, which prohibited slaves from trading on
their own accounts, slave women dominated the Charleston city marketplace.[46] These women hawked produce and finished goods and were
renowned for sharp business dealings. One observer objected that they
"*buy* and *sell* on *their own accounts*, what they please, in order to pay their
wages, and get so much more for themselves as they can; for their owners care little, how their slaves get money, so they are paid."[47] Even more
than laundering, huckstering provided enslaved women with cash profits and a measure of physical and economic autonomy.

White urban widows benefited from the autonomy of slaves, as well,
and were determined to protect their marketing income. When in 1783
new regulations sought once again to clamp down on the activities of
slaves in trades and the marketplace, nine Charleston widows petitioned
their assembly for relief on the grounds that they had "been used to send
their Baskets out in the Streets of Charles Town with Goods, wares, and
Merchandize by their Servants, in Order to expose them for sale and Obtain an Honest Livelihood in defence of their fatherless children."[48] The
widows considered themselves entitled to, and were dependent upon,
the market work of their slaves. This did not mean that the white women
sat idly by. Two of these petitioners were struggling seamstresses; one of
them, Elizabeth Gilbert, also had herself listed as a shopkeeper in the
1790 directory.[49] So it was not necessarily fear of public exposure that

encouraged white women to send their slaves into the market in place of themselves. The expertise and relative independence of their slaves were valuable assets to women in need of cash.

Money and mobility placed enslaved women in competition with free ones. One resolution in 1775 asserted that greater measures needed to be taken "to prevent slaves being suffered to cook Bake sell fruits dry goods and otherwise Traffic Barter &ct in the Public Market & streets of Charles town, and by those means preventing many poor & industrious families from obtaining an honest livelihood."[50] The references to poor "families" and to items like fruit, baked goods, and dry goods, all of which were commonly linked with female activity, implicitly acknowledged competition between black and white women as hawkers of goods on the streets of the city. Black and white women competed for this segment of the urban service economy, and often the enslaved women came out ahead.

When entreaties to the Grand Jury failed, whites charged enterprising black women with theft. Charleston newspapers ran lost and found advertisements for articles like the fan "STOPPED from a Negro Girl who offered it for Sale," in 1774.[51] The day Thomas Corker discovered six fifty-pound bills of credit missing from his desk, he immediately thought of Lizette, an older slave woman belonging to the widow Hester Brown. As he ominously noted in an announcement for the newspaper, Lizette "attends the Lower Market, and frequently has Things to dispose of there; it is therefore very probable, that she may endeavour to exchange some of them [the bills] for Goods to sell again; but it is hoped, People will be careful how they take large Bills of Negros, unless they can prove in what Manner they came by them."[52]

Whites were ambivalent about slaves' agency in the marketplace. Corker called Lizette a thief and suspected that she would use her criminal profits for personal enrichment by purchasing more goods to sell. He further tarred her regular sales activities with the same brush of suspicion, noting that she frequently had "Things to dispose of" at the market. Brown, who relied upon her slave's ingenuity in the marketplace, quickly came to Lizette's defense by agreeing that a slave conspiracy had indeed deprived Corker of his money; however, it was his own slave "Katy [who] was the Thief, and has some Accomplices whom she wants to screen."[53] Enterprise on the part of one's slaves could cut both ways.

Enslaved women did not travel the seas of the Atlantic as part of the "floating proletariat" that their male counterparts did and so have not been recognized in the ranks of Atlantic creoles. But by tapping into the flow of goods around the Atlantic, they solved one of the problems that all enterprising women, free and enslaved, faced: limited access to capital. While historians have focused on their market activities as defiant social statements or emulative gestures of consumption, women like Lizette can best be understood as entrepreneurs experienced at turning goods into money and vice versa. One payoff to her regular trade in goods was access to the "large bills" Corker complained about. Corker's assumption that Lizette would have no trouble using bills of credit to her own advantage challenges the image of poor and enslaved women confined to petty trade and local barter. Clearly, imported goods gave women's activities a wider scope and a surer financial base.

Imports plus access to a marketplace was not a simple recipe for female autonomy, however. In Charleston, female slaves' expertise and contacts as sellers in the city markets involved them in suspected (and real) opportunities for theft; it also facilitated their ability to "steal themselves." Forty-five-year-old Mary Ann's master acknowledged the connections among slave women in Charleston when he advertised her disappearance from his house and speculated that she was still in the city, having probably "borrowed some other Wench's badge to get work."[54] Enslaved Newport women, though, rarely ran away from their owners, in spite of their own access to imports. Newport account books include entries paid for or delivered "per your Negro woman" and Newport mistresses complained about slave theft. But the enslaved women of the northern port lacked the systematic opportunities and extensive personal connections to convert goods to money and freedom. Cash earnings or the experience of driving a hard bargain at a market stall did not in and of themselves translate into meaningful autonomy. The ties that constructed marketplace opportunity shaped the meanings that northern and southern women attached to their business activities.

The availability of imported goods was disrupted by embargo, war, and occupation. During the Revolution, for example, auction announcements for real estate, livestock, and bulk goods replaced the enticing lists of imported goods and services in the newspaper columns of both cities. One foreign critic observed Newport in the late 1780s as "an empty place . . . the shops are miserably stocked and offer for sale only coarse cloth, packets of matches, baskets of apples, and other cheap goods."[55] Retailing intensified the link between female trade and the wider Atlantic world that was implicit in bartering, trading, and selling of home-produced goods. The retailer's connections put her in a position of power, in that she served as conduit of and educator about new and fashionable items from abroad. But hers was also a position of vulnerability, since she, like all retailers, depended on volatile currencies, uncertain credit, shifting demand, and distant supply. Retailers were consumers themselves, of a significant magnitude, and targets of the same suspicions and patriotic exhortations that erupted over consumption in the political crises of the late eighteenth and early nineteenth centuries.

Linking the fortunes of female retailers to specific Atlantic market fluctuations is tricky, since absolute numbers of female shopkeepers and tavern keepers are hard to come by for any city. Women running smaller businesses were less likely to advertise in newspapers or directories and their smaller-scale debts were settled by justices of the peace more often than courts of common pleas.[56] From the available evidence, the diverging fortunes of Newport and Charleston after the Revolution indicate that access to the Atlantic world was key to survival for these women. Pre-revolutionary Newport was home to prominent female shopkeepers whose businesses in imported fabric, housewares, and luxury items involved them in credit connections with the city's largest merchants. Female shopkeepers appeared regularly in court, seeking compensation for book debts too long unpaid. After the war, these kinds of businesswomen disappear from the docket of the Court of Common Pleas and are an infrequent presence as advertisers in early nineteenth-century newspapers. Pre-revolutionary Charleston had many female advertisers in its papers, but few female shopkeepers developed the scale of business and professional connections to bring them into the courts along with male merchants. Book debt and promissory notes, the vital currency of urban trade, account for few female court appearances prior to the war. Late in the century, free women emerged as debtors and creditors in their own right, shopkeepers prominently among them. Charleston's wealth and continued trade ties to England made shopkeeping a viable female livelihood.

Shopkeepers and tavern keepers mixed imported goods with service to produce pleasing selections and convivial evenings around the punchbowl. For their part, women who processed imported textiles literally knit together the consumption of these goods with productive labors. Using their skills in sewing, spinning, and knitting, free women earned credit from local shopkeepers in order to buy imported products of Atlantic commerce. Merchant Jabez Carpenter's stock of sugar, tea, chocolate, and fabric proved a spur to Susannah Reed, who spun a few ounces of candlewick, knitted up five pairs of mittens, and made a pair of thread stockings in 1759 to acquire these items for her table and household.[57] Her work, motivated in part by a desire for imported goods, can be seen as an American contribution to what historian Jan de Vries has called the "industrious revolution," whereby families reallocated female labor in order to acquire more goods in the market.[58]

Reed's handiwork, in turn, entered Atlantic circulation, when the candlewick she spun was dipped into candles made from spermaceti oil and exported in large quantities on merchant ships.[59] The women who earned consumer credit by working on projects "put out" to them were deeply and systematically connected to the markets of Atlantic trade.

Rather than use domestic skills to participate in a local service economy animated by Atlantic trends, these women were directly engaged in Atlantic commerce. Under a "putting out" arrangement, merchants gave out raw materials to women who then finished them in their own homes, on their own time. The cotton that merchant Aaron Lopez put out to be spun by women like Niobe Austins was imported from the West Indies; the trousers, frocks, and jackets that Mary Wood sewed for him from coarse ticlinburgh and oznaburgh could find themselves on ships traveling to New York or Jamaica to outfit slaves, sailors, and other laborers.[60]

In spite of this close connection, neither the specific demands of transatlantic customers nor the specific prices of desirable imported goods dictated the work patterns of women who supplied Carpenter and Lopez. The productivity of Mary Wood, Lopez's most prolific female sewer, ebbed and flowed, so that one month she might make nothing, and another £86 worth of trousers, jackets, and great coats.[61] She came to Lopez's shop frequently between 1769 and 1775, sometimes to drop off finished goods, sometimes to make purchases, sometimes to collect more cloth and trimmings to bring home for manufacture, and at other times to perform a mixture of these activities. Like all of the women who worked for Lopez, Wood scheduled her own work pace and returned clothing to Lopez as she finished it, rather than in batches. When he handed out "Ticlinburgh with trimming for 6 Trowsers," she might return in a week with three pairs of trousers, plus a jacket from the last batch of materials, or four pairs of trousers in five days, and another four pairs a few days after that. The fluctuations in the rate at which Wood sewed trousers indicate that her own work schedule was dictating production rather than the demands of Lopez's customers. While those customers provided the business, their pressure on Wood was mediated through Lopez, the man who took the risk and provided the raw materials for free.

Atlantic markets may not have shaped the pace of women's craft work, but they did influence its availability. After the Revolution, craft work in Charleston and Newport was threatened by the same cheap imports that drew many women into working for money. In 1789, sixty-seven Charleston seamstresses signed a petition asking the South Carolina legislature to increase the tariff on imported ready-made clothing to protect their businesses. They presented themselves as "reduced to indigent circumstances [by the loss of male relatives during the war], and obliged to earn Subsistence for themselves (& some of them for their helpless offspring) by their needles," but unable to find enough work to do so. They blamed "the great importation of ready made Cloaths Such as Shirts Stocks, thin Jaccats & Breeches, Slops & millinary of every kind that your Petitioners can make here . . . [from] a Nation whose policy it is to employ their own industrious poor rather than give bread to foreigners."[62] The petitioners were keenly aware of the international context of their labor; their competition came not from fellow Charlestonians, they believed, but from British women whose earnings were protected by national policies that recognized their value.

Joined together for the purpose of petitioning, the Charleston seamstresses earned money with their needles under disparate circumstances. The majority were probably poor widows and wives; most did not appear in the 1790 city directory and many belonged to families who were not listed, either. At least one of this group was probably a free black woman. Only half were able to sign their names with more than a mark. For a few of these women, the needle trades were a regular, recognized business; for others, it was one of several income strategies, combined with teaching or retailing. The collective nature of the petition was unusual, but the common thread joining women from multiple social circumstances was not, since work like sewing was flexible, could be done with little investment, and drew upon available raw materials: in this case, imported ones. In rural communities this work might still be exchanged among women as barter. In a port city of the Atlantic, those shirts and thin jackets were fixed with a price that had to compete internationally.[63]

The anxiety over import competition dramatized related changes in the economy that reconfigured the context of women's economic activities. A poem in the *Newport Mercury* in 1785 spoke with the voice of a poor widow:

The time was once when I could spin,
And gain my children bread;
What my industry then brought in,
My little babes were fed;
. . . .
The market-men who use'd to call,
With butter, meat, and grain,
Now pass me by, for money's all,
And that they ask in vain;
. . . .
I ask for work, they tell me "nay,
'Tis cheaper to import,"
And while they flaunt in such array,
I lose my whole suport.[64]

The sad picture conveyed in this poem was more an expression of anxiety about the changing economy and women's relationship to it than a precisely accurate description of the decline of homespun or in-kind payments, given that both persisted into the nineteenth century.[65] But the speaker's reference to feeding her "little babes," like the seamstresses' plea for "bread," underlines the fact that women's work for money was not necessarily driven by the desire to participate in the Atlantic economy for the sake of new comforts and imported excitement. Mary Wood may have sewed trousers to buy sugar and calico, but many women saw Atlantic goods as means, not ends. Women's pivotal place in circulating these goods was therefore not necessarily an endorsement of imported culture as much as a willingness to work with it.

Family Ties and Female Earnings

Women who were publicly enlisting the help of others to earn money—those petitioning the government for licenses or appealing to a dead husband's former customers—usually justified their activities by referring to the needs of their own "little babes." They spoke in two registers as they made their pleas. They were apologetic: only the desperate situation of the fatherless children had emboldened the mother to seek the favor of the benevolent official or buying public. They were assertive: as financially responsible adults, they had to find a way to support their families. Women's roles as economic actors were linked, as were men's, to the need to provide for themselves and their dependents. While this was taken for granted with free male employment, free women asserted the connection to secure public sympathy and support. Taking them at their word means untangling the connections of family, trade, and business activity that shaped female work in the urban economy.

Certainly, invoking family responsibilities was no empty ploy. Women's work bridged the demands of Atlantic markets and families in ways that changed both. The classic "family economy" of premodern farming families, which depended on the collaboration of dependents living in the same household under the guidance of the household head, had transformed in the cities of the late eighteenth century into a sometimes desperate collection of strategies for mutual support among kin and non-kin members of a houseful.[66] Instead of farming and trading, individuals worked for often uncertain payments at locations around the city. By the early nineteenth century, industrialization began to shift the terms of employment further, as many kinds of trades moved from workshops to early factories. Each transformation pulled at the obligations of family members toward one another and challenged fundamental ideas about what made men independent or women productive.

Urban working men responded to these changes by adopting a language and politics of artisan republicanism. Although many did not own land, they proclaimed what they saw as their rightful place in the home and polity through ownership of artisan skills and vigorously defended their skilled, productive work from lower-wage piecework performed by women and children. Craftsmen who seemed poised to lose the most from a market revolution championed this ideology loudest in public parades and political rallies. [67] Their goal was to maintain their independence as free men, on which rested their public place as citizens and their family position as ultimate authority.

There was no place for working women under the umbrella of artisan republicanism. Instead, in making their own claims to independence through economic activity, free women chose words that echoed the language of commercial service. Every newspaper of the revolutionary era was filled with the peculiar blend of supplication and assertion common to the retail language of merchants and shopkeepers appealing to discerning customers. Shopkeepers "beg[ged] leave" to inform customers of new arrivals that were "best," "choice," and "a very grand assortment." Service workers had to please, but they also had to stake their claim to skill. The rhetoric women employed to secure their families' livelihood was fully a part of the modern marketplace, however "traditional" it may sound. Words reflected the reality of the fundamental link between female service work and international commerce as much as between service work and family obligation.

For women as for men, family served more than a rhetorical function in shaping work lives. Just as relatives trained free children in craft skills, so, too, did family ties shape the work lives of enslaved women. Mothers, sisters, and fathers provided education in skills that could mean the difference between field work and more autonomous city house work. Masters and mistresses, looking to ease and enrich their own families, capitalized on specialized knowledge that had been passed from slave mothers to their daughters. For that reason, Alice Izard thought her son Henry should keep his slave Juba in his house rather than hiring her out to another Charleston woman. "I only wish she could be useful to you, & learn to be a housekeeper, & Pastry Cook as her Mother is." Alice was confident that Juba's mother would "take care to teach her such things as will make her useful to you, & Emma."[68]

Relationships with kin influenced the kinds of independence that slaves carved out of city life through their work. Numerous runaway slave advertisements in the South linked an enslaved woman's market activities with her personal connections. Margaret Remington's slaves Phillis and Elsey were "well known in town, having been used to sell oysters for these 13 years past" when they ran away; Elsey, at least, was suspected of joining her mother, who lived on a nearby plantation.[69] The frequent acknowledgment of "connections" suggests that enslaved women sustained emotional and economic relationships outside of their owners' homes, often with their own kin. Acting in financial partnership could strengthen enslaved families as cooperative ventures; it could also change the dynamics of enslaved families. On the plantations that surrounded Charleston, male slaves traded with their masters for money more often than female slaves did, perhaps permitting enslaved men to act as the economic heads of their own families. Within the city itself, however, enslaved women were prominent and regular traders and sources of goods for whites and blacks in the urban population, and would not have needed their husbands' intercession. These women's economic contributions to their own families drew upon and may have strengthened their independent sense of themselves. [70]

Free people took extensive advantage of family ties when they needed workers, connections, or investors.[71] Ebenezer Rumreil, a Newport shopkeeper, died in late 1743, leaving his wife, Sarah, as administrator of his estate. Following the common practice of widows, Sarah, after settling his debts, took up running the business and began to sell cloth, thread, pins, and other dry goods in her own name. Many of her husband's former clients continued to purchase from her shop and borrow money from her. Sarah's children helped with the business in a variety of ways. Her daughter, Sukey, made purchases on her mother's accounts in town; sons Ebenezer, Thomas, and Simon each in turn learned the family business by helping to keep her accounts and pursue her debtors before launching into his own venture.[72] After their apprenticeships with their mother, Ebenezer and Thomas themselves became shopkeepers, Ebenezer taking over the dry goods store of another Newport man and Thomas ten years later advertising dry goods for sale in his own shop. Running separate businesses, the family members remained financially linked through credit transactions with other merchants and shopkeepers.[73]

Ties that sustained linked family businesses like the Rumreils' also threatened to pull them down together. In 1767, Newporter Thomas Robinson asked his own brother to intervene in the Rumreil family finances, "my Friend Thos. Rumreil having Requested of me, to desire thy assistnce in obtaining the Act of Insolvency for his Bror. Ebenezer Rumreil." "His whole Family," Robinson explained, "lives now upon his mother who is a widow & Considerably advanced in years." Robinson likely spoke for the whole Newport community in praising the widow's hard work and regretting the obligations that an imprudent son had entangled her in: "She was left a widow with a Family of small children which she brot. up Reputably by her industry and is at this time bound to pay the bigest part of her sons debts & is not of ability without distressing herselfe to pay the Remainder."[74]

Dispersal of business expertise within a family was supposed to ensure the enterprise's persistence in the wake of a father's or mother's death, though it could not guarantee a widow like Sarah Rumreil an easy life.[75] In the colonial period, taking up the family business was advertised as evidence of competence and experience, regardless of the gender of the family members involved. Abigail and Mehitable Downs announced their coffeehouse business with assurances that "from long experience that they have had, in conducting the same, under their mother, they shall be enabled to render the utmost satisfaction to any gentlemen who may think proper to make trial of the same."[76] Charlestonians Margaret and James Oliver announced that they would carry on their mother's butcher business, and sought the patronage of "their late mother's friends and good customers."[77] Customers and local officials responded with both charitable acknowledgment of the deceased and the presumption that the new owner was competent. The South Carolina House of Representatives even stated that their decision to appoint the widow Ann Timothy as the state printer was "in Consequence of the Services rendered to it by her late Husband," the former state printer, who had himself inherited the business from his widowed mother.[78]

Charleston couples in the late colonial period sometimes practiced an alternative to the family business by establishing separate but mutually enhancing enterprises. William Adams and his wife took out a joint advertisement in 1767, offering his services as writing master and hers in making clothing, teaching children to sew, and washing and starching fine fashionable clothing. The pair also collected boarding income from gentlemen and schoolchildren willing to live in their Elliott Street cellar.[79] Like other pre-revolutionary couples, the Adamses were capitalizing on a unique appetite for acquiring a variety of social graces in one location that was emblematic of the early, expanding years of Charlestonian culture. Newport readers were never enticed with the prospect of one-stop shopping at a husband-and-wife establishment in the same way. Although husbands and wives pursued different occupations—a tailor might be married to a schoolteacher, or a joiner to a seamstress—and any couple might take in boarders in addition to other enterprises, they did not advertise themselves as a multitalented family to potential customers. The family connection was an asset to those who carried on the same business, but evidently not for independent ventures.

After the Revolution the open advertisement of both inherited businesses and husband/wife purveyors of gentility declined. The population upheavals of the revolutionary period may have dispersed and discouraged long-term family businesses. The economic climate was changing in other ways, too, as the number and specialization of businesses increased. Those who had the money to advertise their trade promised specialization rather than versatility. While family ties remained important in the funding and operation of businesses, they were no longer touted to entice potential customers. In some ways, the family connection went underground.

Husbands and wives in Newport had little reason to tout their individual businesses, given the assumptions about men's and women's lives encoded in the prevailing law of coverture. Throughout the colonial period and well into the nineteenth century, courts used this English common-law principle to define the legal standing of free women. Under coverture, free married women were declared to be "covered" by the legal identity of their husbands. They could not make contracts, incur debts, sue, or be sued on their own behalf. Unless they made special arrangements, they did not own or fully control property they brought to marriage or acquired during marriage.[80] This fundamental legal principle threw up many obstacles to free women's enterprises, since it placed economic responsibility and ownership of capital in the hands of a husband over a wife. At the same time, the concept of coverture hobbled husbands and wives with each other's debts.

Husbands and wives who proclaimed their separate businesses in Charleston, however, operated in a legal climate that was unusually receptive to the idea of independent economic activity in marriage. South Carolina, along with Pennsylvania and, at the end of the eighteenth century, Massachusetts, recognized that separating the finances of free husbands and wives was sometimes the best way to shore up a family's ability to support itself and keep it off the poor rolls. While a seriously indebted husband could find it near impossible to obtain credit, his wife, if her property was secured from his debts, might be able to make new and valuable business connections, thereby sustaining the family. To facilitate these arrangements, a series of statutes created the legally recognized identity of "feme sole trader." First adopted in South Carolina in 1712, these statutes drew on another English legal tradition, known as the "Custom of London," in reference to the many married women who traded on their own accounts in the capital city. Under feme sole trader laws, a married woman could carry on independent business ventures, sue and be sued for debts, and dispose of property on her own, provided she had the overall consent of her husband.[81] To the community and the legal system, she became a "feme sole"—in other words, a "woman alone," treated in economic matters as if she were unmarried.

Although most free women in South Carolina did not seek out feme sole status, the assumptions revealed by the petitions of those who did— that husbands and wives might have separate pursuits, that the general economic health of the family benefited from female enterprise, that a couple might need more than one source of credit—were widespread. When they requested legal recognition as femes soles, women and their husbands typically offered a general argument that it would be "conducive to the interest of [the] family" for them to maintain separate accounts. Sometimes, they detailed specific financial hardships driving the wife into desperate measures, but the overall impression these documents give is of routine, rather than exceptional, economic realities.[82] Even colonies (and later states) without explicit feme sole trader laws maintained some legal doctrines that helped free women support themselves and their children in the absence or failure of their husbands.[83] None of these provisions was meant to champion women's rights, but they did recognize potential conflicts in the economic interests of married couples and saw female earnings, however undervalued, as part of the solution.

Divergent legal cultures shaped the working strategies of women in the Atlantic service economy. Ann Cross, the Charleston tavern keeper, maintained her feme sole trader status during her marriage to Paul Cross. Since her husband was a slave trader and merchant frequently away on slaving ventures, it was far more practical for her accounts with local merchants for rum, beer, sugar, or cheese to be in her own name. She managed her own stock and paid her own debts. In contrast, Abigail Stoneman, the Newport tavern keeper who operated in a community without feme sole trader laws, closed her tavern, sold her billiard table, and moved away from Newport when she remarried in 1774. Both women used their earnings as part of a family strategy. They reinvested their profits into their businesses, expanding their inventories with new imported goods and improving their services for the Atlantic transients in their cities. Ann Cross, who had feme sole status, also used her own earnings to pay for the education of her son from a previous marriage, Robert Little. She may have felt a particular responsibility to pay for Robert's school because he was not the offspring of her current marriage.

Cross's desire and ability to earmark some portion of her profits was typical. Although wages were frequently enfolded into the family's budget, a broad range of women had specific, individual plans for their earnings. In 1802, Newport resident "Black Rachel" spent twelve days washing to earn the money to purchase a cherry Pembroke table from Samuel Vinson for £1.16. Free black Sally Martin used her earnings as a pastry cook to purchase the enslaved Felix in 1814. Jane Ball stated that she conducted her poultry sales because she "wanted the profits to get other matters," especially tea and writing materials.[84]

Jane Ball's enterprise provided her with "egg money"—the small sums of discretionary personal income that free women in early modern England and colonial America expected as their due even in marriage. Urban and rural free women throughout the American colonies experienced a degree of economic autonomy as a result of local trade. Most of their purchases with this kind of money were either for food or, like Ball's, for imported small luxuries. Free women and men constructed a blend of independence and interdependence in their "family economic systems" that emerged from practical considerations and shared Anglo-American ideas about the division of resources and power among members of the same family.[85] The urban marketplace injected additional intermediaries. Jane Ball, ensconced on her plantation for much of the year, sent her poultry and eggs to her son, but he did not sell them. Instead, he and his mother had to wait for their city slaves, Hagar and Mary, to get the best price in the marketplace, a wait that at least once caused Jane to grumble that the state of her finances would improve "if I could get any one to dispose of my little truck."[86] Since she knew that Hagar and Mary were knowledgeable marketeers, however, she did not ask other family members to take on the job themselves. She had to wait on the negotiations of the enslaved part of her household.

When the *Newport Mercury* announced tavern keeper Abigail Stoneman's marriage to Sir John Treville, it saluted her as "a lady descended from a reputable family, of a good genius, a very polite and genteel address, and extremely well accomplished in every branch of family economy."[87] These complimentary words were a poor description of her aggressive, entrepreneurial business practices and the eclectic composition of her "family." In framing her urban tavern, with its dancing and gaming rooms, as a model of thrifty housekeeping, the declaration instead looked back to older understandings of free women's housework as a valued contribution to the family enterprise.[88] The reality had shifted—Stoneman charged money for feeding people, and sued them if they let their tabs run on too long. Prior to her marriage she lived in a house that contained at least two other white women and two blacks, probably slaves who worked in her tavern.[89] And yet the newspaper hailed her as an accomplished, genteel housewife who used her social standing and good manners to welcome guests and oversee the financial health of a household, just as free women in Anglo-American society had done for more than a century.

The dissonance we can hear in the newspaper's words marks the revolutionary period in which Stoneman and the other women of this chapter lived as a transitional one in terms of public discussions of women, family, and paid work. Had Stoneman been born a generation or two later, it is unlikely she would have been hailed as a businesswoman at all, since "female gentility" and "family" were seldom linked with "economy" by the 1820s. The preferred "accomplishments" of nineteenth-century ladies were of the decorative rather than remunerative kind, as was reflected in the sentimental language of separate worlds for "economic" free men and "domestic" free women.[90]

It would be a mistake, however, to confuse one thread of nineteenth-century literary culture for the tapestry of working women's lives in the late eighteenth and early nineteenth centuries. Historians have

discovered that despite the condemnatory political language of work-
ingmen's organizations in the early nineteenth century, not all artisans
faced "proletarianization" and deskilling in the age of manufacturing.[91]
By the same token, not all free women gave up on entrepreneurship in
favor of unpaid nurture to serve their families under these same pres-
sures. In fact, family responsibilities regularly pulled women out into the
Atlantic marketplace.

Family ties shaped any woman's engagement with the Atlantic port
economy, but with considerable flexibility and variety. For the Ball slaves
Hagar and Mary, as well as for free blacks like Sally Martin, who used
her earnings as a city cook to buy the freedom of a relative, the service
economy that developed in Charleston provided discretionary funds they
would be far less likely to have in rural areas. These earnings could be
marshaled to support kin ties that were under constant threat from the
system of chattel slavery. For poor free wives, running a service business
might be enough to pull a family out of a husband's debt. Other women
perceived work as a means to escape a struggling marriage altogether,
and willingly announced their self-divorces in favor of self-support.[92] The
presence of new people and new goods did not always revolutionize family relationships, but it changed women's prospects for economic autonomy significantly, even if they reinvested the proceeds in dependent ties
rather than public markers of independence.

Women in port cities responded to economic change by turning to the
resources of the Atlantic community to earn money; as a group, they
created and sustained an Atlantic service economy. The contours of the
service economy took shape in the unique market culture of each city.
The existence of feme sole trader laws in South Carolina, for example,
which permitted married women to keep their debt and credit separate
from their husbands', may have encouraged separate enterprises within
free families more broadly. Prior to the Revolution, such separate enterprises were prominently advertised—not as partnerships or as a specialist
and "help," but as multiple special services available in a single location.
Rhode Island did not have this legal provision and as a result free women
did not trumpet their family connections unless they were taking up the
same line of work and all (seemingly) pulling together in the family enterprise. The scope and shape of slavery also had a significant impact
on all women's work lives. Charleston's larger slave population meant
that enslaved women's labor played a greater role in household earnings
strategies. A female slave selling and buying in the marketplace might
create more time for the women in her owner's family to sew clothes for
income. Custom also shaped the ubiquitous urban practice of providing
for boarders. Newport women who took in boarders could negotiate and

charge separately for washing and mending clothes, tasks that were enfolded within the "women's work" expected of providers in Charleston.

Although each city's service economy took shape in a particular context of law and custom, the influence of international commerce was paramount. Female proprietors were more common in Newport before than after the Revolution because the city lost the mercantile ties to Europe that fueled the shopkeeping business and because it lost much of the population that had supported the food and entertainment business. Millinery and mantua-making remained lucrative in post-revolutionary Charleston because ties to English goods and training were quickly rebuilt. The pattern was repeated in numerous branches of the urban economy, both in services and in emerging manufacturing niches. For example, the large fortunes accumulating around Charleston encouraged white families to pay for an education in refinements for their daughters, which created opportunities for female schoolteachers in the southern city earlier than in trade-focused Newport. In both cities, competition from sewing and craft work from abroad threatened female livelihoods. As major ports, Newport and Charleston had faster access to potential markets for women's work; Aaron Lopez probably exported most of the ticlinburgh trousers that Mary Wood made. They also were the first to receive competitive imports, which might suit the shopkeepers but devastate the seamstresses.

Urban women's lives as earners were linked to their lives as consumers on several levels. Whether selling their goods or labor, they sought out cash or credit to use in the city marketplace. The kinds of relationships they forged as consumers, in turn, shaped the meaning of their labors. When a Newport woman sewed up a pair of breeches in exchange for tea and calico, she was making a departure from traditional exchanges of eggs for wool. The goods she sought were imported, the person she exchanged with planned to sell the breeches to unknown third parties, and the place of exchange was public and heterosocial. The coin of women's transactions might remain the same over many decades: women washed clothing for Sarah Osborn in exchange for her schooling their children; fifty years later, other women washed clothing for Samuel Vinson in order to purchase stylish furniture. But the context and content of transactions had shifted. Cash accounts acknowledged the variety and value within women's work and imported goods connected timeless female labor with a changing economic and cultural climate.

The reverse is true, as well. The women who created entrepreneurial niches in this Atlantic service economy sustained the trading world by feeding it, clothing it, reproducing it. In the process, female industry partook of unexpected collaborations in the urban economy, such as those between landladies and tenants, or between enslaved women and occupying soldiers. Most of these collaborations were unequal and often one party was looking to exploit the other; independence was unattainable and impractical. Taken together, however, these combinations determined the economic landscape of port cities as much as the well-trod paths from wharf to counting-house.

Chapter 3

Family Credit and Shared Debts

In 1776, Sarah Cantwell responded indignantly and in print to her husband's claim that she had run away from him, taking his credit and good name with her. In the pages of the *South Carolina and American General Gazette* she asserted: "JOHN CANTWELL has the Impudence to advertise me in the Papers, cautioning all persons against crediting me; he never had any Credit till he married me: As for his Bed and Board he mentioned, he had neither Bed nor Board when he married me; I never eloped, I went away before his Face when he beat me."[1] Point-by-point refuting John's claims and displaying her disgust with his pose of aggrieved husband, Sarah linked "credit" to both material possessions (which she had ✔ and he lacked) and financial reliability, which she confidently felt she possessed independently of her husband; in fact, he had benefited from association with her "credit" reputation. Sarah's concern in penning her rebuttal was not merely a point of pride: to function in the daily economy of Atlantic cities, people needed credit, and a woman like Sarah could not afford to be cut off. Doing business in the eighteenth century required the constant extension of credit, whether one was a merchant who imported fine furniture or a shopper who selected a yard of ribbon. Networks of credit bound London merchants to colonial wholesalers to individual retailers to customers to family members and neighbors.[2]

By separating from her abusive husband, Sarah Cantwell put her credit network in jeopardy. Like most free married women, Sarah was a feme covert, restricted under law from borrowing or lending money on her own account. It did not matter whether she was thrifty and prudent compared with her profligate husband. For Charleston's milliners, butchers, or merchants, the ability to account for one's debts was paramount, and since law made the husband, not the wife, financially responsible, most shopkeepers took the precaution of entering debts in their account books under the names of those who could legally be required to pay. Thus the shops at which Sarah Cantwell purchased flour, buttons, or knives would record her debts under John Cantwell's name. Gender, in the context of marital status, trumped "character." At the same time, Charleston proprietors expected married women to make purchases on credit as a matter of course. Wives, daughters, servants, and sons all made purchases and payments on behalf of the joint account; through such practices, a concept that can be called "family credit" prevailed in the urban marketplace. When a man made a public, legal declaration such as John's, he hoped to overturn this expectation and sever his wife's part of the credit web.

In terms of the extension of credit in the revolutionary era, ability to pay ultimately mattered more than gender. The law marked married women in a particular way, but tradespeople regularly extended credit to single women and facilitated the transfer of credit among women and men through a system of third-party reimbursement. Single women and widows who had proved themselves reliable borrowers received credit just as men did, and, like men, could be thrown into debtors' prison. A free woman whose husband had died was held accountable for his debts and had to appear in court as executor, administrator, or devisee of his estate.

There was, however, a specifically gendered element to thinking about credit in the larger sense. "Lady Credit" was a familiar figure in eighteenth-century Anglo-American political discourse, used by polemicists on all sides of debates over public and private debt. To promoters of commerce, she was a well-bred gentlewoman, virtuous and pure, a source of bounty for her country; to detractors, she was mercurial at best—a "Phanatick" subject to ruinous "false fits"; at worst, she was a duplicitous "whore."[3] A female allegorical figure captured the aspects of credit that were particularly mysterious and frustrating for people increasingly reliant on commerce. Credit provided the means for entrepreneurial innovation and economic growth, but dependence on credit made people subject to the whims and manipulations of others. Extending or receiving credit could expose city dwellers to considerable financial risk in an age of personal liability. To recover one's credit and good name, once lost, seemed as impossible as restoring a lady's honor, once tainted.

"Credit" therefore described an embedded marketplace—one in which financial arrangements were guided by personal relationships and personal relationships had a strong economic element to them.[4] Creditors needed to judge the character as well as the financial stability of the people they loaned to, because credit was both a relationship and a contract. The balance between the two elements of credit, however, was shifting in eighteenth-century society. Although informal, personal arrangements of loaning and borrowing persisted, new written tools, such as promissory notes, bills, and bonds facilitated more long-distance lending and borrowing between individuals who did not know each other well. Historians of Britain and America have found that civil courts faced an explosion of credit cases over debts that neighbors and strangers were unable to settle among themselves.[5] Tracing a simultaneous decline in women's debt litigation over the early eighteenth century, some have suggested that the new forms and contractual approach to economic life were hostile to female participation. Cornelia Hughes Dayton concluded that, in the shifting world of credit, "the economic spheres of men and women were diverging in critical ways before the nineteenth century and the separation of home and workplace."[6]

Because the expansion of commercial society in the second half of the eighteenth century depended on many individual shoppers' and retailers' access to credit, tracking women's credit practices is essential to understanding consumer culture in Atlantic port cities. If women were cut off from access to formal credit in the late eighteenth century, they would indeed have been forced to the margins of the consumer revolution. Instead, in the court records of the seventy years between 1750 and 1820, at the height of the Atlantic consumer economy, there is no evidence of increasing detachment of women from the business of everyday life. Fluctuation and persistence describe urban women's involvement in what Dayton calls the "litigated economy." More significant, behind the raw numbers is the story of how commercial culture, by demanding credit, drew women as well as men into complex, diverse economic relationships.

The Litigated Economy and Tools of Credit

Credit, as a familiar, daily phenomenon, crystallized in three kinds of written agreements: book debt, bonds, and promissory notes. Whether these documents recorded years of mutual trading or an impulse purchase of one last round at the local tavern, they also dominated the dockets of the courts of common pleas, which handled civil cases in each colony or state. In the revolutionary era, debt collection was a routine part of court proceedings that rarely involved courtroom confrontations. By the time cases reached the court, most plaintiffs had already been through several increasingly formal efforts to settle their complaints, from face-to-face negotiation, to hearings in front of a justice of the peace, to the initial salvo of purchasing a writ. The majority of defendants failed even to appear at court, which meant automatic judgment against them.[7] Of those who initially responded to their court summons, many opted to settle the issue out of court. Prior to the Revolution, only 57 percent of civil cases filed in the South Carolina Court of Common Pleas resulted in judgment.[8] Courts stepped in for recordkeeping and enforcement as communities expanded and became more specialized.

Litigation was an everyday part of the credit economy, and court records provide a helpful vantage point from which to understand how women confronted debt and how credit was gendered. Of course, there are important caveats to the kinds of answers that court records provide. First, bringing a complaint to court took money and effort; the records, therefore, reflect only a small portion of the many economic transactions that filled the lives of the inhabitants. Second, enslaved men and women were excluded from this type of redress, since they had no legal standing to bring suits, though they did purchase goods on account and periodically loan money to free and enslaved neighbors.[9] Finally, the legal status of free married women tended to hide their names and participation from legal proceedings. Nevertheless, while court records may present a profile of the more resourceful and most delinquent market participants, they do not depict a hostile world dramatically at odds with the rest of the borrowing and lending community.

Patterns of litigation offer clues about not only changing courts and laws but also the overlapping economic story. For example, the economic and political crises of the 1780s are apparent in the dramatic drop in civil cases at the time of the Revolution (Figure 8). Newport and Charleston were both occupied by the British army for extended periods during the war. Daily life was in turmoil; few made it to court, even when a sitting court could be found. The overall trend after the Revolution is likewise clear: civil cases rose sharply in Charleston and remained high, while Newport failed to regain its prewar level of activity.

"Women's cases"—those that involved women as plaintiffs, defendants, or interested third parties—differed much less between the two cities in terms of overall percentages of the court docket. The striking fact about women's cases is that in both cities, they were an enduring segment of the court's business (Figure 8). Women's part in the litigated economy persisted because women's use of credit endured the economic transformations of the revolutionary era. In spite of subordinate legal status, women continued to use, and be used by, the instruments of credit that were at the heart of port economies. Their interactions with these credit forms testify to the diversity of what credit really meant to Americans. Credit appeared in long-term, unwritten agreements between neighbors, in merchants' negotiations with suppliers, in the speculative investments of the wealthy, in the mundane purchases of the poor, in the labor exchanges negotiated by or over slaves, and in the cooperative efforts of relatives to settle estates and secure the name and financial standing of kin.

Although the meanings were diverse, credit tools—book debt, bonds, and promissory notes—served two basic needs of market participants. They tracked exchanges in a world with little circulating money, and they provided a means of investment and growth. Each met these needs in particular ways: account books through the convenience of a single

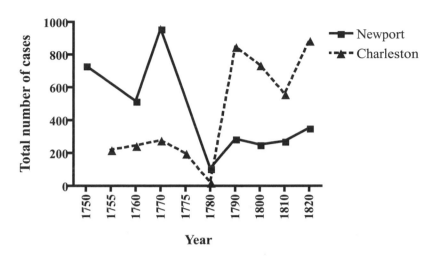

A

Cases in the Courts of Common Pleas

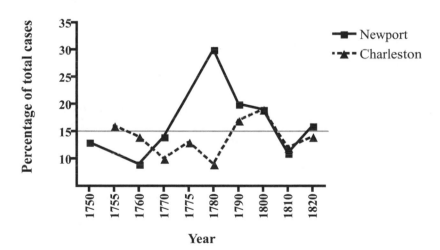

B

"Women's cases" in the Courts of Common Pleas

Figure 8. Table A and B. These data were gathered from the Judgment Rolls and Petitions and Decrees in Summary Process of the South Carolina Court of Common Pleas at the South Carolina Department of Archives and History and the Docket Books, Record Books, and Case Files of the Newport Court of Common Pleas at the Rhode Island Judicial Archives.

running tally, promissory notes and bonds with the security of legally binding signatures and the promise of interest payments. The individual features of these tools reveal different ways of thinking about the nature of trust in an expanding economy and suggest the designs of the woman who used them.

Of the three dominant forms of credit in revolutionary port cities, book debt was the oldest and most familiar. It was long standing, mutual, and open ended, like most early commercial interactions. Account books recorded charges and reimbursements that could take place over years, with no specific obligation to pay at a particular time and no expectation of interest payments. A change in fortunes, legal suit, death, marriage, or move prompted reckoning between the parties, compelling plaintiff and defendant both to present to the court a full list of the date and cost of each service provided or item obtained. The role of the courts was to assess information provided by both sides and make appropriate adjustments to settle all matters between them. Historian Bruce Mann observes, "Books were not conclusive evidence of the debts they recorded. They were, instead, merely a starting point for discussing the range of dealings between debtor and creditor in open court."[10] Adjudication of book debt thus bridged older methods of verbal contract and the growing specificity of written accounts.

One of the many cases of Newport tavern keeper Abigail Stoneman illustrates the mix of verbal and written accounts typical of book debt relationships. In 1771, Stoneman relocated briefly to Boston, where she continued to take in boarders. As often happened in urban housefuls, talented borders created business opportunities, and she hired one of them, William Blodget of Providence, to serve as her accountant, paint portraits of herself and her daughter, and decorate her house. Their relationship was trusting and wide ranging, covering a variety of informal arrangements and transactions without the force of written agreements. But within the year, the relationship soured, and she sued him in Newport to recover three months' worth of board and liquor.[11] Stoneman reconstructed her version of their financial relationship for the courts, presenting an account of £14.2.0 lawful money that he owed her, minus some payments she had received on his behalf from another woman. Fortunately for Blodget, one of his Boston friends knew that verbal agreements were chancy; he later testified that "while sd. Blodget was in Boston, sd. Stoneman threatened to sue him, which occasion'd my making minutes of as much of the transaction as I knew; and I fully rememr. that there was a large Ballance in favour of sd. Blodget." He submitted a written account of charges that Stoneman owed Blodget, amounting to £25.9.4 lawful money and acknowledging only £6 due for board from Blodget. In penning his account, he alluded to a source of the tension between the two: a displeased Stoneman had required Blodget to re-paint the headdress, face, and drapery in his portrait of her. The root of their disagreement, like the book debt they had with one another, was simultaneously professional and personal. After deliberations and an ap-peal, the court-appointed referees decided in favor of Stoneman over the offended artist, but only for the nominal fee of one shilling, plus the costs of suit and appeal.

Women's involvement in book debt flourished when they were active participants in daily, face-to-face transactions. Free Newport women en-joyed this atmosphere prior to the Revolution, when book debt accounted for about 40 percent of their court cases.[12] Their active use of book debt marked them as consumers, workers, and investors, sometimes simulta-neously. Women's purchases, for example, could constitute investments in their own businesses. Abigail Pinnegar, Newport tavern keeper, used book credits with her suppliers to obtain the rum and sugar she needed to make punch for guests at her tavern (Figure 9).[13] Book credit was what stocked the Atlantic service economy, by ushering imported groc-eries into the homes and businesses of urban women. Charleston women were slower than those in Newport to tap into this source. While South Carolina law encouraged female enterprise by permitting free married women to conduct business as if they were single, southern business-women before the Revolution rarely sued their debtors. Although the pages of South Carolina newspapers offered a tempting array of goods to women and men, female Charleston shoppers were seldom brought to court over delinquent accounts. In the pre-revolutionary courts, Charles-ton women came to book debt as administrators of men's estates, not as calculating entrepreneurs or overextended spenders. It was not until the nineteenth century that Charleston women began to use and go to court over book debt in significant numbers.[14]

What made book debt more common for northern women in the eigh-teenth century and southern women in the early nineteenth century? The records of goods and services exchanged, folded into the court case files as evidence, provide some clues. High levels of female book debt in Newport courts prior to the Revolution were in large part due to busi-nesswomen suing on their own credit. After the war, these women had moved or fallen into poverty, and the long accounts detailing multiple trips to urban shops dwindled in the court's files. The humbler services of boarding, renting, and teaching remained, marking the diminish-ment of commercial opportunities for women in the northern city. In contrast, Charleston women after the Revolution took new advantage of purchasing and selling goods on account. Prior to the Revolution, the few Charleston women's book debt cases were for rum, rice, nursing, and slave wages. In the early nineteenth century, accounts recorded a

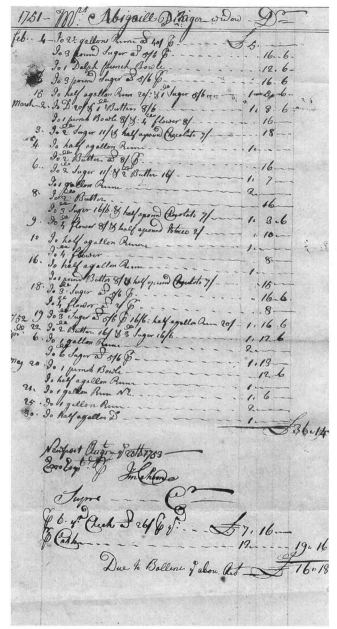

Figure 9. This account details the rum, sugar, and other necessities that Abigail Pinnegar purchased from James Cahoon, as well as two of her payments. Newport Court of Common Pleas 1753, November Term, #418; *Cahoon v. Pinnegar.* Rhode Island Judicial Archives.

much wider variety of goods and specialty services, as well as multiple cases of boarders and renters who had reneged on their bills. Charleston women's involvement in book credit as lenders and borrowers grew as they became more firmly integrated into urban services and retail purchases. The strength of rental and retail businesses in particular was one of the most important determinants of women's participation in litigated debt.[15] A denser population of potential customers and plentiful shopping opportunities in the early nineteenth century created ideal circumstances for book accounts.

Free women regularly loaned and borrowed on book debt, which meant that they came to court as both plaintiffs looking to be repaid and defendants who had failed to meet their obligations. The profiles of female plaintiffs and defendants were often quite different, however, and these profiles more precisely pinpoint the place of women as lenders and borrowers in the credit economy. Female defendants in book debt cases were sued for dry goods, alcohol, and staples they had purchased. While moralists wrung their hands over the profligate use of credit for foolish ends, delinquent female defendants who had bought goods on credit were largely familiar, unremarkable customers. The debt that brought widowed Phebe Strengthfield to court in 1760 was no wild splash-out for ribbons and fancy shoes, but rather a purchase of Irish linen and cotton check the previous year for which she had already paid a third of the total charge.[16] Her debt was hardly the residue of heedless consumption; it was, however, clear evidence that credit extended by merchants and shopkeepers opened the world of imported goods to women.

Female plaintiffs, in contrast, were concerned with the provider side of the Atlantic service economy, bringing suit over unpaid rent, board, and nursing services they or their slaves had provided. In 1755, Elizabeth Huchins had to sue to recover £150 from Nicholas Lewis for "Meat, Drink, Washing and Lodging found and Provided at your Request, for your Servant James Bishop, and for Serving and Mending said Bishop in his Sickness at my House, for 37 Weeks and 2 days at four pounds Currency Pr. Week."[17] These women did not use credit to enrich their material lives; rather, the expectation that services would be provided on credit when cash was scarce used them.

The transactions of female plaintiffs reflected the fact that the very flexibility of book debt made it easy to exploit when service work was the currency of exchange. Women hired to provide domestic services had a clear sense of the overall value of their work, demonstrated by the weekly rates they charged. But within the bounds of an agreement, the duties could always expand if they were not carefully itemized. While a hogshead of rum had a single price for a finite quantity, the tasks and expenses included in "Meat, Drink, Washing and Lodging . . . Serving and Mending" were fluid and negotiated between a worker and her employer. The "credit" these women had to extend might be fixed in terms of the fee, but not necessarily in terms of what that sum represented. Because no cash had exchanged hands up front, those negotiations might take place long after the work had been done, introducing the distance of time to the ambiguity of expectations. As we have seen, landladies like Sarah Tucker knew to take the precaution of itemizing their services for their boarders, so that the washing, mending, ironing, and provision of candles and firewood to a sick customer would each get its due.[18]

The apparent exactness of credit transactions recorded in books and on scraps of paper obscures the calculations and disputes over the value they represented, particularly when labor was included in the exchange. Attempts to fix the value of enslaved women's work were especially difficult. Abba, Mary Bedon's slave, went to work for Mary Calibuff for six months in 1759. The £36 debt that Calibuff owed Bedon for the enslaved woman's work went unpaid for at least a year before Bedon sued.[19] From Bedon's point of view, she was extending credit by loaning the labor of property she owned. She probably knew, for example, how much Abba was worth on the slave market; she also may have had a good sense of the value the enslaved woman's work brought to her own household. However, Bedon's sense of Abba's worth was not the definitive measure of the credit extended to Calibuff. Every day, servants and slaves negotiated tasks with their mistresses, implicitly adjusting the value of their work credit. Even though a woman like Abba was excluded from the formal institutions of the litigated economy, the use of book accounts in valuing women's work meant that she could be instrumental in determining the values contested in court and the marketplace.

"Paper" credit tools such as bonds and promissory notes tried to resolve some of the ambiguities that plagued book debt. Unlike book debt, bonds were used for investment and could be unrelated to the exchange of goods or services. They were for people with capital to spare or property to mortgage and so were more common in wealthy areas like Charleston. The legal features of bonds made them a limited and impersonal form compared with book debt. They specified a time of repayment and accumulated interest charges. They were transferable, which allowed the debt to travel away from the original debtor-creditor relationship. Court proceedings over bonds were straightforward; they evaluated the document's authenticity but not the larger credit relationship between the parties. Most bonds established a penalty worth double the amount loaned if the bond was not paid, permitting the lender to sue for this much higher sum (though it was not always awarded).[20] In other words, bonds relied less on mutuality and custom and more on specified terms.

Written bonds appealed to women with funds to invest but little interest in the active management of a business; such women abounded in Charleston. Free southern women enthusiastically embraced bonds, and bond debt was the most common type of civil case that brought Charleston women to court in the eighteenth century, constituting 64 percent of women's cases in 1770, 75 percent in 1775, and 60 percent in 1790.[21] Well-to-do widows loaned money by bond and then let the bond run beyond its due date, collecting interest payments as income and turning the loans into "virtual annuities."[22] What was an accessible form of income for the investing woman became an important tool in capital formation for the city's businesses. Investing women were particularly active in the first decades after the Revolutionary War, when women who had loaned money on bonds dominated the court docket of women's cases.

It is little surprise that wealthy widow investors were vital to Charleston's economy, since wealthy women had played similar roles in cities around the Atlantic world for decades.[23] It is surprising, given assumptions about female economic standing, that so many Charleston businesswomen were able to borrow money with bonds. In fact, in cases brought to court, Charleston-area women borrowed money as frequently as they loaned it. Single businesswomen like Elizabeth Carne, a shopkeeper who kept a tavern in the 1750s and 1760s, regularly borrowed money from fellow Charlestonians on bonds. In the 1750s, she took two short-term loans (for less than two months) on bonds from a Charleston merchant for £1,000 and £221.9.0 South Carolina money. By 1765 she was sufficiently flush to loan the equivalent of £2,100 to Charlestonian Paty Holmes. She probably had a substantial financial relationship with Holmes—as a butcher, he may have also been one of her suppliers—because in 1767 she, Holmes, and his wife, Jane, together borrowed £100 from Charles Stevens Stocker. Carne also borrowed money from a planter in St. Thomas's Parish, in this case, backed by a mortgage. Elizabeth Carne's bonds were not distant investments; they were transactions that linked her to the urban commerce that flowed daily through her establishment. As a woman who "keeps good ENTERTAINMENT for MAN and HORSE," she used bonds in the way that Newport businesswomen used book debt, to stock and operate her part of the service economy.[24]

In the unstable economic climate of the postwar period, women spread out their risk as lenders and their obligations as borrowers by taking on male co-signers. While in the late colonial period about one-third of women co-signed with men on their bonds, in the postwar years, three-quarters did so. Seen in isolation, this might appear to be evidence of women withdrawing from direct involvement in credit. But bond practices were undergoing many changes in the difficult years after the Revolution, as lenders tried to gain more security and control over repayment. For example, the length of time allowed before payment was due on a bond increased. Late colonial loans tended to be for short terms of a year or less. In the first decades of the early republic, however, debtors had at least one year to repay the money; some had as long as six years.[25] Lengthening the terms of the bond acknowledged the difficulties of speedy repayment in a time of financial instability. At the same time, by specifying longer terms at the outset, extenders of bonds hoped to gain greater control over repayment than was possible under the earlier system, when short-term bonds were allowed to continue past their due dates in exchange for interest payments.

Alone or with financial partners, free Charleston women benefited as recipients of the culture of investment they helped to fund. Charleston's wealth created pools of capital for investment, making the bond a regular part of many individuals' financial lives. The true significance of bonds as tools of female investment cannot be fully explored in the context of the court of common pleas, however. Much capital accumulation in the Charleston area was in land and slaves, and studies of free southern women's wills indicate that property in enslaved people was their greatest repository of wealth. In fact, one study of women's inventories in pre-revolutionary South Carolina found that a majority of the women who invested in bonds (or the related form of mortgage) were not wealthy elites, but women of fairly modest means.[26] Written bonds provided a means of investment to women who could not afford to invest in traditional and preferred forms such as land or slaves.

Bonds were on the decline in New England by the mid-eighteenth century, and Newport women never warmed to them as a means of support. A few female lenders brought cases before the courts, but women seem not to have benefited as borrowers on bonded debt. The low rate of bond holding in Newport when compared with Charleston probably had little to do with gender. If bonds were truly a widespread means of obtaining capital in Newport, we would expect to see bonds bringing female executors to court over the debts of their deceased male relatives. But neither women nor their male relatives used bonds with frequency. Local lending and borrowing seem instead to have been recorded by the shorter-term promissory note.

Like bonds, promissory notes and due bills (a closely related variant of notes, also called bills obligatory) delineated a single credit transaction and earned interest.[27] A signature on a note was legal evidence and could be challenged only by a defendant claiming it was not her note, or that she had already paid; mutual negotiation was not part of promissory note adjudication. Notes usually represented a shorter-term investment than bonds, requiring payment plus interest in a few months at the latest. Notes were also assignable, allowing them to circulate as currency, which they did, more commonly than bonds. In Newport and Charleston, this mobile tool of commerce gained popularity between 1750 and 1820, becoming a more important part of women's credit lives over time.

Prior to the Revolution, urban women appeared almost always as the plaintiff in court cases that involved promissory notes, and the typical plaintiff was a widow trying to recover money she had loaned to a man of the city. In 1750, Newport widow Meribah Jones sued the administrators of John Gidley's estate for a note he had signed in 1743, promising to pay her "£44.10.3 in goods on demand, that is English goods out of my store or to pay her in cash the above sum in the year after date."[28] After the Revolution, Newport women still appeared primarily as plaintiffs; in other words, they used notes to loan money but did not secure funds of their own. These women partook of the expanding credit economy—in fact, many of the promissory notes recorded money due over the exchange of goods or services—but only so far as they were willing to extend trust to others. Charleston women, in contrast, began to appear more equally as plaintiff or defendant in these cases, suggesting a broader and more flexible involvement in the world of circulating notes. As lenders, women just had to have money in some form, which was more a financial question than a cultural one, and so less dependent upon gendered ideas about men and women. As borrowers, free Charleston women had to secure the trust and standing demanded of a "person of credit."

That female Charlestonians were able to secure this standing in the economy is evident from the facility many had with the flexible potential of promissory notes. For women as much as for men, portable credit instruments greased the wheels of a commercial, yet cash-poor society where close, trusting ties crossed with far more impersonal exchanges. The most striking example of skill in endorsing and recirculating notes involves the cases of Sarah Smith and Roger Smith in 1800. Sarah Smith, who it seems was not Roger's wife but likely some other kin, was represented in court in 1800 at least thirteen times.[29] Almost all of her cases pertained to a series of promissory notes signed by Roger Smith to her in the late 1790s, which she immediately endorsed over to Charleston merchants. In four cases, she endorsed multiple notes to the same merchant partnerships. In this way, women could act as credit intermediaries for their male kin or friends. Over these few years, Sarah loaned Roger close to $8,000, drawing upon her credit with Charleston merchants such as Adam Tunno and James Cox. She also became a legal target; many of the creditors sued both Roger and Sarah in separate suits over the same notes and were awarded their claims, plus interest. Sarah had resources of her own, including rental properties, and she incurred some debts apparently purely for her own use.[30] Her activities as an independent woman of credit were routine and no cause for alarm; her gender was

not at issue in her credit arrangements or her lawsuits. It was her activities as credit intermediary for the elusive Roger Smith that provoked
Charleston creditors to band together in late August 1799 with a fusil-
lade of suits.

The contrast in the ways that northern and southern women employed
promissory notes suggests that there was considerable room for cultural,
regional, and other influences to determine what these new credit forms
meant. For Newport women, notes formalized a debt incurred in the
provision of goods and services. When Ann Hill agreed to board the
daughter of Mark Robinson, a Newport house carpenter, in 1769, she
made him sign a note promising to pay her £3 old tenor per week until
the child was seven years old. After eighty-three weeks, Hill used the note
to sue him for the costs.[31] The note provided her greater security of payment than a verbal agreement followed by a book debt case—soon after
she brought the suit, she withdrew it, presumably having received payment. The terms of the promissory notes themselves suggest this limited,
case-specific understanding of credit in Newport, since notes before and
after the Revolution were frequently signed to be paid "on demand with
lawful interest" or "with lawful interest until paid." Charleston notes, in
contrast, almost always specified the duration of the loan, with interest to
accrue after that date if the payment was not made.[32] They were designed
to serve as investments and embodied a more abstract, anonymous understanding of credit value. Charleston women saw the credit extended
on a promissory note as a loan; Newport women were more likely to view
it as a temporary expedient acceptable when cash was not immediately
available.

This variability in the use and meaning of credit instruments was true
across the economy. The words often used to understand credit instruments (impersonal as opposed to personal, or active as opposed to passive) are imprecise in capturing the way city dwellers actually used and
thought about them. While promissory notes were "impersonal" in that
they were legally fungible, women and men attached them firmly to people and personal exchanges. Book debt (which required the exchange
of goods and services) could be characterized as a more "active" mobilization of credit than a bond or note (which tracked the circulation of
money), but these "passive" methods of earning income fit the entrepreneurial schemes of many southern women. Therefore, it is not possible to classify book debt, bonds, or promissory notes as "masculine" or
"feminine" by their basic nature. What is apparent, in the details of how
people used the tools of credit, is that the flexibility and mutuality of a
tool such as book debt both benefited and took advantage of women in
particular ways. The struggles of women in the Atlantic service economy
to be paid for specific tasks within the category of "women's work" were

intensified by the vague, open-ended quality of the book debt many employed to track their transactions.

What was the solution for urban women at the mercy of deferred payments and flexible debts? In her study of middling English families, Margaret Hunt has argued that the rise of bonds, notes, and annuities helped pull women out of the daily business grind of book debt and into "safer" incomes. As eighteenth-century English businesses became more expensive to establish, women emerged as a new class of investors who no longer had to cobble together funds for business ventures.[33] There is little evidence of a similar tradeoff in the Charleston of the early republic. Free Charleston women, either on their own or together with relatives, continued to have access to credit as lenders and borrowers; in fact, women added promissory notes as one more tool for generating income. Notes were extended for longer periods of time and had the potential to act more like bonds by providing capital or interest. At the same time, book debt cases rose, indicating that the spread of investments did not preclude face-to-face exchanges of goods and services involving urban women. Notes and bonds offered little solace to Newport women, who could neither mobilize book debt nor get many new enterprises off the ground in the early years of the nineteenth century. Credit instruments embodied certain kinds of financial promises, but they also were strongly shaped by the market realities of the economies through which they circulated.

Networks of Borrowers and Lenders

In any port city, a credit tool was only as effective as the relationships it hammered together. One pamphleteer in 1786 wrote that "credit is the confidence which mankind place in the virtue and good character of its object. . . . Credit and honesty are in their nature correlatives, and must and forever imply and support each other."[34] Since social and financial worth were correlated, extending credit required nuanced calculations about risk and trustworthiness—not just of the instrument but of the person signing it. For men, the question of whether one was a worthy risk for advancing money depended on public face and accountability. Credit information—who would pay, who was a risky investment, who was on the way up or down—was vital currency in letters between merchants. In one sense, nothing could be more personal than credit, since it was constrained by individual reputation and an insolvent debtor could have his very body hauled away to prison for his defaults. In practice, however, credit and debt were fundamentally social. A wealthy and powerful man's credit could extend to friends and family and persist even after his death. From her travels in New York, a widowed Alice Izard wrote home to her son in Charleston, "Your Father has left such a character for punctuality, & honorable dealing here, that I might easily ruin myself from the facility with which I find credit. I should be very sorry to do anything to discredit his name."[35] The credit reputation was attached to the dead man's name, but its employment and perpetuation were in her hands.

Whether in the face-to-face context of urban neighborhoods or the transatlantic reach of mercantile trade, relationships with familiar, reliable associates were crucial to a credit-based economy.[36] Men and women created these networks through lines of kinship, shared ethnicity, vocation, religion, and friendship. Some alliances were permanent; others were fleeting, particularly if they lacked institutional support, and death terminated many strong bonds. Family was often the core of an individual's credit network, but many men and women had wide-ranging contacts and moved from one individual to another in search of credit. The scope and complexity of women's credit networks demonstrate how their economic activities were embedded in urban social and business life.

Tavern keeper Abigail Stoneman's credit relationships were intensive and mutual. The men she sued over the course of years of civil suits had frequently sued her on previous occasions. Thomas Bannister, Stoneman's landlord in the early 1770s, sued her for seventy Spanish dollars' worth of unpaid rent; she and her new husband sued Bannister in the same year for an account from 1768 to 1773 for broken dishes, food, drinks, lighting, and other charges totaling £19.7.9 lawful money, as well as for a loan of £2.8.0 Stoneman had extended Bannister.[37] Her accounts with Newport merchants, craftsmen, and laborers document an interconnected web of credit and payment. Stoneman's 1767 debts to shopkeeper John Miller included £48.17.0 in old tenor that Miller paid to a Mr. Wyatt as part of her order, and £60 paid to James Niyon's order, delivered to her. Stoneman herself in 1765 paid £100 to Joseph Borden, £120 to John Easton, and £193.5.0 to John Scott for Timothy Waterhouse, Jr. In those years, she was a regular client of Waterhouse's, purchasing cloth, dry goods, and wine from him; he returned payment in molasses delivered to John Scott and money to George Remfen and Thomas Wood. While Stoneman, like most businesspeople, spread out her debts among multiple suppliers, she also extended credit to and received credit from a regular group who appeared on both sides of each other's balance sheets. Her associates—merchants, gentlemen, mariners—were drawn from many of Newport's leading commercial families, including the Coggeshalls, Eastons, and Richardsons, but also included less prominent Atlantic traders.

Credit ties like Stoneman's were the best bulwark against the risks of commercial trading in the revolutionary era.[38] Blending social and economic elements, they provided reliability and forbearance when needed. The fact that such relationships were social and economic was the source of their appeal, though it constrained a creditor's behavior. Joseph Manigault counseled his brother Gabriel to extract a bond payment from Mrs. Middleton indirectly through her son, "as I wish to avoid any thing which might be construed into a demand of the debt; having often perceived how shy people are of you, if it should not suit them to pay immediately."[39] Manigault wanted to collect on his loan but through experience had learned the importance of preserving social relationships with his fellow elites by staying flexible about the legal specifications of credit.

Strong, elite, mutual credit ties required reciprocity, which was possible only when both parties had something to offer. Abigail and Mary Pinnegar, mother-daughter tavern keepers in Newport, ran a smaller operation and had fewer mutual credit and debt relationships. Sometimes, especially with boarders, they could establish such connections. When Newport mariner James Carter sued in 1754 to recover cash and credit he had extended to Abigail, she brought out three years' worth of charges for Carter's board and lodging, as well as clothing she had provided him.[40] Pinnegar's relationship to James Carter relied on the daily personal interaction of the houseful and involved small loans over time on both sides. These kinds of mutual face-to-face credit relationships are the type most associated with colonial women, but they were the exception for the Pinnegars. Because they were tavern keepers, mother and daughter accrued substantial debts with suppliers of rum and bread, and they signed and received promissory notes with butchers as well as mariners, yeomen, and local widows. Their relationships were extensive, but debtors and creditors seem to have been largely separate groups. Pinnegar suppliers extended credit (and came to court as disgruntled plaintiffs) but did not borrow money from the mother-daughter partnership. Customers, who were brought before the court as defendants, rarely sued the pair over unpaid loans because, presumably, they did not lend to and borrow from the same individuals.[41]

Instead, the Pinnegars' credit practices created local networks through third-party reimbursement rather than mutual trading. Pinnegar accounts are filled with suppliers who accepted payment from third parties who had shopped at Abigail's store. Many Pinnegar customers did not pay their own bills; instead, they sent some other person into the tavern months later to make good the debt. In this way, individuals who never appeared in court together were linked through a shared debtor or creditor. The Pinnegar women, by virtue of the credit connections they independently formed in the course of doing business, linked single transactions into a web of debt across the city. Transactions were opportunistic rather than long-planned, indirect rather than mutual, but the result was an interconnected, social marketplace.

Ann Eleanor Vanrhyn, who kept a shop in Charleston from the 1780s to the 1820s, had intensive credit relationships with her customers, but her credit network differed from the model provided by Abigail Stoneman as well. Vanrhyn extended multiple loans to customers such as Mary Elliott and David Deas, each of whom signed both a bond and a promissory note.[42] Credit relationships with customers led to credit relationships with their kin. In the 1790s Catharine Simons, her daughters, and the other executors of her late husband Benjamin's estate all kept separate accounts with Vanrhyn and her partner Ann Savage. Each made numerous purchases at the store, sometimes on the same trip, sometimes shopping alone.[43] Vanrhyn vigorously pursued her debts through the courts after a suitable grace period, but since she rarely appeared as a defendant in court, we know little about her ability to borrow money from the people to whom she had extended credit. Vanrhyn's accounts with her suppliers were settled without resort to the civil courts; as a result, there is little evidence of the kinds of dense borrowing and buying networks in which Abigail Stoneman was involved in Newport prior to the Revolution. That the Charleston shopkeeper was deeply involved in the economy of Charleston retailing is clear. Her sales reflect a wide variety of shop inventory, which would have required merchant connections willing to extend her credit. When her estate was inventoried in 1828, it included $6,000 worth of stock goods in her store, hundreds of shares in state and national banks, twenty-six bonds from twenty-two individuals, and numerous promissory notes.[44]

The striking pattern that emerges from Vanrhyn's one-sided litigated accounts is of credit relationships composed of several threads, involving women as well as men. Most of the shoppers in Vanrhyn's stores were women. The majority of her suits, however, were against men, often the husband or father of the avid shopper, making her intensive relationships more wide ranging in fact than is apparent under the letter of the law (Figure 10). The records of other retailers tell a similar tale. In 1752 and 1753, Martha Mann made seven visits to sole trader Mary Cooper's shop in Charleston, purchasing an assortment of cloth, trimmings, gloves, tea, and china, racking up an account of close to £50. For six years, the debt went unpaid. Finally, the shopkeeper went to the courts for satisfaction and, in serving out her writ, transformed the terms of the credit relationship. In the lawsuit, shopper Martha Mann's husband John was named the sole defendant responsible for the debt; shopkeeper Mary Cooper's husband John was added as a plaintiff.[45] A commercial transaction between two women became a court case involving a man and a married couple. Numerous debt cases between a man and a woman tacitly involved

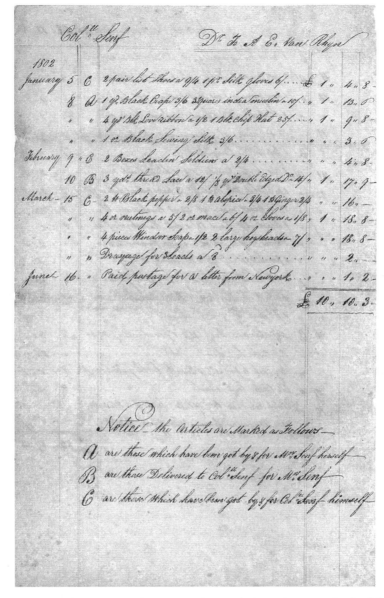

Figure 10. Shopkeeper Ann Eleanor Vanrhyn coded purchases on the Senf family account according to who made them and for whom the goods were purchased. This account is under Colonel Senf's name, but, as the annotation shows, he made purchases for himself (category C) and on his wife's behalf (category B). Mrs. Senf also came to the shop herself (category A). Charleston District Court of Common Pleas, 1824, #474a; *Vanrhyn v. Breithaupt*. South Carolina Department of Archives and History.

another woman who had initiated the debt with her shopping or labor. The transformation of the debt in the court's legal context obscured the activities of the marketplace; at the same time, though, the court extended the reach of marketplace credit transactions by involving parties who could have been an ocean away when the first skein of thread was debited from an account. The court's records therefore illuminate the fact that even a seemingly straightforward, binary lender-borrower transaction took place within an expanding web of connections.

Across this web, men loomed as an implicit presence in the feminine atmosphere of a millinery shop by virtue of their names in account books. Slaves haunted the court docket as the proxy shoppers who had initiated a debt. The shopkeeper's credit relationship with a family had several facets—one with the customer, whose preferences and habits were known, and from whom she demanded cash or permitted the courtesies of credit, and another with the individual who would be legally held responsible if the relationship with the customer broke down. Customers were a "network" of one kind, linked by the transaction but also by exchanges of information; debtors formed another kind of more purely instrumental tie. The customer herself, entering a store or workshop, was tied not only to the purveyor, with whom she haggled over terms, but to the financial source of her own credit, whether by sentiment, kinship, or command.[46] Sometimes, shopkeepers ran credit interference between the various parties. Ledgers from Britain reveal shopkeepers who kept two versions of a "family credit" transaction—one acknowledged to the male head, another for the wives and female servants who purchased items: a hat cost eleven shillings sixpence, but only "to tell 8 s."[47] Historians have long recognized that the pervasive presence of credit created a marketplace where personal considerations of "character" set the terms of the transaction; what becomes evident in looking at how men and women actually used credit to make purchases is just how many "characters" could be implicated in a single transaction.

Many women's account histories defy easy classification into networks. Certain occupations tended to fragment rather than consolidate commercial ties. Martha Bolton, a Charleston widow who ran a tavern and ferry, appeared in court sixteen times in the 1790s and early 1800s, mainly as a defendant for money she had borrowed with promissory notes and bonds. She was involved in suits with twenty-seven people, only one of whom appeared twice. Bolton had extensive financial associations around Charleston, enhanced by her business, which provided transportation to the city and lodging and entertainment for the many transient visitors to the southern port. In November 1789 she cosigned a two-month bond with Mary Hibben to pay Hyman Solomon £84.18.5 sterling with interest. Bolton paid off the bond in 1795, then went to

court to obtain payment from Hibben.[48] Contact with a constantly shifting clientele shaped Bolton's credit standing, which was not developed
within or contained by a particular network of individuals. Unlike the
highly skilled male cabinet makers of Newport, who cultivated a closed,
loyal clientele, tavern keepers and other female service providers took
and extended credit as they could.[49] It was not their gender per se that
denied them a close, reliable financial network, but the nature of the
work that women tended to do in the Atlantic service economy.

Bolton's credit standing, however dispersed, did provide her with capital funds to operate her business. Newport widow Mary Searing's broad
financial connections were less happy. She appeared in at least fourteen
cases from the 1760s to the 1780s, only once involving the same man, in
an appealed case. No single group of financial associates emerges from
the plaintiffs, defendants, witnesses, endorsees, or debtors named in her
estate inventory.[50] In Searing's case, multiple associations were the product of an entrepreneurial spirit born of dire necessity. The Atlantic service
economy presented numerous opportunities for Searing, who supported
herself by taking boarders, grinding chocolate, and selling sugar, milk,
and dry goods. In the process, she loaned and borrowed money and contracted with local craftsmen for food and carpentry. Like the Pinnegars,
she spread out her indebtedness, keeping bread accounts first with Godfrey Wainwood, then with Richard Johnson. She leaned on family ties
and rented slave labor to invest in her businesses.[51] Searing and the many
women like her were not isolated from credit connections, but neither
did they profit richly from them. Women patching together a livelihood
by providing services to the urban population had to use credit to stay one
step ahead of destitution, and extensive transactions rather than close-
knit ties were the result. Although tavern keeper Abigail Stoneman's alliances fit a familiar model of credit pioneered by wealthy men, given the
shifting opportunities of the urban population and economy, Searing's
strategies were likely representative of a larger group of women.

Tavern keeper Mary Pinnegar struggled too, not because she was isolated from credit networks, but because they were imperfect. Active as
a trader through the 1750s and 1760s, by the summer of 1769 she was
jailed in Newport as an insolvent debtor. The inventory of her estate,
in addition to recording the backgammon tables and "Signe & Retailing Board" that had been hard-won investments in her business, noted
a book of accounts, many "unsettled."[52] When the men and women to
whom she extended credit failed, she failed along with them. Debtors'
jail was humiliating and dangerous—Pinnegar joined a handful of fellow
debtors and more than one hundred supporters who claimed that the
jail and surrounding grounds were too confining and threatened their
health. They were right. Within the year, Mary Pinnegar was dead.[53]

Litigated debt reveals no separate female world of credit networks, since women's accounts were more likely to be with men than with women. Although newspaper and other records suggest that female partnerships were common, only a few of these alliances appear in the court records. Part of the explanation rests in the ways that women's changing marital status influenced the intersection of the market and the court. Suits between women were not unheard of, but for a female credit exchange to appear in the courts, both parties had to be legally independent. In 1810, for example, Harriott Elliott Maxwell sued Susannah Egan McDonald for a $1,500 bond the two women had signed in 1803.[54] As widows, both Maxwell and McDonald had legal status in the eyes of the court, and since neither had remarried, the court record preserved their transaction as a matter between women. Had either remarried, their original female exchange would be transformed into a case involving men in the courts. Litigated debt also preserved just a slice of the complex credit entanglements that bound individuals to their neighbors; it is likely that many credit relationships among women existed in the "memory economy" of verbal agreements between neighbors that were remembered, but never captured in official records.[55] Nevertheless, the records that do remain clearly present a heterosocial picture of credit rather than one of gendered isolation.

Few women sued or were sued by people from distant counties or parishes, other colonies, or European cities; their litigated debt is a picture of local negotiation. But the long chains of credit that structured the Atlantic economy as a whole quickly cast these local relationships out in an international context. Even drawing an account with a local merchant could entangle women in international credit connections. When Charleston merchants James and Keating Simons went out of business in 1789, they assigned their list of creditors over to the London merchant house of Lane, Son, and Fraser. More than ten years later, the London merchants were still trying to collect from these 107 debtors, which included fourteen women under their own names and doubtless many more as family administrators.[56] Thus, just as the Atlantic economy created a new, international market for female work and new sources of materials to process into valuable goods, the credit connections on which that economy rested reached down to implicate women's and men's local reputations for financial probity.

"Family Credit" and Collective Debt

As John and Sarah Cantwell, the separating couple who opened this chapter, well knew, familial ties were some of the most important and perilous links to credit and debt. Credit connections often formed and broke over family connections. Shopkeeper Sarah Rumreil and tavern keeper Abigail Stoneman, widows who took over husbands' businesses and established long litigation records, both had financial dealings with some of the same men who loaned to and borrowed from their husbands and sons. Family members paid off the debts of kin and created new obligations in the process. Remarriage forged new connections, as husbands were named in suits springing from their wives' financial affairs prior to marriage, and husbands and wives entered new financial agreements together. In 1767, Charlotte Mathews loaned Thomas Knights and another St. Andrews Parish planter £373 lawful South Carolina money for a year. When she sued to collect the money in 1770, she was no longer acting alone; she and her husband, James Skirving, brought the suit together.[57]

Death created new credit relationships that were particularly relevant for women. Charlestonian Hepzibah Rose Christie and her new husband, James, became embroiled in cases involving debts previously incurred by Hepzibah, James, and James's former wife, Mary.[58] Many free married women faced debt litigation as administrators or executors when their husbands died, and their court appearances in the service of a family member's estate capture the simultaneously individual and collective nature of credit.[59] Half of the court appearances of Charleston-area women in the eighteenth century involved action taken on behalf of another's estate, a pattern that declined only after the turn of the century, and Newport women's involvement as administrators peaked at half of their court cases during and after the years of the Revolution.[60]

Estate administration was not a passive duty. Administrators and executors had to collect and pay debts, sell off land, disentangle financial agreements, and show persistence in the face of court continuations and countersuits. If they acted wisely, they could persuade creditors to forgive or extend past debts of the estate. If they spent heedlessly, new debts for funeral expenses could pile on top of existing debts. These responsibilities were complicated by the fact that suits against administrators often concerned debts that the deceased had incurred many years before death. Newport widow Elizabeth King was sued in 1750 for lawyer's fees her late husband had accrued as many as eleven years earlier.[61] Wealthy Charlestonian Frances Pinckney and her male relatives were called to court in 1790 as executors of a deceased executor to answer for a bond that Miles Brewton had signed nineteen years earlier.[62] In fact, estate administration could extend credit ties long beyond the lives of the original transactors. In numerous administration cases, one group of administrators sued another group. The original parties might have died, but the credit relationship remained, at least in the courts.

The finances of the administrators also became intermingled with those of the deceased. When an estate was not large enough to cover its debts, administrators and executors could be held personally liable to pay penalties and the costs associated with the suits brought against them. From their standing as financial manager of another's estate, administrators could accrue additional credit or enter more deeply into debt. Women and men signed new bonds, loaning or borrowing money to meet the circumstances of their administrative responsibilities. Jane Jones and Joseph Jones were executors of the estate of Thomas Jones when they signed a bond promising to pay the Ford brothers £2,000 lawful money in 1762. When the Joneses still had not paid by 1770, Jane and her new husband, Thomas Singellton, were sued and ordered to remit double the amount of the original bond.[63] The labels "Executrix" and "Administratrix" after a woman's name on a court document thus did not mark her as an empty proxy for economic activities. They testified to her real participation in the tangled world of credit.

Coverture added another tangle. A female administrator acting on behalf of an estate was often no latecomer to the financial transactions under question. Because of the legal restrictions on free married women, any goods or services they provided would be credited to their husbands' accounts. Widows could therefore find themselves settling accounts as administrators for board, washing, and mending they themselves had provided while married. For nine months in 1797, mariner John Burlingham's wife, Elizabeth, and their two children boarded at the home of merchant Thomas Cottrell by an agreement between the two men. During those months, Hannah Cottrell was no doubt instrumental in supplying their boarders with food, clothing, and other necessities. The following year, Thomas died, and Hannah was released by the law to make contracts in her own name, which she did, loaning money at interest to at least one fellow Rhode Islander. But when she went to court to sue Burlingham for the cost of boarding services, she acted, in the eyes of the law, as Thomas's widow and executrix, not on her own behalf.[64] From the point of view of the parties involved, a woman like Hannah Cottrell was representing both her husband's economic interests and her own. Many female administrators were playing this double role in court, either explicitly or indirectly. A female administrator could be sued for purchases she had made on her husband's account; she could also be held accountable for loans she had not signed.

The credit economy demanded men's and women's ongoing involvement in the financial entanglements of people long dead. In the Charleston area, where early marriage, frequent remarriage, and large families were common among whites, groups of siblings were often named as executors/administrators and were called to court together. For most of the second half of the eighteenth century, female administrators were more likely to share their duties with others than to face the task alone. The real burdens of estate administration in a city of great fortunes, multiple residences, and early death made joint administration a practical decision.[65]

The group estate administration cases of colonial South Carolina suggest that the concept of "family credit" was particularly strong in this community. "Family credit" embraced a number of practices and conventions, but it rested on the idea of a shared pool of financial and social credit, backed by the force of law. Its influences, as a way of conceptualizing credit and debt, can be seen in both personal and business accounting practices. Families all over British North America and the new United States kept joint account books to serve as collective record of their "family credit." Out in the Connecticut Valley, physician Reuban Champion kept a ledger recording both medical services he provided and clothing his wife, Lydia, made for their neighbors; individuals were identified as "debtor to us."[66] The urbane Robinson family in Newport had family account books in which multiple members recorded money they spent, earned, loaned, and borrowed. The handwriting might change, the kinds of work and goods differed according to age, gender, and ability, and yet as a whole such books recorded a joint construction.[67]

Although we often think of a family's credit as deriving from the public reputation of the head of household, family credit was a mutual creation of relatives, associates, and tradespeople and was often securely rooted in the shop rather than by the hearth. Women in every port city made purchases on family credit at city stores, and their labor and sales paid off the debts of their families' accounts.[68] In their account books, shopkeepers sometimes recorded that "yr wife" or "your son" had come to select and collect the goods. Those who failed to note the name of the individual transactor were no less willing to accept payments from and extend credit to multiple individuals on a single account. When the debts between shopkeeper Mary Searing and John Almy came to court, Almy's side presented a neat account detailing the debts that Searing owed him, weighed against his own debts to her. Only because Searing submitted her own, more detailed record do we know that the £184 worth of milk, cloth, tea, and cash came from Mrs. Elizabeth Almy's transactions, not John's.[69]

Shopkeepers and tradespeople expected legally dependent women to use and contribute to men's credit accounts. Mary Crandall not only bought Irish linen from Aaron Lopez on her husband Lemuel's account but also spun cotton and reamed sieves to provide the credit for them both.[70] While it was legally "his" account, the credit experience of the Crandalls was collective, in terms of deposits and withdrawals. His reputation for probity mattered and so did her labor. If a family came apart, as in cases of "self-divorce," when a husband published warnings to local merchants not to permit his eloping wife to continue to draw on the family account, the collective was disaggregated. The resulting statements followed a clear formula; they maligned the wife's reputation ("[She] has behaved herself in a very unbecoming and scandalous Manner"), defended the husband's by asserting that she had acted "without any provocation," and dissolved the family credit account. Such announcements frequently charged the wife with thoughtless overspending and, as Sarah Cantwell sharply pointed out in the *South Carolina and American General Gazette*, completely neglected the wife's substantive contributions. In the daily conduct of the marketplace, of course, a wife's contribution to the family account was acknowledged financially and socially. In the eyes of the law, however, the benefits of the "collective" account reverted to her husband. Her only recourse was to physically remove the items that her labor had produced, as when Mary Wenwood left Godfrey and, in his words, "stripped my house of sundry articles much to my prejudice."[71]

Families that stayed together could sometimes manipulate ideas about family credit to escape their debts. When Mary Bedon sued Stephen and Mary Calibuff in 1760 for the work her slave Abba had done, she named Mary Calibuff a feme sole trader. Among the defendants' responses to the court was the claim that Mary did not have feme sole status, and so the case should be dismissed. Women from New York City to Providence to Philadelphia used similar tactics to escape legal dunning. Free couples in Charleston actively sought out feme sole trader status for wives as a separate and fresh source of credit when husbands' debts had ruined their own standing. In part, these manipulations were about gender: the law embodied one set of assumptions about men and women, but individuals used its inconsistencies and oversights to suit their own needs as husbands and wives.[72] In part, though, their actions revealed a social understanding of credit. By establishing a new credit line for a free wife or by retreating under the cope of coverture, city dwellers moved between collective and individual conceptions of debt as much as between male and female ones.

Among Charleston elites, "family credit" was part of a linked set of strategies focused on strengthening and exploiting family ties. These strategies, involving intermarriage, business partnerships, and mutual financial assistance made it possible for this group to hold onto political, economic, and cultural power throughout the late colonial and early national periods with remarkable tenacity.[73] Charlestonian Henry Ravenel's ledger book documents one of the most sophisticated deployments of family credit in the practice of bond discounting. By this method, Ravenel assumed the bonded debt of one relative and applied it against the debt of another person who owed him money. Acting as a clearinghouse

for debts of family members, a patriarch like Henry Ravenel could re-
duce interest payments between members of his extended family as well
as bind some of them closer to him by assuming their debts to outsiders.
Participants in the family credit circle of the Ravenels were not equals,
but they were able to contribute to, and draw from, a social and economic entity larger than themselves.[74] A strong patriarch such as Ravenel
could harness the disparate elements of family credit into a powerful,
unified enterprise; for more desperate families, tensions over who contributed to and who had the right to oversee expenses on a joint account
tore at family connections.

While family ties structured women's participation in the litigated
economy, the relative prominence of estate administration among their
transactions fluctuated. Historians of colonial America have found in
some regions that eighteenth-century male testators increasingly chose
male executors over their own wives, either because of female financial
ignorance, or possibly to "protect [genteel] women from the cares of
commerce."[75] If this were true generally, and women were less likely to
be named executors over time, we might expect female participation
in the civil courts to decline at a similar rate. But there is no clear decline in women's court participation in Newport and Charleston, and so
estate administration per se is probably not a good measure of female
economic ability. The demographic consequences of war likely led to
more female administrators and more female involvement with litigated
debt. In Charleston, the nineteenth-century increase in female debt litigation was due to women acting on their own debts. While it may be that
women were less often chosen as administrators in the late eighteenth
century, several factors indicate that there was no general feeling of female inability in the face of growing commercial complexity. For one
thing, those who did appear as administrators were more likely to be
acting alone than women of their mothers' generation. Even as female
administration cases declined, moreover, the number of cases involving
women suing and being sued on their own behalf rose.

Estate administration and family credit are therefore best understood
not as symptoms of free women's financial marginality but as emblems of
an embedded economy. Credit transactions overlay social relationships
that could help or interfere. Consider Newport bricklayer Daniel Smith's
£50 bond (calculated in the old tenor currency) with his brother. After
his brother's death, Smith offered to pay his sister-in-law £40 in exchange
for the return (and therefore cancellation) of the bond. But Deborah
Smith, although she accepted the money, kept the bond and sued for
repayment in 1750, prompting not only legal protest from Daniel, but
two countersuits, claiming additional debts that his brother had owed
to him (or, more likely, his wife) for mending of "Sea Clothes," washing,

sewing, and boarding.[76] Beneath every confident claiming of credit lurked the constant danger of debt, frequently laid at the door of one's closest relations. In spite of the expansive credit context—new tools, new institutions, new international connections—again and again, sex and family laid people low. Wives overshopped; husbands left town; uncles defaulted. Insolvent debtors increasingly cited "sources beyond their control" as the culprit in their downfall; often, however, it was those ties most closely and personally connected that were at fault.

Gender, Character, and Credit

Credit was on the mind of every urban woman, whether she was looking for work, buying goods, or lending money to a relative. Credit ties shaped her ability to negotiate urban life and even, perhaps, what she looked like as she walked through the city streets. In June 1800, the *Newport Mercury* joked: "The new female fashion of dispensing with pockets, adds considerably to the *credit* of the Ladies; for being now without any convenience for carrying their money, the trade's people cannot be displeased at the want of *prompt* payments, as such a conduct would only serve as a reproach upon their own *inventive taste.*"[77] The paper played on two meanings of the word "credit"—both the sense of purchasing without paying and female shoppers' reputation for ingenuity—that captured the intertwined concerns of too little cash and too much uncertainty about financial reputations. The women described were canny players in a marketplace dominated by credit purchases. The shopkeepers, as creators and purveyors of fickle fashion, fell victim to their own need to extend credit to stay in business. The satiric passage also highlights the specifically gendered ambiguities of credit and its uses in the revolutionary period. On the one hand, credit was used to obtain goods that many felt were frivolous and wasteful, altogether typical of female indulgence. On the other hand, credit meant power, often in the hands of those unable to obtain political power.

Credit was on the minds of politicians, too, in the revolutionary period, because each time port residents bought goods, put in a day's work, or cleared a ship from the docks, they spread debt. At the time of the Revolution, white South Carolinians owed more per person to British creditors than any other mainland colonists.[78] While the colonies' indebtedness to British merchants was an appropriate state of affairs under the mercantile management of empire, in a republic it was politically unacceptable, for the nation and for individuals. Debt fostered dependence. The boycotts and embargoes of these years were attempts to break dependence on outsiders in favor of independence by curtailing commercial debt.

Dependent connections could be read as socially positive or socially destructive. On the positive side of the ledger, credit enmeshed an individual in society through the obligation to pay or the obligation to loan to the needy. Credit was the emblem of the personal trust that held communities (or even nations) together. In her revolutionary-era essays and plays, Judith Sargent Murray depicted dependence in a credit-based economy as "not simply a feminine state, but a *human* state" that could be tapped for public benevolence.[79] Sober use of credit encouraged rational calculation, forbearance, charity, and compassion; society profited from the presence of debtors and creditors. On the debit side of the ledger, credit threatened to disrupt the virtue and vigor of a society precisely because it spread dependence, and this consequence preoccupied republican thinkers in the late eighteenth and early nineteenth centuries. Rather than celebrate the way that credit bound together members of a society, these men saw debt as another form of enervating dependence, binding people to the demands of patrons rather than the selfless good of the community.

If credit risk in the form of mercurial "Lady Credit" generated gender anxiety, so too did the dependence that credit bred. By championing dependence as a "human state," Judith Sargent Murray was right, but few political theorists of the early nineteenth century followed her lead. Most stressed that dependence was a condition for white women and slaves; increasingly, to be in debt was to be unmanned. Anxious talk about the perils of ever-expanding debt was highly gendered and sexualized, from the pages of American newspapers down to the private letters of wine merchants who fretted to prevent "a disgrace happening to the yet unsullied Credit" of their businesses.[80] Many men felt torn between their need to seek out credit patronage and their desire to eschew "effeminate" dependency as they negotiated the late eighteenth- and early nineteenth-century economy.[81]

Although "credit" might have been depicted as female when merchants bemoaned their losses or wits poked acid fun at national monetary policy, however, actual women were not inherently too flighty or unstable to engage in the credit relationships that structured the Atlantic economy. Consumer culture and service work drew them deeply into the credit economy as debtors and creditors, either as part of families or on their own. In the seventeenth century, free women's reputations, and so female credit in the general sense, rested on sexual continence.[82] The experiences of litigating women and even the fictional pocketless female shoppers hailed in the *Newport Mercury*, however, indicate that the more commercial eighteenth and nineteenth centuries offered additional sources of credit for women, including family connections, their own histories of payment, and their crucial role in using and promoting goods. This wider base of financial credit suggests new possibilities for public understanding of female "character."

The pockets of free women in the colonial period were fabric bags, tied around their waists over full petticoats (Figure 11). Filled with the "small, easily lost, yet precious" items associated with housewifery (keys, seeds, yarn), pockets have been described as emblems of the "social complexity" of women's work.[83] When they shed these pockets in keeping with the new neoclassical styles of the early republic, free women implicitly acknowledged an economic transformation whose gender implications were still uncertain. As cash began to supplant barter and bank loans replaced neighbors' loans, an instrumental impersonality emerged in the marketplace, reflected in the records of the civil courts. Previously, the courts had watched over the long-standing book of account debts between neighbors. By the late eighteenth century, they found themselves flooded with technical cases concerning promissory notes that had circulated far beyond the confines of a face-to-face economy. Specific terms and interest penalties replaced mutuality and implicit promises to pay. Credit as contract prevailed over credit as relationship within the courts.[84] All of these changes have prompted historians to describe the eighteenth century as a time when a premodern world of deferred payment and barter gave way to a modern world of risk-taking that was essential for economic growth.[85] Would women, understood as perpetually dependent by their communities, find new places in these emerging economies of credit?

The relationships revealed within women's debt cases underline the persistence of social and familial factors in the marketplace and challenge the idea that economic change was moving resolutely toward impersonal capitalism. For many women, new instruments were linked with familiar exchanges. Free women in Charleston used promissory notes as they and their relatives had used bonds for many decades. Women in Newport employed promissory notes to secure the exchanges of goods and services that had long been central to the urban economy. Some women sought credit to support entrepreneurial risk-taking; others found credit a means of survival in an economy where most payments were deferred.[86] The change in the culture of credit was slow and partial. As Margot Finn has discovered in the small-claims courts of eighteenth-century England, the institutions that were designed to modernize credit relationships by replacing custom with law instead "repeatedly registered and affirmed entrenched social beliefs, identities, and practices."[87] Evidence from women's cases makes this point from the perspective of those who used credit to negotiate the urban marketplace. For them, the tools and the institutions themselves did not define what the changing market economy meant. Instead, the relationships in which these tools were embedded shaped their use and the larger understanding of credit.

In the daily experiences of city dwellers, dependence did not close people off in a subordinate limbo; it opened the door to participation in the marketplace and in society. Each time a woman made a purchase,

Figure 11. A pocket is clearly visible as part of this woman's undergarments. "Tight Lacing, or Fashion Before Ease," after a painting by John Collet. The Colonial Williamsburg Foundation.

witnessed a loan, helped a relative collect on an old debt, or worked for someone in anticipation of future wages, she created or strengthened economic connections to the credit-bound urban market. Her connections could lead to opportunity or greater vulnerability. The same system that enabled boardinghouse keeper Mary Searing to run up a bread tab left Bethia Clark in the lurch when lodgers sailed out of port without paying.

Chapter 4
Translating Money

A sheaf of promissory notes distributed throughout the city marked a woman as a person of credit but not necessarily of wealth. From tax lists with only a sprinkling of female names to poorhouse rolls dominated by them, official city records tell a tale of relative female poverty. These records support conclusions that have guided our understanding of women and money in the eighteenth and early nineteenth centuries: that most free married women's wealth was controlled by their husbands; that many unmarried women were too poor to possess enough property to be taxed; and that those unmarried women who did have taxable wealth tended to have less, overall, than men.[1] Legal restrictions and contemporary ideas about gender conspired to make the fully autonomous woman of independent wealth a relatively rare creature and her struggling, dependent counterpart a familiar one in urban port cities.[2]

Given the laws of coverture (which denied married women economic autonomy) and dower (which granted widows the right to use only a portion of the estate), free female relationships to property and female participation in commercial culture were often contingent and mediated through male capital and male economic activity. Enslaved women lacked even this connection, since under law they had no property rights, and only the use of money permitted to them by their owners. From the standpoint of these structural limitations, it might not even make sense to talk about "women and money," because rank—membership in a planter family, in a community of artisans, a group of day laborers, a family of slaves—mattered more in placing individuals within the wealth structure of the city than did gender.[3]

But urban women of many ranks used money every day, because city economies and connections depended upon money. Female city dwellers shared a combination of legal disabilities and fluid occupational identities that meant that women, free and enslaved, were less likely to be wealth holders, but they were regular wealth users. As a group, most women encountered money not as pieces of gold or acres of land but as inked lines in an account book, paper money in hand, or the value of their own or their laborers' bodies. In other words, "money" meant "earnings" and "prices" to them, translated into common units of value.

Those units of value were in the process of profound flux in the late eighteenth and early nineteenth centuries, a period often referred to as the "transition to capitalism." Banks, paper money, wage labor, and corporations all became common features of the economy and shaped how people thought about the daily use and political consequences of money.[4] In the years after the Revolution, private enterprise replaced colonial government control of the economy and commercial banks replaced a public money system. If personal credit—whether book debt, bond, or promissory note—threatened to enslave individuals to the whims of others, cash promised to set them free. The rise of the cash nexus seemed to offer impersonality and uniformity, since the value of a one-dollar note did not depend upon the bearer's deference to her neighbors.

The experiences of urban women clearly demonstrate, however, that the same kinds of ties that made daily use of credit possible bound cash itself to personal considerations. The result was a far less transparent, freeing medium than abstract thoughts about money suggested to men eager to proclaim their "independence." After all, ten shillings in the pocket of an enslaved woman was no ticket to freedom if she was forced to spend the money on her home plantation. Women's experiences of money as a product of relationships between individuals rather than between the individual and the state underscore how socially bound cash was. In some cases, cash dissolved hierarchical ties, but in others, it reinforced them, because even this most fungible and transparent form of money was what Viviana Zelizer calls a "socially created currency, subject to particular networks of social relations and its own set of values and norms."[5] New forms of money did not escape their social context; they gained meaning within those contexts. The human intention that moved money from one hand to another also defined it.

The fact that social relationships always shaped the cultural significance of money was an important continuity in women's lives from the colonial through the early national period. What changed was that ideas about money became a central way for women to understand the social connections that bound city dwellers together. Advice literature and family diaries have revealed that English homes in the eighteenth and early nineteenth centuries became increasingly "monetized" as women, in particular, applied the business techniques of record keeping and regular auditing to track wages of family members and budget for regular consumer expenditures.[6] In rural America, this way of thinking about profits and losses in domestic life was slower to develop, especially among women, who continued to conceive of relationships as reciprocal and cooperative, even when work and goods were exchanged.[7] Cities, however, were different. From the economic arrangements that created housefuls, to the Atlantic service economy's market valuation of women's work, to the constant presence of enslaved people whose bodies and labors were directly translated into cash value, the environment of Atlantic port cities led women to view their lives and their connections in newly financial terms.

The Many Forms of Money

Early Americans had two ways of thinking about and using money. The first, which scholars sometimes call "imaginary money," or money of account, was recorded in account books. The entries in these books noted the value of goods or labor in common units, like pounds or dollars, but the sums did not correspond to physical bills changing hands. Imaginary money was closely linked to credit because it served as the currency of book debt. The second form of money that Americans used was "real money"—coins, paper bills, and commodities. "Real money" was the physical representation of value, and in the case of currency, could not only settle transactions but also circulate throughout the economy. It was closely tied to credit, too, through financial instruments like promissory notes, which exchanged hands and could be assigned to others in new transactions.[8] Urban women's familiarity with each marked their integration into commercial culture, since whether they were paying shopkeepers in candlewick or selling chickens for cash in the market, they had to master monetary concepts of value.

Real money circulated in various forms, including foreign coins and paper bills of many descriptions. The presence of multiple foreign coins and paper bills in the economy meant that women, like men, who bought and sold, loaned and borrowed, had to be able to understand and use more than one form of money. It took several tries and multiple scraps of paper for wealthy Newport shopkeeper Sarah Rumreil to enumerate precisely the various bills, notes, and coins that John Shearman and Daniel Dunnavin had stolen from her desk one night in 1762. Breaking in through the back window, the two men made off with a "Work'd Pocket Book" containing:

£53 in old tenor bills
£0.16.0 in lawful money of the colony of RI
£0.2.9 in lawful money of Connecticut
£9.4 in New Hampshire old tenor
several pieces of O.T. Bills

a silk purse with:

> 32 small pieces of silver
> 13 pistereens
> 3½ Spanish milled dollars
> 1 cobb silver
> 2 half French crowns
> 5 shillings sterling

a linen bag with:

> 2 tickets for the Newport 2nd class lottery
> 2 tickets for the Newport 3d class lottery
> 4 tickets for the Newport 4th class lottery
> 1 ticket for the Providence Library
> 2 tickets for Roxbury
> 1 ticket for Boston
> 1 ticket for the county of york[9]

The sheer volume and variety of Rumreil's holdings were remarkable, but more interesting was the way she grouped different kinds of money in each container. From the humble linen bag to the elegant silk purse, each separate receptacle and its contents reflected a particular kind of money and, indirectly, suggested a particular kind of consumer.

Rumreil's silk purse, filled with silver coins, English shillings, and pistereens, marked her as a successful, elite American. Knowledge of foreign currency was not exclusively the province of the rich; women who worked in service businesses, for example, were familiar with foreign coins because of their Atlantic clientele. Mary Sous ran a small business retailing rum in mid-century Charleston. When her supplier demanded payment for the hogshead he had sold her, she gave him a doubloon to cover part of the cost, promising the balance when she was able to sell the rest.[10] While retailers like Sous might understand and use foreign currency, they did not stockpile it. Wealthy elites, in contrast, could view a cache of foreign hard currency as a bulwark against hard times or a legacy to pass on. The inventory of Charlestonian Martha Savage listed, in addition to paper money, Spanish dollars and pistoles, Portuguese and German pieces of gold, and sterling silver coin.[11] These international collections of currency depended upon wealth and direct involvement with foreign commerce; women as a whole had less of all three. As a result, most women in daily activities did not use foreign coins and had little regular exposure to foreign currencies, unless they were called to court to settle debts incurred by their more internationally involved male family members.

The diverse contents of Rumreil's "work'd pocket book" and linen bag (colonial paper money and lottery tickets) would have been more familiar to the average city dweller. Multiple forms of paper money were common in the urban streets, though contemporary complaints about the scarcity of cash suggest they were not common enough. Paper money could be private (issued by a bank and backed by reserves from subscribers), but until the nineteenth century, it was typically an IOU issued by a colonial government to help finance a war, redeemable in the future for coin or, more often, tax credit (Figure 12). From the beginning, this kind of paper money, also known as fiat currency, was a battleground

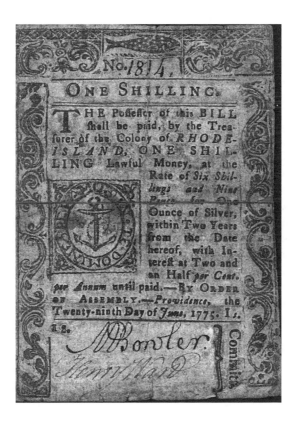

Figure 12. June 29, 1775, Rhode Island note. Reproduced from the original held by the Department of Special Collections of the University Libraries of Notre Dame.

over power and trust. Who had the power to control forms of money—colonial governments, or the central British government, exclusively? Could colonial or state governments be trusted to repay their debts? In the years of the early republic, as the creation of money fell increasingly into private hands through institutions such as banks, many wondered if these chartered institutions could be trusted to stay in business, much less repay the debts that enabled them to issue their own forms of paper money. The fact that the state or a private bank could issue "money" above and beyond what it held, and that the state could, and did, change the value of currency already circulating in the economy, made people profoundly uneasy about what money really represented and unlikely to store it up in large quantities.[12] Small denominations (such as Rumreil's sixteen Rhode Island shillings) were useful for local transactions and would not have remained in the pocket book for long.

The greatest fear with paper money was that it could lose value, since it was not inherently of value itself. Elizabeth Thurston tried in 1782 to redeem bills of public credit emitted by Rhode Island in 1750 and 1760, emphasizing that she should be paid "at their real value when emitted," plus interest.[13] Rhode Island and South Carolina currencies both depreciated over the eighteenth century. Rhode Island even retired its inflationary "old tenor" currency in favor of a new one in 1763. The experience of constant inflation may have been one of the reasons that bonds were not popular among eighteenth-century Newporters. Most of the depreciation of South Carolina currency took place in the first half of the century; by the time of the Revolution, the rate of seven pounds in South Carolina currency for each one British pound sterling had been remarkably stable for several decades. The financial demands of the national war effort threw all economies into disarray. Depreciation of Continental bills of credit during and after the Revolution threatened the complete breakdown of the paper money system, as creditors refused to accept the bills for transactions.[14]

Paper money was physically as well as economically unstable. When Newport widow Mary Thompson's pocket book caught fire, it contained more than £27 of paper money, £16 of which were "Bills of Credit emitted by the Colony of Rhode Island." Fortunately for Thompson, the General Assembly replaced her burnt fragments with new bills.[15] Paper money, whether bills or bonds, was difficult to keep track of in tumultuous times. Abigail Barker had a bond for 952 pounds, 14 shillings old tenor from Rhode Island's general treasurer Joseph Clarke, on behalf of the then colony in March 1762 to be paid the following year, but a decade later she related a breathless tale of its disappearance. Forced to move as British ships ominously filled the city's harbor, "during the hurry & confusion she with others was in at that time in the Town of Newport, she by some accident lost said Bond in her removal." Pressing on, Barker explained that "as the money due thereon was what she relied upon for her support, when by Age or Infirmities she should be rendered incapable of earning her livelyhood she requests the Assembly would be pleased to direct the General Treasurer either to pay her the money due thereon or to give her a Bond for the same as will be most agreeable to them."[16] Rather than insist on the presentation of the physical form of the money, the Assembly honored the spirit of the promise and granted her request, but only after resolving to advertise for the bond, to ensure that Barker had not endorsed it over as currency.

Paper money required political calculations about which bills of which colonies should be accepted, and at what value. Urban proprietors, who were often forced to accept diverse forms of payment, struggled to set boundaries. One Meeting Street storekeeper in Charleston announced in the tumultuous 1790s that he would accept: "country produce at generous price, continental or public securities, bonds under the installment law, or the purchaser's bond with approved security; a small part cash will be required."[17] Not every woman could keep up with such calculations. Abigail Barker's 1762 bond had been intended as an annuity. Just as Charleston women salted away savings in private and public bonds, thereby ensuring financial maintenance for themselves and a badly needed source of capital for businessmen and politicians, Barker invested some of her own savings in the Rhode Island treasury in hopes that the interest she earned would support her in old age. Thirty years after her initial investment, she had "lost her reason" and could not translate the state's promise into her own maintenance. Thomas Robinson, the man who was supporting her, had the government transfer this responsibility and access to him.[18] Paper money, in other words, made particular demands on its users—organization, good record keeping, solid legal representation—that many could not meet, particularly women who could not control their living arrangements and needed male representatives to speak for them in court.[19]

Women who did appear in court over civil cases had to make savvy financial judgments as they translated purchases, loans, interest payments, and goods into a common currency. Over the course of the revolutionary period, favored and official currencies changed regularly. In Rhode Island, old tenor bills of public credit or "current New England money" in the 1750s gave way to lawful money in pounds or Spanish silver milled dollars in the 1780s and 1790s, and dollars in the 1820s.[20] Charlestonians shifted from transactions conducted mainly in "current money of the province," calculated in pounds prior to the Revolution, to sterling money in the 1790s, to dollars by the 1820s.[21] The resulting conversions and calculations—between old and new currencies, as well as between currencies of different states and different countries—were a perpetual problem in colonial North American commerce. Enterprising publishers came out with "ready reckoners" filled with conversion and price tables for those unable to perform the calculations themselves.[22] An urban woman understood financial life in this language; her exposure to paper monies, bonds, and shifting currencies in daily commerce meant that she used and understood money not only as an "imaginary" concept but as a changeable, manipulable object. Through her experiences with depreciation, old and new official currencies, and exchange values, she would have seen herself as operating within a larger economic system. In other words, the changing language of currencies implicated female transactions in commercial trends more generally. While their rural counterparts could perhaps conduct barter in a world where a "shilling" had enduring meaning, city women had to learn to manage a world where value was perpetually negotiated.

Entities that issue money believe that coins and bills speak to their power, trustworthiness, history, and values. A five-shilling note issued by the state of South Carolina in April 1778, just after a devastating fire, featured the image of a phoenix rising from flame and ash, promising a rebirth that, unfortunately, was soon to collapse under British army occupation (Figure 13). The illustrations on money acted as a widely

Figure 13. April 10, 1778, South Carolina five-shilling note. Reproduced from the original held by the Department of Special Collections of the University Libraries of Notre Dame.

accessible kind of "public imagery" that leaders strove to control, but this control was never complete, since those who used the money infused it with their own values.[23] The same can be said of the many kinds of paper and hard currencies of the late eighteenth and early nineteenth centuries. A paper bond certificate might seem to represent impersonal, modern money, since it earned interest and bore penalties if the debtor failed to pay after a specific length of time. Handwritten notations on the back of Charleston bonds, however, reveal that they were paid not just in the "lawful money of the province" promised on the front but in a combination of cash and rice that sometimes conformed to the repayment schedule, but often did not. Particularly in the decade following the Revolution, commercial transactions involving women and men could still be closely connected to tangible goods as well as more abstract ideas about value.

During a period in which "everything changed" in terms of political economy, currency, and assumptions about the marketplace, individual users could be stubbornly persistent in the ways they handled those pieces of paper. Old conventions were stretched to accommodate new forms of money; newer, commercial instruments often bore the residue of economic relationships cemented with commodities and barter. The validity of any form of money lay in the willingness of trustworthy people to use it, more than printed promises of worth. The result for urban women was that gender, race, and rank continued to shape the daily use and meaning of money.

Cash as a Socially Coded Currency

For all its perils, paper money did have the benefits of portability and flexibility; it could be folded into a pocket and could be used in disparate transactions. Mary Thompson's pocket book full of bills burned as it sat inside her desk, but it also would have been convenient to carry around for use in transactions. Charlestonian Elizabeth Hunt was probably carrying the "Irish-stich POCKET-BOOK, containing some small money, a note of hand and receipts that will be of no use to any person but the owner," when she lost it in the summer of 1765.[24] Well-to-do and middling families enclosed bills with letters to pay for goods they had requested from distant cities. Slave women carried bills with them to exchange in the course of business at a variety of market stalls and street corners.

As they physically carried money around, women could also assign it over to others. During the Revolution, the South Carolina government issued certificates to its creditors in place of the increasingly worthless colonial paper money. Rather than hold onto these IOUs, free Charleston women used the certificates to conduct transactions of their own. Government certificates, like paper money and like private bonds, circulated in the economy through the hands of women as well as men. Wealthy Frances Susannah Pinckney assigned one of her several public "indents" for £3,000 principal, £210 annual interest over to William Parker a year after it was issued, "having received from him full value."[25] The many women who held indents of far lower value could do the same, taking their paper certificates with them as they moved through city streets.

The mobility and transferability of cash was both its greatest asset and its biggest threat to the established commercial and social order. Armed with paper money, buyers and sellers could do business with those they did not know well enough to trust with credit in the form of book debt. Transactions could flourish in the more impersonal context of mobile urban populations. As historian Gordon Wood notes, paper money "had a corrosive effect on traditional patronage dependencies" because it could be detached from the long chains of credit that bound the community together.[26] Money borrowed from a bank through a paper certificate did not come with an added charge of social deference.

For other kinds of dependencies—those between women and men, those between servants, slaves, and masters and mistresses—the picture is more equivocal. Cash in hand certainly facilitated transactions for those unable to receive credit on their own account. But using cash, as opposed to trading goods, required skills of numeracy and the ability to tell true from counterfeit forms, which could place the less educated at a disadvantage. Cash was also vulnerable to confiscation and manipulation by the powerful over the powerless. South Carolina planters used cash both to motivate slaves and to control their economic activities. By the "planter's custom," enslaved workers were sometimes paid cash rather than plantation credit for crops they grew on their own time. The nominal transparency of the cash they received failed to liberate them as consumers because their money was earmarked for a specific destination controlled by a master. [27] Planters frequently coerced or compelled cash-holding slaves to spend their money at plantation "stores" rather than at urban shops, marking that money for exchanges that took place in a context of domination and supplication rather than service and autonomy.

Earmarking was only one way that money was socially coded. The relationship between cash and credit, in a store and under the law, determined how individuals used money by linking economic decisions with social ones. Although frustrated merchants presented cash and credit as opposites in their advertisements, promising discounts for those willing to pay immediately, it is more accurate to see them working together. In shops, periodic infusions of cash could breathe life into malingering credit accounts; conversely, credit dollars earned through outwork could be cashed in by women looking for a little liquidity. Under the law, enslaved and free married women had no right to their own credit; cash could serve as a vital tool for purchases outside of fathers', husbands', and masters' oversight.

The more than two hundred women who did business with Newport merchant Jabez Carpenter in the 1750s and 1760s needed both cash and credit. The particular mixture each used depended on her relationship with Carpenter, her own wealth, and her ability to exchange work for money. Infrequent customers who purchased single items or small amounts paid in cash, either on the same day or after a brief grace period. "Nurs Huddy" bought a pair of women's shoes in the fall of 1755 for £4.12, and twenty days later paid the cash in full, her only transaction recorded with Carpenter.[28] At the other end of the spectrum were women who did more than £100 worth of business with Carpenter, most as both customers and suppliers. Over years of regular transactions, these women paid for their purchases with a mixture of cash and credit he received on their, or a third party's, accounts. Abigail Sanford's purchases were periodically balanced by "a ballance due in my [Carpenter's] favour," Sarah Martain's by yearly discounts with Francis Honeyman. In some cases, the credit women earned came from years of their own work. Mary Dumoy supplied mittens in exchange for imported fabric and thread.[29]

Women of all ranks used ready money and delayed or third-party payments in some combination. What account book entries reveal is that the place of cash in each person's life was shaped by income and social position. A poor woman gathered together a small sum of cash when she wanted to purchase a pair of shoes or a half-pound of tea. Since she had no source of credit, cash was the ticket to participation in the marketplace. A woman with space enough to grind chocolate or spin candlewick could initiate regular transactions in goods that produced store credit. She brought cash into the relationship only when she had collected enough through other means to pay off a larger portion of her debt. A wealthier married woman, widow, or businesswoman already had the long-term credit to run up larger debts before arranging a reckoning. The well-to-do in Charleston, for example, tended to run up a series of credits before paying "cash in full" for their purchases.[30] Cash was used variously as a replacement for credit, a stop-gap measure, or a periodic gesture of reckoning. Its flexibility came not in transcending social constraints but in working within them.

For all of Carpenter's customers, as for other urban women, cash was grounded in two very concrete concepts: the value of their labor, and the prices of goods that they wanted to buy. Cash earned through local work or selling produce could be exchanged for desirable goods. Since women were more likely to be paid in cash, and to use cash in stores than men were, for women in particular, cash was labor value and prices. Rural women in colonial Virginia, including slaves, free wives, and daughters, were cash customers in local stores because their work gave them the money (in the form of cash) that the law prohibited in the form of credit.[31] Work in the Atlantic service economy was a common source of cash for women. Tavernkeeper Ann Cross, who ran a busy cash-and-credit business before the war, purchased her supplies every few days, each time receiving a receipt acknowledging full payment.[32] Since this would not be possible with an all-credit clientele, Cross must have been able to obtain fairly regular cash payments from her customers, which she in turn used to supply her business.

Bolstered by a measure of interest-free credit from their own suppliers, merchants continued to offer informal store credit to worthy customers into the nineteenth century. Henry Muckenfuss's female customers typically paid "cash in full" several months after their purchases; this practice did not change according to the relative size of their balances. Mary Shields purchased just $3.72 worth of rice, currants, vinegar, and sugar over the course of a year but brought cash to the shop only in late December. His largest female customer, Jane Strawberry, made purchases six times in a year and paid in two lump sums totaling $201.10.[33] These women used cash the way other men and women used reciprocal credit accounts—long periods of accumulation, with periodic reckonings.

Free and enslaved women negotiated a mixture of cash and credit when paying off the debts of husbands and masters, as well as their own. The entries "By cash dld. yr wife" or "Cash rec'd of his neegro woman" are common in eighteenth-century account books.[34] Wealthy Charlestonians had their slaves carry cash from the countryside to the city and vice versa, and asked them to purchase and sell goods in the marketplace on their behalf with cash. Enslaved women and men performed similar tasks in the city's shops, paying installments on free male credit accounts. Handling, carrying, and paying out cash were part of understanding a money economy.

Carrying cash on behalf of a mistress did not, however, obliterate the social distinctions between a slave and her owner; the presence of cash did not necessarily render economic exchanges independent of their social nexus. Many cash transactions, even in the early nineteenth century, were not products of distant, "rationalized" relationships but in fact still densely interwoven with emotional, social, and political concerns. Family members used cash in repaying debts to each other. Mary Nichols eventually sued to retrieve the cash she had lent to Herbert Nichols and his family while they boarded with her in the 1760s and early 1770s. She had even been forced to "hire" cash herself "in the time of their sickness . . . and laid out in Necessaries for his Wife's and Family's Use."[35] Cash, not just credit or gratitude, was the coin of family transactions because cash was demanded by those who provided the "necessaries" of life.

The close tie between cash and labor value meant particular perils for free married women that increased over time. In Newport, for example, as throughout New England, free women's petitions for divorce increased at the end of the eighteenth century, with the typical woman citing the need to protect her earnings—"the fruits of her industry"— from a husband who had deserted her. Without legal protection, these earnings could be claimed by any such wayward husband on his way back through town. As historian Elaine Forman Crane notes, he would have been unlikely to make the effort for the bartered goods that dominated female economy in the seventeenth and early eighteenth centuries.[36] Cash payments for work—portable, transferable—gave women currency, literally, in the urban economy. They made the value of women's work easily translatable and newly vulnerable.

The social power of cash earnings was potentially greatest for enslaved women. Jane Ball kept her Charleston account with her son in "cash," which allowed her to direct him to "give Hagar & Mary [her slaves] 1/2 Dollar a piece out of my cash" for their efforts in marketing the fruits of her plantation dairy.[37] Since she hoped that such a payment would inspire their industry, she must have known that they had good use for cash in the city. Female slaves who washed clothes and cooked meals for the soldiers stationed in town or on Sullivan's Island also collected cash, as did those who sold goods in the Charleston marketplace. By paying cash to the slave herself, rather than using her work to earn credits with her mistress, employers and customers facilitated a measure of autonomy for enslaved Charlestonians—an autonomy supported by the courts, which upheld slaves' property rights in bonus wages.[38] Cash gave enslaved women spending power that many whites themselves lacked and, if they could keep it from the hands and appropriation schemes of their owners, a means to assert some independence.[39] As slaves knew all too well, however, using money in the marketplace was often just as socially and culturally constrained as earning it.

Converting Money, Translating Value

Frustrated at her longtime tenant James Dupre's failure to pay his full rent, Ann Ferguson went to his house the first day of October in 1818 and seized his slave, Jim. Dupre protested, but the court supported her view of an enslaved person as walking money; the jury found that Ferguson was due the late rent and interest payments and ruled that she could keep possession of Jim or be paid the $565.70 due.[40] Ferguson's actions bore one of the hallmarks of economic autonomy—the ability to convert one kind of asset into another. Rank largely determined whether and how men and women could make such conversions. The majority of the urban population had just their own labor, foodstuffs, and consumer goods to trade for currency. The more well-to-do also had real estate, property in other people, bulk commodities, and financial investments.

The flexibility with which any woman approached money was a product of her overall wealth. Wealthy families had multiple strategies for shifting around forms of money, either by generational transfer of property via inheritance, assuming each other's credit burdens in exchange for cash or property, drawing on credit accounts with third parties to repay each other for purchases, or consolidating real estate holdings by offering widows cash payments to relinquish their dower rights. For most women, however, money was not something stored up but something gained piece by piece and used soon after it was acquired. Earnings paid for rent, food, or store accounts. A few shillings became a set of buttons, which might in turn become a few shillings again, or some eggs. Money was real, but it was transitory, and was always closely connected with prices in the urban marketplace.

Gender, too, played a role in the kinds of financial conversions possible. Women were the most likely members of their communities to convert material goods such as clothing into money through pawning, in-kind payments, or local exchange. Free and enslaved women had extensive access to and knowledge about cloth and clothing, which gave it particular value in their material and financial lives. Gender-based legal restrictions made other kinds of conversions very difficult; only by a special act of the government could most free women turn real estate into ready money. The most common reason for Newport women to petition the General Assembly, except during the dire circumstances of the Revolutionary War occupation and its aftermath, was to obtain permission to sell the property of dead, missing, underage, or mentally incapacitated husbands, brothers, or children in order to pay off debts or support themselves. When Robert Audley's four daughters wanted to sell the Newport lot and the house on it that he had bequeathed to them, two of the women needed special permission from the General Assembly of the colony to do so. Sarah Mason was married, and her husband John had been lost at sea on a sloop headed for South Carolina four years previously. Although she was almost certainly a widow, she was still considered a feme covert, and was unable to sell property without the participation of her husband or the involvement of the colonial government. Her unmarried sister Constant was not quite yet twenty-one, and so also required special permission to make the sale.[41]

Female Charlestonians with land but little cash likewise had to seek permission from the assembly to circumvent restrictions of coverture.

In their petitions, women did not challenge a general male prerogative over land or the law's determination to treat real property separately from other forms of money.[42] Their narratives of desperation and "last resort" portray a sense that real estate, although fixed with a price and exchangeable for money, was different. Real property was not something they considered ready-to-hand for paying debts.

Real estate was the most masculine form of capital, and law and custom worked together to keep capital in the hands of free men. The working women of the Atlantic service economy who struggled to patch together services for the urban population had to find ways around the widespread perception that capital was to be accumulated and deployed by free men. Historian Margaret Hunt found that among middling English families in the late seventeenth and eighteenth centuries, boys were given small sums of money to practice investing in business ventures with, whereas girls were expected to view money as something they could deliver to a future husband in the form of a dowry. "Men got capital; women were, at least in theory, merely a conduit for capital to flow to other families."[43] This distinction guided family arrangements among the middling trading classes, from work assignments to inheritance patterns. When a free widow remarried, for example, the property left to her use often reverted back to her children; even when she did have access to capital, it was for use, and not permanently hers.[44] Women who never married might not even temporarily find usable forms of capital.

Under certain circumstances, women did hold and use capital on their own behalf, not merely as "conduits" between men. Women setting themselves up as feme sole traders (who could legally keep their money separate from their husbands) in Charleston usually pledged a small stake that they had scraped together from the contributions of friends and relatives.[45] Others had capital in ownership of a house or business, enslaved workers, and, increasingly, financial instruments such as stocks and bonds. Gendered patterns of daily life, however, continued to shape the ways women could use the capital they had. If she could keep up the property, a woman with a house could obtain rental income, which was always a possibility in mobile cities, but difficult if the owner herself was on the move. Elizabeth Hathaway and her four children fled Newport for Massachusetts during the Revolution. The house they left behind them, located on Easton's Point, fell into disrepair and "decay," such that "no person capable of paying Rent will tenant it." The straitened circumstances of the war had contributed to their woes: "not since the Evacuation of the British troops" had she "received Rents sufficient to keep it in repair."[46] In the devastating postwar years, the slow recovery of Newport meant that few could afford to pay rents, leaving even women with capital investment in homes without means of support.

At the death of a husband or father, some women inherited both a shop and tools of a trade; carrying on the family business was a common way for middling urban women to support themselves. But a workshop and tools functioned as an investment only if a woman could add the necessary labor. Marcy Stevens's husband had left her a shop room that measured fourteen feet by twenty-six feet in Thames Street—the heart of commercial Newport—and the tools of his trade as a cutler. Unfortunately, she was unable to "devise any profit from it whatever," either through renting the space (it needed too many repairs) or through her "own industry," which brought in only a "little" to support her four children. In fact, the shop and the attached rooms were further burdened with annual dower payments due to her mother-in-law that threatened to "consume the whole" of the property. For Stevens, the best option was to convert the capital into more liquid money; she petitioned the general assembly for permission to sell her husband's legacy.[47]

For substantial portions of the free urban population, enslaved people were a form of capital, returning income to their owners and retaining a certain value. Well-off southern widows were especially likely to have most of their wealth invested in the bodies of people that they owned.[48] Even women who did not have large estates often had their greatest wealth in the bodies of their slaves. So when Rachel Laurence died in 1767, of her £307 inventoried estate, £290 was in the value of two slaves.[49] It was not unusual for free women to inherit enslaved people rather than real estate. Newporter Phebe Bull ended up in county jail for her dead father's debts in 1794. As she explained to the General Assembly, "the bulk of the Estate given her by her said Father consisted in Negroes, some male and some female part of whom died soon after, and the remainder when the British Troops evacuated Newport left her and went with them to New York and became a total loss."[50] The enslaved people "became a total loss" to her by becoming their own masters and mistresses under the provisions of the British army. Phebe's remaining estate was humble, consisting of a few pieces of furniture and cookware, as well as six Queen's Ware plates.

A free woman saw in her slave a form of money that was vulnerable to the dangers that all human bodies confronted; it was, however, relatively easy to convert slave wealth into another form as needed. The implications for the way people thought about money were profound, since all kinds of daily transactions "were backed by the idea of a market in slaves, the idea that people had a value that could be abstracted from their bodies and cashed in when the occasion arose."[51] With potential sale perpetually hanging over them, enslaved people learned from early in life to think about themselves in a doubled way—as a person and as a commodity. When they could, enslaved people used this doubled vision for their own purposes. While freedom could be "stolen" or "awarded," it could also at times be "bought," either by a family member or by paying one's own way. Because self- or kin-purchase was a legitimate avenue to freedom, sales were sometimes more symbolic than profitable. Widow Susannah Cochran sold Tissy, Maria, and Emma to Sarah Hawie for the nominal price of five shillings "and for natural affection" on the part of Sarah in 1806. By 1811, "Tissy Hawie" had become a free black woman. When she proceeded to purchase her daughter, Maria, from Sarah Hawie, she had to pay $370, a sum representing real labor value, despite the formerly cited "natural affection" that Sarah had for both of them.[52] The sale of a person was always a real financial transaction. As they negotiated freedom for each other, the Hawie women also used their sales to move and exchange money.

Where free white women sought exemptions from the laws of property to support their families, enslaved women and men tried to use those laws to reconstruct theirs. For their part, free black women in Charleston who bought and sold human beings found themselves on both sides of the "doubled vision" of slaves. For some, buying slaves meant purchasing family members out of slavery and into freedom. Louise Florance, a free black woman in Charleston, paid another woman $230 for her daughter Nanite, who was described as a "mulatto" on the bill of sale. Other free blacks, like whites, invested in enslaved people for a return in the form of labor, as was probably the case in May 1807 when Joseph Loveille ("a black man") and Rosette Finley ("a yellow woman") bought "an African slave named Mary" from Jacob Babett for $300. For still others, slave ownership was a source of cash: Barsheba Cattell, a "free woman of color" in Charleston, sold Rose and her child to Jacob Wulf for $850 in 1818.[53] In all of these cases, individual solutions failed to systematically challenge the legal system's racial and gender hierarchies.

The end of the Revolution did bring systematic change in Newport, as a gradual emancipation law freed the children born to enslaved mothers after March 1, 1784. These children would continue to serve their mothers' masters, without wages, until adulthood, but their bodies could no longer be cashed in by owners in need of funds. Their parents had no such protections. Free Newporters started to sell off their slaves to southern states during the Revolution, a practice that continued into the nineteenth century in spite of laws designed to curb it.[54] Hoping to preserve her investment and fearful of her female slave's independent attitude, one Newport mistress petitioned the court in 1810 for permission to send her slave to South Carolina, where she would live perpetually under the threat of sale.[55]

Potential investors looking for a new, non-human form of money with easy liquidity found stocks. Women had been investors in England from

the beginning of the eighteenth century, riding stock bubbles and col-
lapses with the rest of the population, but bank shares became notable
in American women's probate inventories and correspondence only in
the nineteenth century. Male relatives frequently facilitated these investments, such as Ruth Hadwin Williams's brother Benjamin, who wrote to
her from Newport, "Bank Stock is profitable. I hope to send thee more as
soon as another dividend is made."[56] Given their need for usable forms
of money, the initiative to seek out these new financial instruments could
easily be female, particularly in a city like Charleston, where several generations of women had depended on private investment through bonds.
When the Charleston Ladies' Benevolent Society organized in 1813,
they were not content to collect and redistribute clothing and food to
the poor. Instead, the female-headed society, which conducted most of
its own business matters, invested in bonds, bank stocks, and public securities to increase their funds.[57] Women in many cities embraced new
forms. By 1811, women held 8.5 percent of the accounts at the Bank of
North America.[58]

Stocks and securities held out the promise to women that they would
convert their investments into larger sums, but of course risk lurked behind hopes. "Jonas informed me that bank stock is so high, that he could
not advise me to purchase it, but that a new *fire insurance company* was
likely to be soon established, where he thought money might be deposited to advantage. He says it will be more productive than private notes
of hand, & that there is *no doubt of its safety*." Abigail Robinson wanted
to trust her brother, but expressed doubts about "the propriety of placing the few hundred dollars on which I chiefly depend for support in a
fire insurance company—where very destructive fires are so frequent as
they are in N York.—Perhaps the premiums are proportionate to the frequency of their occurrence."[59] An unmarried woman approaching her
sixtieth year, Robinson was caught between her desire for a more "productive" investment and her fears that a scheme based on the inflam-
mability of another city presented too great a risk for the "few hundred"
dollars' worth of capital she relied on for her support.

Investment safety was a vital concern at a time when money seemed
unstable and bank and insurance shares had yet to prove their security. This was all the more important for those with small amounts of
money—among whom white women and free blacks were disproportionately represented. Free people of color, Newport founders of the African
Union Society, heard an address from the Convention of Deputies from
the Abolition Societies assembled in Philadelphia in 1796, which advised
them that "your money will be safest and most beneficial when laid out
in lots, houses, or small farms."[60] In spite of the legal obstacles and practical difficulties of management, real estate remained in many minds the

safest form of capital. Urban women's limited ability to partake of this "safe" investment was therefore keenly felt. They had to be gamblers and dealers, creative and persistent in their efforts to extract small sums from the transactions of daily life.

Female Mastery of Money

The advice literature for young ladies that proliferated after the Revolution charged free women to see themselves as mistresses of money, rather than let it be masters of them. Instead of letting purchases on easy credit or available cash slip away, women were to manage these decisions actively, following the guidance of the pamphlets' (often English) authors. It was an ungrateful daughter and a disastrous wife who allowed extravagance or thoughtlessness to overcome her and thereby failed to marshal the value of her or her male relatives' money. Ann Taylor, one such author, began her section on "Domestick Economy" with "a simple calculation, which forms a sage, but neglected maxim, '*A penny a day is thirty shillings a year.*' Were this habitually kept in view, how many superfluous expenses would be curtailed! It would raise the character of that degraded thing a *penny*, to its proper value; pence would accumulate till they became pounds; and, like a well disciplined troop surrounding our possessions, would prevent insidious depredation, and often keep poverty at bay."[61]

Advice writers advocated various techniques for achieving this mastery, including keeping written accounts, gathering and double-checking receipts, and having a general sense of what items should cost, so that young women could not be deceived by a tradesman or servant. Mrs. Chapone advised genteel young women to practice their calculations: "Many articles of expence are regular and fixed; these may be valued exactly; and, by consulting with experienced persons, you may calculate nearly the amount of others: any material article of consumption, in a family of any given number and circumstances, may be estimated pretty nearly."[62] Numeracy, arithmetic, and estimation, firmly linked in colonial minds with commerce, remained valuable female skills even after mathematics gained a new kind of intellectual legitimacy in the decades following the Revolution. While advanced mathematics, as a practice and habit of mind for developing reason and logic, came to be added to male, but not female, curricula, as a practical matter of commerce and daily transactions, some basic facility united urban women and men.[63]

Again and again, by charging free women to live within their husbands' income, these tracts presented money as something belonging to men, but managed by women. Thoughtless women failed to remedy their ignorance about household funds; their passions controlled them, and as a result they could be ruined by money and debt. The active management style that was advocated assumed that women would understand debits and credits, would see the benefit of paying for items immediately rather than on credit, which often carried higher prices. In that sense, they were supposed to master money by remaining quite preoccupied with it. Even though Taylor sang the praises of the domestic woman, she envisioned the "domestick sphere" as one of knowledge, not ignorance and confinement. "A prudent woman ought to be made acquainted with her husband's affairs; she has an indisputable claim upon his confidence; with him she must stand or fall: he should not, therefore, conduct her blindfolded to the edge of a precipice, and plunge her, unsuspecting, into the gulf below."[64] As husbands' lives became more bound up in money and the market, so too must wives keep pace.

Taylor had high expectations for her female readers. Her most bracing advice, however, was reserved for lower-class women, who were upbraided with the lessons of capitalism: "A LIFE of indolence is injurious both to body and mind; and were it not so, it is unreasonable to expect food and clothing, with other accommodations, for nothing. These are things which much be purchased by some means; and those who have no property or fortune, must earn them by their labour: and to Providence they ought to be very thankful, if they have the use of their limbs, and senses, with health and strength, to enable them to do so."[65] While not particularly sympathetic toward poor women, her message about managing money in order to keep within one's means was consistent across classes: "suppose your father has twenty shillings a week, and spends but eighteen (which I hope is the case), he is really richer than one who has ten times as much, if it is not equal to what his situation in life requires."[66] This kind of message was fundamentally conservative in stressing the importance of mastering one's place in the social hierarchy through prudence and thrift.

At the same time, thrift demanded knowledge and calculation, whether a woman had pennies or hundreds at her disposal. Specific sums in specific denominations had to be tracked and accounted for; custom could not be relied upon. Taylor modified the opening salvo from her pamphlet for mistresses when addressing female servants. Rather than using the metaphor of money as defending troops, she focused on what money could buy. She urged serving women to save every scrap of food, because "A penny-worth of bread may be easily wasted every day, and that is thirty shillings a year!"[67] Martial imagery was a reasonable way to reach young ladies who read histories; for those with a more rudimentary literacy, money as prices was the common ground. But no one escaped the charge.

The poorest were not trusted to be thrifty on their own, even with the guiding advice of domestic manuals. Parish officials and Overseers of the Poor, who managed charitable contributions to the urban poor, viewed cash as a dangerous tool in the hands of the ignorant or incompetent, and therefore poor relief payments were very different from wages. While earnings could theoretically be spent anywhere, poor relief handouts could not. The parish officials at St. Philips in Charleston meted out specific sums on a case-by-case basis. Mary Dubberly was "lame, with the rheumatism and unable to work"; the charity she received was limited and specific—the parish paid her rent and gave her a pair of shoes.[68] Small allowances from the parish were earmarked for specific purposes: "for Cloaths," "for her children." Those who resisted this earmarking were punished by having even that small discretion in spending taken away, as when the wardens "Agreed, That the Allowance to Mrs. Savey be stop'd. from this day & she be only allow'd such Relief as the Church Wardens shall Think proper."[69]

Over the course of the late eighteenth century, city officials up and down the Atlantic Coast worked to put an end to the overburdened and inefficient "out relief" payment system and replace it with almshouses and work houses. The change in policy reflected demographic changes in cities that faced rising numbers of the permanently impoverished, as well as changing ideas about what made a poor person "worthy" or not. In exchange for relief from starvation and illness, almshouse residents were supposed to give all aspects of their lives over to the overseers, who chose what they wore, how they were fed, and where their children would be sent to work. Many found the degree of supervision too onerous, and left the almshouse whenever better weather or improved health made life on the street more bearable.[70] The shift from "out relief" to almshouse also indicated a belief about the power and danger of money. Those who distributed "out relief" allowances hoped to model thrift and calculation, like Mrs. Taylor and her ilk, but they feared that the poor were unable to master such a system. Women like Mrs. Savey, who so frustrated the Charleston church wardens, spent by her own calculations, which did not accord with theirs. The exasperating liquidity of a money allowance was too much for parish officials to bear and they moved to limit her discretion. By switching to handouts and tightly earmarked grants, however, these officials could not completely thwart Savey's financial autonomy. Charity shoes could be pawned.

Abigail Robinson, a Newport Quaker, kept a series of account books that would have made Mrs. Taylor and Mrs. Chapone proud. She used her accounts not only to practice frugality but also to bring order and mastery to her life. Upon the death of her father in late 1817, Robinson began a new account book titled "Account of family expenses since my dear Father's decease." The first page of entries included payments for food, lamp oil, freight, storage, and carting foodstuffs, payments to the doctor who had visited her father, and $7.75, the largest single payment, to William Vernon for burying her father. Taking control of the financial details surrounding her father's last illness and his burial may have deflected the emotional burden of losing both parents within months of each other. Her actions reveal the ways that economic life offered women an intellectual and emotional outlet. In addition to resigning oneself to God's will, or finding comfort in correspondence with sympathetic kin and friends, a woman could take control of her financial life to combat feelings of helplessness and loss. Margaret Manigault thought that the "poor little privations, which must I think be painfully felt in some instences" made by her headache-plagued sister-in-law "might add to her happiness if she thinks them useful."[71] Active financial management, whether in the form of record keeping or penny pinching, yielded psychological and social benefits.

Settling the accounts of a dead relative, while no doubt a chore for many, could also confer a sense of mastery upon a woman as she took charge of the family's well-being. Women who were denied these responsibilities were relieved of court appearances but stripped of the meliorating effects of financial work. After her husband's death, Alice Izard spent many hours and sheaves of paper trying to arrange for her own financial survival, the estates of her children, and the legacy of her husband. But since much of the work was done by male relatives, she was unable to control the course of events in the way that she wished. This was a trial for a wealthy woman like Izard, who through years of experience had gained mastery over a wide range of financial matters and was able to manipulate money in her own mind. In 1807, she wrote a letter to her son Henry, bristling with financial savvy:

I know very well that if I insure only $10,000 on my House, I can only be entitled to receive that sum on case of accident, & that was what I wished to have done. We shall see each other before it is necessary to renew the insurance, when we will talk the matter over. I am glad there was no mistake about Beck's Child, & that you recollected that her youngest is mine. . . . I wish I could conclude my Letter with agreeable accounts of the Rice you shipped in the Brig Speculator; but unfortunately it is a good deal hurt. . . . The forty five Barrels were sold, provided they were landed in good order, at five dollars pr Cent. The sale of course did not take place. Pray, my Son, let this be a warning to you to insure for the future.[72]

Accounts, insurance, rice sales, the value of property in enslaved workers—all were well within Izard's grasp, as she tartly informed her son. Women's primary responsibility for the stewardship of family resources has typically been seen as evidence of free women's subordinate social position. Casting their lot with family economic stability over individual enrichment, they were, in the eyes of some historians, "tools of and steadfast promoters of patriarchy."[73] Perhaps, though, it was a source of pleasure and self-confidence to settle financial matters. Since many free women's economic health was embedded in that of their families, taking charge of the family's possessions did work to preserve their individual well-being. A widow who tended an estate before passing it along to her children was also preserving her own freedom.[74]

Securing this kind of "freedom" was certainly not always a pleasure. Multiple petitions to the colonial and state legislatures in the revolutionary era speak to the dire financial straits of women asking for help with this task. Mary Brightman pleaded with the General Assembly to be permitted to return with a few household items from Tiverton to Newport, where her husband was with the British, or at least have her cow restored to her. "To hear my infant cry for milk will be very hard," she told the General Assembly, since "I suppose you are a father and to hear one of your infants cry for food and to have none to give it would be heart breaking work."[75] Defending the family's possessions occupied many hours for female relatives of departed Loyalists in Charleston after the Revolution, as they sought to shore up their own and their family's financial footing by claiming property that had been confiscated.[76] To make their case, many women had to argue that their political allegiance was distinct from that of their Loyalist husbands, and that they therefore deserved to be treated as economically distinct. It was a difficult position to take, particularly in Rhode Island and South Carolina, which among all the former colonies were strictest in linking political and economic interests of the family with the male household head. Statutes in both states denied any wife of a Loyalist man rights to even her own dower property.[77]

Sharp contrasts mark the picture of female "mastery" of money in the revolutionary era. Sometimes, pleading ignorance was the best defense. Those same Loyalist women hoping to reclaim seized assets stubbornly declared their ignorance of land values and the financial entanglements of their husbands.[78] Peggy Carr, a servant who worked in the house of wealthy Newporter William Ellery in 1800, used a similar tactic when her employer demanded that she return his accidental overpayment. As the aggrieved Ellery noted in the incriminating account book, "she acknowledged that she served with me at 4/ per week, but said she did not know money and she should not repay the $3.00."[79] These tactics worked because many people at the time did harbor beliefs that women as a group could not master money. Writing to her sister-in-law about her own husband's business losses after the Revolution, Catherine Read commented, "The Men think we don't feel those things because we do not penetrate into the ill consequences attending it." However, as she indicated in her letter, she was well aware of some of the complexities of finance in the early republic; the situation "was more mortifying because the loss was equal to ready Mony."[80] Jealous observers of Charleston's enslaved marketers found their financial acumen, in the face of presumed racial and gender inferiority, particularly galling.[81]

Women of different classes and different temperaments clearly had different degrees of mastery over their financial lives, but urban life demanded some facility with money from everyone. Not every urban mistress used account books to keep track of her servants' wages, but given the frequent loans and advances exchanged between employer and employee, many probably kept some kind of account. Not every woman collected receipts to document purchases, but many had to be ready to reconstruct the transactions of the Atlantic service economy. When Rebecca Allen wanted reimbursement for boarding the impoverished Mary Allen and her child, she needed to present an account for the $10.00 (five weeks at $2.00 per week) that was allowed to her out of the poor tax and agree to a $1.58 deduction for the quarter cord of wood the town had given the household.[82] Enslaved women who carried money for their mistresses, earned wages and bonuses in cash, or saved funds to purchase their own freedom needed sufficient "mastery" to negotiate a legal system hostile to their possession of cash. Money would become more, not less, important in the lives of women in the nineteenth century as cash wages and set prices for consumer goods became increasingly prominent parts of life. Peggy Carr might prefer an oral agreement with William Ellery, but her daughter would be unlikely to strike such a deal with her employer if she went to work in one of the new textile mills springing up around Rhode Island.

Commerce and Conscience

By the late eighteenth century, commerce had become a common idiom for understanding all kinds of human interactions, and some historians have suggested that commercial paradigms dominated Americans' lives. The language and concepts associated with money, purchasing, and trade were serviceable tools for authors of all stripes. The indefatigable Mrs. Taylor advanced her cry for economy from the saving of bread crusts to the saving of souls: "if economy in worldly matters is indispensable, of how much greater importance must it be in your spiritual concerns! . . . If pence accumulate and become of value, listen to the clock, and note the fleeting moments, how rapidly do they amount to hours; hours to days, and days to months and years!"[83] For patriots, too, money and trade were a lingua franca for reaching disparate colonists. On the pages of the colonies' newspapers, the British imperial crisis of the 1760s and 1770s was framed around "an elaborate story of misunderstood American consumers."[84] Vulgar shoppers run amok were to blame for injurious taxes.

Personal correspondence mirrored political rhetoric in reaching for commercial metaphors. Making the familiar charge that she had not written as often as she should have, Mary Morton wrote, "I know very well, Eliza, that in this Commerce the balance will be vastly in my favour. . . . Our traffic will consist of articles we can spare & still have enough left for domestic consumption; thou art unusually qualified for the friendly communications of an epistolary intercourse; & I am favoured with sufficient talents to know their value."[85] Personal visits were exchanged in a manner that echoed obtaining goods on credit. Ann Simons invited her friend Mary Singleton to Charleston with the words: "remember Mary— that you have not Paid the interest of your debt to me on the account of visits. I should be sorry to be thought mercenary on any other bill but the one in question—and I do confess the spirit of a usurer on that."[86]

These repeated public and private references were more than literary devices. A commercial consciousness served to explain as well as illustrate. In speaking of the "balance" of letters or the "account of visits," literate women alluded to the account books in their own minds. Neighborly exchanges had long been supported by a current of calculation, but urban women's words suggest something more expansive than convivial reciprocity. References to "domestic consumption" and usury connected the imagined ledgers in their minds to larger debates about finance and economics.

For urban women, knowledge about money in the form of prices, in particular, conferred a broader frame of reference for ideas about community and human relationships. As the family marketers, women were keenly aware of prices. Wealthy or well-connected women could put their knowledge of international prices to profitable use. Abigail Robinson was not confined to local rural women in the Newport marketplace when she wanted to purchase butter. Her cousin in New York, "where I understood it [the price] was lower than it was here," arranged for a credit purchase of "between 40 & 50 dollars, in twenty months which has been a saving to me of, from ten to twenty cents on a dollar."[87] An interest in prices and saving money encouraged women with resources to look beyond their communities and contemplate the contours of the larger economy. In fact, given the state of commercial markets in the revolutionary era, this kind of knowledge and its transmission along social networks was vital. Networks provided the knowledge people needed to figure out how new goods or new forms of money would fit into their lives. Women and men depended upon them.

The price information that city dwellers shared also served as a measure of community well-being. In the midst of the War of 1812, Ruth

Williams heard from her kinswoman back in Newport, "N Port is very dull, I cant tell thee anything cheerfull about it—numbers have removed, many more thrown entirely out of business. . . . Mutton has been 12 & is now 10 cents pr pound Beef very high Butter 25 the standing price of Indian meal 8/ pr bushell it has been 10/. was it not for the high price of provisions we should do as well as for several years our finances are the same but it makes a great difference tho desire not to complain when our Neighbors are so much worse off."[88] Quoting prices to each other, women both conveyed information of practical use and captured a picture of community health and stability in brief, stark terms. Prices served as a cultural shorthand that women all along the coast could interpret.

Export commodity prices served a similar dual function for Charleston elites. While they accumulated vast estates, all members of elite families kept an eye on the international markets for rice and, later, cotton. The majority of their letters, whether written by women or men, contained some reference to the sale of rice. Often, the discussion centered around business affairs of direct interest to the participants. According to Joseph Manigault, Mrs. Middleton promised him, "as soon as [she could] sell her rice, [she would] pay her bond; but I can assure you that there is no demand for Rice at present."[89] Margaret Manigault's agent in Philadelphia informed her that her rice "happens however to be as unsaleable here as with You, owing to the embargo," and suggested other ways for her to repay him "rather than that it should be Unpaid, which would be Unpleast. to us both."[90] Rice was accepted as commodity money, and its fluctuating price was crucial to the fortunes of men and women.

Commodity price information could also create a sense of connection—of being "in the know" about a wider world—even between those who did not plan to act on it immediately. This was one of the ways that money, in the form of prices, served a symbolic function in the lives of people who might not control much of it personally. Lydia Simons's November 1776 letter to her brother John Ball at Kensington reflects an unsure hand and limited formal education, "I will be glad if you will cum for me next Tuesday week or if that day dont sute you any day that week, for I asure you I all most long to see home and you all," but these deficiencies did not preclude a knowledge of, and interest in transmitting information about, commodity prices. "Sault sells at 25 Shillins a bushil," she informed her brother, telling him that their father would obtain a supply, "and Ozns that is 9 Shillins People thinks it will be 7.6 soon."[91] Simons was passing on useful information as well as signaling her participation in family concerns. Free women, like men, saw the price of rice, and by implication its quality, as an important marker of South Carolina's identity in the Atlantic world.[92] In their letters and conversations, they reinforced their own participation in this outward-looking identity.

An expansive commercial consciousness was usually not explicitly rec-
onciled with the emerging discourse of domesticity. At the same time
that early nineteenth-century booksellers were peddling Mrs. Chapone's
vision of a financially shrewd housewife, they were also flogging a new
kind of literature that proclaimed money-making a "contagion" that "true
women" of the white middle class were well rid of.[93] Pursuit of profit,
these writers believed, required men to shed their consciences. In their
homes, the "domesticity" literature promised, middle-class white women
could preserve the values of love, compassion, and charity that were
threatened by cold hard cash and an impersonal money marketplace.

But city dwellers knew that dollars and domesticity had to coexist. For
urban women, compassion and calculation often leaned on one another,
as in the case of the rising female benevolent societies in American cities,
including the Charleston Ladies' Benevolent Society and the Newport
Quakers' "gleaning society." These organizations drew well-to-do women
into the homes and finances of their neighbors, where they passed judgment, cajoled donations, and organized investments, lotteries, and raffles
of their own.[94] Free women's early involvement in these private societies,
and their access to wealth, gave their public roles a financial cast that co-
incided with the domestic and religious meanings of their work. Domesticity, benevolence, and commerce were all useful discourses for urban
women trying to make sense of social relations in the new United States.

Poor working women and enslaved women were pointedly excluded
from the rhetoric of "domesticity" and simultaneously distrusted as managers of money. Jeanne Boydston has argued that the emergence of "the
peculiarly intense and sentimental" American domesticity was in part
a reaction to the increasing economic importance of poorer women's
waged work.[95] The challenges to household unity raised by arrangements
such as the houseful, as well as new labor demands of a volatile economy,
were deeply threatening to many urban residents; domesticity promised
respite. Money matters, however, could not be left to those women compelled to earn it.

The familiar story of women and money in the revolutionary era has
been shaped by studies of free women's property rights. From this perspective, little changed for free white women in cities like Newport and
Charleston between 1750 and 1820, who faced the same climate of constraint with limited loopholes and exceptions. The property rights tale of
restriction and marginalization finds its complement in the nineteenth-
century middle-class discourse of domesticity. The period witnessed
often dramatic economic transformations in the way people worked,
earned money, and organized themselves. In response, the language of
domesticity promised middle-class and well-to-do families a haven from

the cruel calculations of the marketplace, presided over by women whose work was grounded in affection.[96]

Money was not, however, an abstract, corrupting force, it was something people used every day in a commercial society, whether exchanging cash for goods, plotting capital investments, or viewing their possessions and their fellow Americans with a calculating eye. The meaning of money was situational. Cash transactions, for example, could signal economic marginality or thriving commercial activity. Poorer people obtained cash in the form of payments for work and spent it in small increments for life's necessities. Retailers accumulated and used cash to pay suppliers and expand their businesses. Among slaves, possession of cash was linked to self-assertion and material display.

Women's thinking about money in the larger sense emerged from the situations in which they used it in their daily lives. Female petitioners' practical experience with financial hardship forced them to consider the cash value versus investment value of property their families owned, calculations that depended on particular circumstances and the seaport economy as a whole. Daily participation in a labor market that paid in paper money thrust currency issues and the political debates surrounding them into the consciousness of mistresses and servants, and gave white and black women more access to and a greater stake in urban commerce. Negotiating the various forms that money and currency took in the late colonial and early national periods required a flexible understanding of values and exchange. Watching the price of flour rise and fall with the commercial and military success of the port city linked family, community, and national health with cash values in the minds of throngs of female shoppers.

There was no sweeping legal change in the economic status of city women in this period when so much did change for their male counterparts. In the early years of the new republic, white urban artisans armed with wages and tools, but no landed property, argued successfully that their masculine economic agency entitled them to the political power of the vote. Free women who worked for money were not granted the same independence. But the cumulative effect of daily experiences with money, prices, and earnings was a culture where the home and the market were bound together by commerce, with women often tying the knots. In their homes, as in the marketplace, women had constant, varied exposure to numeracy and cash as they transformed work into money into goods and back again. An urban woman was always thinking about ways to quantify her relationships and the work that she did. In this way, in spite of their legal dependence, women were quintessential commercial actors, well versed in negotiating the human connections that shaped the meaning of money.

Chapter 5
Shopping Networks and Consumption as Collaboration

In March 1775, Eliza Pinckney packed a trunk with limes, aprons, paper, and cloth to send to her daughter Harriott Horry. Pinckney tucked the trunk's key into a newsy letter that reported on her labors:

> Jones sent me word a few days after I came to town that the stores had been serched and he could not get a bit of fine washing pavilion Gause any where; I afterwards sent old Mary with directions not to miss a store, and to let them know it was Cash, and after two or three days serch she got me some coarse stuff . . . I sent her to Cape (I am glad you mentiond him) and have got 40 yards of fine Pavilion washing gause; 'tis more than your quantity but they wont cut it and it will do to mend it. It is 15s. per yd.[1]

Hunting down Harriott's gauze required a network of knowledgeable individuals: the man who scouted the scene; the trusted female slave who haunted city shops for days; the savvy daughter with good connections; and the mother who coordinated and judged their efforts. Pinckney's description portrays shopping both as unpaid work and as a social activity that enmeshed several levels of society. The shoppers she depicted were critical and tenacious, cooperating to comb through the available goods for what they wanted. The search itself was a product of interactions between and within Charleston's social classes and depended, to some extent, on high-born and low-born sharing a common consumer language.

Pinckney's letter, with its evidence of the collaborative and mediated nature of shopping, tells a story about consumption that few newspapers at the time acknowledged. The advertisements in the *South Carolina Gazette* or the *Newport Mercury* promised shoppers vast selection—so many goods it was "too tedious to mention" them all—with no controls over which goods would be sold to whom. Merchants were peddling a heady mixture of choice and independence, hoping to attract customers with their vision of abundant, liberating commercial life. Such tactics certainly worked on political writers, who adopted the trope of "consumer choice" as a new way to think about political power in

America. If a consumer had the right to shop around for a better deal, they suggested, so too did a citizen contemplating the government.[2] But what did "choice" mean for the people who searched for Harriott Horry's gauze? No one in Pinckney's depiction strode alone into a shop, armed with cash, confidence, and a sense of entitlement. Instead, her account suggests that power was spread unevenly over a consumer network made up of dependent ties. Some held the purse strings. Others performed the leg work, balancing commands and judgment. Still others provided opinions—solicited and unsolicited—about goods, shops, and money. Choice was not coiled desire, released by the right merchant, but an accumulation of advice, information, and purchasing power.

Consumer networks were a practical response to the uncertainties of supply and quality in urban marketplaces. As pivotal members of these networks, skilled female shoppers of all ranks were at the center of the city's economy, tracking and paying off debts, identifying and evaluating new financial connections. Drawing on conversations and connections with other shoppers, they perfected the economically valuable skills of comparison shopping, budgeting, and evaluation, and collected the social dividends of a job well done. Their methods and their manner were strikingly at odds with the spendthrift female shopper of Anglo-American popular culture, a frivolous creature who wasted "men's" money and shamed her community. Critics railed against her in advice books and editorials, charging her to "strip off your trash . . . and ruin your husbands no more," stop shopping, and "sweep out the house, d'ye hear!"[3] Entertaining as such cranky diatribes were, they neither reflected nor directed actual behavior, since most urban Americans knew that shopping was serious business.

What these ubiquitous tirades did reflect was the increasing presence of shopping women in the marketplace. When all of a family's items came from the same merchant's stores, the husband frequently made the necessary selections, though women could do so. In frontier Kentucky, for example, fathers often bought all of the goods for their families, from leather to laces.[4] Beginning in the cities stocked by Atlantic trade, however, general provisioning gave way to "shopping." The term "shopping" was new in the 1760s, used to describe the practice of going into several shops to examine goods and make purchases.[5] The new word described a new reality in consumer culture of the late eighteenth century. More people bought, rather than made or traded for, daily necessities, which were available at more kinds of shops, stores, warehouses, and market stands. Women, long in the business of locating, supplying, and tending to daily necessities, became highly visible shoppers, since food and clothing made up the bulk of family expenditures.[6]

The economic and social implications of female shoppers' activities were often contradictory. In a wide range of venues—from market stalls to riverbanks and from parlors to auction houses—the act of shopping orchestrated relationships between individuals who lived in the same house and those separated by an ocean. Those relationships, fraught with tensions over money, race, reputation, and power, produced results that writers airily ascribed to "consumer choice." The final purchase was not the only result of shopping networks' labors, either; there were also new debts, new alliances, and new opportunities to command the work of subordinates. As a fundamentally collaborative practice, shopping embodied the limits, as well as the possibilities, of commercial culture for women.

Creating Shopping Networks

Old Mary's business was the business of hundreds of people every day in the port cities of the late eighteenth-century Atlantic world. From the wealthiest merchant to the humblest servant, people used brokers, intermediaries, connections, and proxies to obtain and pay for their goods. Because this shopping was seen as valuable work, professional agents were rewarded with commissions and continued business for successfully gauging the needs and desires of their clients.[7] Below the formal relationships spread a web of unpaid proxies who also referred to their work as "commissions," even when it originated in a favor for a friend.[8] Like commission merchants and professional brokers, unpaid proxies collected money and purchased goods, keeping careful account of the money they spent. Every day, women and men shopped for clothing, housewares, books, food, medicine, and agricultural products; wrapped them up; and sent or carried them to the final customer. The packages they assembled and the letters they attached traveled along informal shopping networks that enabled people to provide themselves with cash and goods. No orderly net of individual knots and evenly spaced strands, these shopping networks were more like a beginner's knitting project, made of thin threads and well-worn cords, small loops and thick tangles, as individuals of different ranks and relations connected to each other in their investigation, pursuit, purchase, and use of goods.[9]

Family and friends formed the first layer of an individual's shopping network, providing the credit and care that shopping at a distance required. When judgments about quality and style were crucial, shoppers needed to share a common sense of "value" with their proxies, and members of the same kin group were a logical first choice.[10] Kin connections were also the main source of credit and cash loans well into the nineteenth century, providing the foundation for all kinds of economic endeavors, including shopping.[11] Since family and a slightly wider circle of close friends were key sources of money and goods, any individual's ability to acquire depended in part on the financial and social resources of peers. Charlestonians from the extremely wealthy Pinckney family could request expensive purchases from each other and count on generous credit; Newport's "Nurs Heddy" had to scrape cash together on her own quickly to pay for her shoes.[12] Rank influenced how women mobilized credit and cash; it also shaped the scope of their shopping network resources.

Strikingly, these horizontal ties were spliced with vertical threads that drew individuals from different levels of society into any given exchange. Consumer networks consisted not only of senders and receivers but also of intermediaries—relatives, acquaintances, ship captains, servants, slaves—who transported goods, passed along requests, loaned money, and performed the work of making or obtaining goods. These individuals, like peers, had to be entrusted with a substantial amount of financial and aesthetic authority. Philadelphian Mary Morton informed her mother in Newport that "Our Bella, who is a very good hand at the business, has been almost all day indeavouring to match thy Bengall, & procure a couple of pieces alike for frd Sisson. I believe she has searched every probable store in town, & I think has succeeded pretty well at last."[13] From hundreds of miles away, Morton's mother provided general directions and a swatch of fabric to use in matching but left it to her daughter's servant to choose the stores and evaluate different grades and colors of Bengal cloth. In turn, Bella's choices shaped the consumption patterns of women in distant cities.

The local medium for creating consumer networks was talk. Urban residents "instructed" and "advised" one another and "enquired" about goods. Credit came from verbal agreements recorded after the fact in the pages of account books. The density of the urban population provided a wide field for such face-to-face interactions. Like gossip, consumer information was exchanged in confidences, which were easily lampooned by critics. In Royall Tyler's play about late eighteenth-century Americans, *The Contrast*, foolish, fashion-crazy Charlotte hears about a new cap from her aunt's slave Hannah, who "has a brother who courts Sarah, Mrs. Catgut the milliner's girl, and she told Hannah's brother, and Hannah, who, as I said before, is a girl of undoubted veracity, told it directly to me, that Mrs. Catgut was making a new cap for Miss Bloomsbury, which, as it was very dressy, it is very probable is designed for a wedding cap."[14] Audiences who laughed at this breathless recounting laughed in part because they recognized themselves. Shopping information was passed among servants, slaves, retailers, customers, friends, and relatives. Verbal requests for goods depended upon a shared language of consumption to facilitate purchases.

Written correspondence enabled the well-to-do to extend networks further still. Literate men and women wrote extensively about goods and shopping to their contacts, and their literacy turned them into consumer networks' busiest links. In fact, the majority of middling and elite women's letters contained a commission request, sample of goods, or reports of marketplace success or failure. Whereas community ties in the tenuous settlements of the seventeenth century depended on physical proximity and tended to be homogeneous, frequent communication between cities in the eighteenth century meant that connections could be more far-flung. Literacy and an increasingly sophisticated vocabulary of consumption made it possible for people to trust more distant connections.[15] These changes were most significant for women, who were less free to travel than men. Newporter Abigail Robinson regularly passed along money and requests for goods from neighbors to her sister Mary Robinson Morton, who lived in Philadelphia. To fill these commissions, Morton drew upon her own local acquaintances. In the letter that accompanied one typical shipment, she wrote: "Thou wilt observe by the finery it contains, that it is not all drawn from my own stores, but that I have levied contributions upon some of my friends."[16] Rather than accept the wares offered by local shopkeepers and craftsmen, urban people used these written exchanges to identify and acquire specific desirable goods from around the Atlantic rim.

Personal economic networks echoed and overlapped with merchants' professional networks. Merchants themselves depended on correspondence shopping for large orders from Europe and could also be tapped for special requests by wealthy clients. When Mrs. Ferguson wanted a new pair of brocade pumps in 1788, she gave Charleston merchants Peter Leger and William Greenwood one of her old shoes as a pattern. They forwarded her shoe and her request to their London firm, writing "only give directions (to Mr Hoes the Maker) to make the Pumps above ordered much longer Quartered than the old Shoe that they may Buckle lower & pray let them be the neatest that can be made."[17] Leger and Greenwood relied on specific descriptions and what they hoped were common understandings of quality and style to meet Mrs. Ferguson's particular requirements.

Informal shopping networks were in the business of creating this common understanding about goods. Unlike advertisements, which were for the benefit of the seller, shoppers' words provided opinion and commentary: Was this cloth good quality for the money? What kinds of people were using the fabric? For what purposes? Discussions ranged from how to acquire goods to how to use them. Women described at length the proper construction of a cap ("you must not run a string in it, but fold it lengthways as you would a bit of muslin") or the appropriate accessories ("you must wear a skull cap or braid of hair").[18] They even drew pictures in their letters to illustrate the shape of a watch chain or drape of window hangings. Detailed, personal, and critical commentary created a shared understanding that gave intermediaries the knowledge to make last-minute judgments depending upon what was available. Margaret Manigault informed her mother that "as for hand[kerchiefs] such as you desire, they are quite out of the question, but something that my sister will like I make no doubt of finding."[19]

Samples, including snippets of fabric and finished goods, were the circulating illustrations of consumer language. These objects, pinned into a letter or clutched in the hand of a servant, were crucial in an economy that depended on proxy agents to make selections. Between consumers and proxies, a sample served as a promise of goods to be delivered and a teaching object, bolstered by the words of fellow discriminating shoppers. Samples also helped clarify the limits of a proxy's purview. A sample in the hand of a proxy was a tangible reminder of the authority and desires of the ultimate consumer. In the case of servant proxies, the sample could "speak" to sellers directly, leaving less to the memory or discretion of the intermediary. For peer proxies, samples smoothed a potentially contentious encounter. In 1799, Newporter Abigail Robinson placed an order for crepe with Elijah Waring in Philadelphia by sending him a sample of the type she wanted. Since her sister Mary Morton would collect the cloth for her, she sent another sample to her, suggesting that if the cloth Waring furnished: "is not just like it, and is of a good colour please to take it even if the quality is inferior, provided that the price is in proportion to it—but if the colour & quality should be materially different, & not such as we should like I think we are under no necessity of taking it, as he engaged to send for one *like this*." Robinson provided Morton with the standards by which she should judge the transaction, as well as some physical documentation for the merchant. The arrival of substitute goods was a source of potential friction between the merchant and his customer. Just how far could Morton, in her role as interpreter, express dissatisfaction on behalf of her sister if the crepe was inferior? "I am far from desiring thee to do anything that will be unpleasant to thee, or unhandsome to him," Robinson assured Morton. [20]

Merchants and shopkeepers did the same in their business letters, exchanging information, reinforcing social ties, performing services, and evaluating goods.[21] They pasted samples into muster books to illustrate varying patterns and qualities of silk (Figure 14). Like women writing to friends and relatives, merchants made very specific requests about goods, insisting that only certain colors of fabric and grades of wine were acceptable. In practice, professional and personal networks operated similarly and crossed at many points. Abigail Robinson and Mary Morton, for example, had a personal shopping network so extensive that retailers tapped into it. When Robinson sent Morton a few handkerchiefs one fall, she enclosed "some patterns of India Camblets which William R Thurston requested me to send thee—they contain 18 yds in a piece & cost 35 dollars a piece—he does not find a quick sale for them here, & thought

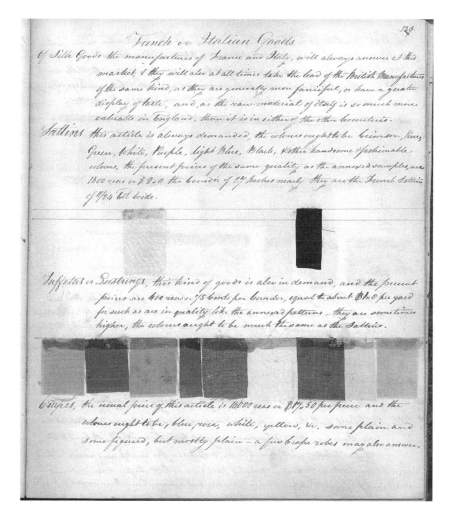

Figure 14. Merchants and consumers attached fabric samples to letters. This merchant's samples have been collected into a book and annotated with market information. Samples page in "Trader's Book, 1797–1809." Courtesy the Rhode Island Historical Society (RHi X17 173).

some of thy friends might probably like to have them."[22] Thurston, who expected the recipients to pay for these Camblets, used his personal connection with the Robinson women to publicize goods for sale and reach potential customers. In doing so, he placed his stock and control over his profits in the hands of women who were neither shopkeepers nor merchants.[23]

Consumer networks made commerce possible. The free labor they provided facilitated expanding exchanges without increasing costs. The news they spread allowed customers to share market information and participate in purchasing decisions. In the late eighteenth and early nineteenth centuries—when goods proliferated but specialized shops were limited and rural establishments few and far between—shopping networks were essential to sellers as well as to buyers, and businesspeople took advantage of them. The exchanges between consumer and professional networks were frequent and familiar, drawing on a similar language of commerce, yet there was an inevitable tension between buyers and sellers, reflected in the ways each talked about goods. No matter how skilled their own assessments, businesspeople ultimately had to please their customers, even against their better judgment: "however convinced we may be of the body and essential goodness of our wines," wrote merchants Newton and Gordon, in the end they had to "please the palates of our employers [customers]."[24] Aunts showed no such deference.

The Economic Functions of Shopping Networks

Most purchases in the eighteenth century were made on credit, and a credit-based system fundamentally shaped what it meant to shop, from the merchants who first imported the goods to the people who brought them home. A few people had the independence, financial reputation, and wealth to obtain credit accounts of their own. They paid for the privilege with anxious vigilance over their public credit or suffered the consequences.[25] For the rest, mediated access to credit—through a husband, neighbor, or master—was the rule. Children and free married women gained indirect access to consumer credit through the family accounts that were discussed in Chapter 3. The rest of the population, including servants, widows, single and even some married women, relied upon a system of third-party reimbursement to pay for their purchases.

Third-party reimbursement was a regular part of shopping on credit that depended on the strength of economic networks and the seller's willingness to bank on them. Merchants, shopkeepers, and artisans acted as financial intermediaries in these transactions, by allowing one customer to pay for another customer's purchases. Payment might come in cash, goods, or mutual accounting with the merchant, and it typically took place some time after the goods left the store in the hands of the consumer. Family members commonly used shop accounts to reimburse each other. Alice Izard advised her daughter Margaret Manigault to purchase some fabric for her brother's shirts at Mr. Lesesne's shop in Charleston, instructing her, "If it should not be convenient to you to pay for it, you should tell him to place it to my account."[26] Although Izard spoke with the self-assurance of a wealthy woman for whom payment was a matter of "convenience" rather than calculation, women with far fewer resources took advantage of third-party payments within their families. For example, the wife of Newport Rider, a black customer of Jabez Carpenter's, paid part of his bill with a discount of her own.[27] Poorer women also extended and received third-party reimbursements beyond the scope of kin ties. In 1759, Deborah Hayden's account with Jabez Carpenter had three entries: in June her account was debited for a pair of shoes for Ruth Center, in August she bought two pairs of shoes herself, and in November she picked up £5.7 worth of "sundries." She paid for the sundries in full on the spot, but the shoes (those she wore herself and those Ruth Center wore) stayed on her account until Joseph Proud paid them off the following January.[28]

The practice of third-party reimbursement transformed dependent social and economic ties into consumer access. Women from across the spectrum of society—acknowledged in an account book as "Nigra," "D. Reeds Dautr.," "Amey Peirce," or "Mrs. Pollen"—could, by virtue of a credit connection with Robert Crooke, purchase fabric, buttons, and groceries at the same stores he frequented and charge their purchases to his account. These women forged credit connections with Crooke through service work, then "cashed" them in at Newport shops. Like English servants who received local store credit against their wages, their very dependency in the marketplace facilitated consumer choice by providing access to credit and, therefore, fashionable goods.[29] People who lacked dependent ties of employment or kinship also lacked this avenue to acquiring goods.

When they drew upon third-party reimbursement or family credit, female shoppers were forced, at least indirectly, to consider the power and preferences of their financial backers when choosing what to buy. Free married women, legally unable to contract their own debts, took advantage of the "law of necessaries," which gave a woman the right to buy certain goods without her husband's express consent, even if the couple were separated.[30] Which goods were "necessary," of course, was up to the community that upheld the law, not the woman herself. Her economic and legal status placed her choices under local scrutiny if the marriage fell apart. It also made these choices an obvious emotional and legal sticking point between estranged spouses. Husbands who published newspaper announcements warning shopkeepers and tradespeople not to credit their "runaway" wives on the family account often accused the women of violating an implicit agreement about necessary purchases by buying too much or too foolishly.[31]

Shopping proxies exercised an even more qualified kind of indirect access to consumer credit, since they could not themselves use the goods they acquired. Proxies served an economic function somewhere between errand girl and autonomous consumer. Some consumers called upon proxies only for general provisioning, preferring to select and purchase more expensive goods themselves. When Captain Peter Simon's wife needed handkerchiefs or pins from shopkeeper Sarah Rumreil, she sent one of her servants, slaves, or children. But when she wanted twenty-six yards of Holland cloth, she went to the store herself to ensure that the quality was worth £130. Her purchases were marked by higher-quality goods and high overall price. With rare exceptions, the Simon family sent slaves and servants to make regular, low-value purchases and reserved larger purchases of finer articles to the mistress of the house.[32]

Other families delegated shopping tasks more freely to their slaves and children. Robert Crooke's account with Rumreil demonstrates a broad credit network that enabled more than twenty individuals to receive goods that were charged to him.[33] Crooke and his daughter came to the store from time to time, but two of his enslaved workers, "Caty" and "Sayer," did most of the household shopping, and one or the other usually visited the shop several times each month, as Rumreil's notes "dld Caty" or "pr. Sayer" indicate (Figure 15). Caty and Sayer were entrusted with purchasing yards of fabric, dozens of buttons, and multiple skeins of thread. Caty twice picked up earrings and once an ivory fan, which at £24 and £11, respectively, were among the most expensive individual items on the account. Overall, this household treated shopping as a transaction that could be managed by white or black members, free or slave, who possessed judgment and reliability.

Like all proxies, Caty and Sayer acted as the economic agents of the people they shopped for. From a legal point of view, what mattered was the identity of the account holder. When Rumreil's patience wore out, she sued Robert Crooke to recover the cost of the women's selections. Since selection, acquisition, and payment were separate processes in eighteenth-century shopping, the economic power proxies wielded within the shop did not translate directly to social power. The earrings Caty collected would not adorn her ears and testify to her discernment. Similarly, when the wealthy Ann Simons unpinned a note worth $10 from her friend Mary Singleton's letter and carried it into a Charleston shop to buy fabric and ribbon for Singleton, she flexed financial power only indirectly and did not improve her own wardrobe in the transaction.[34]

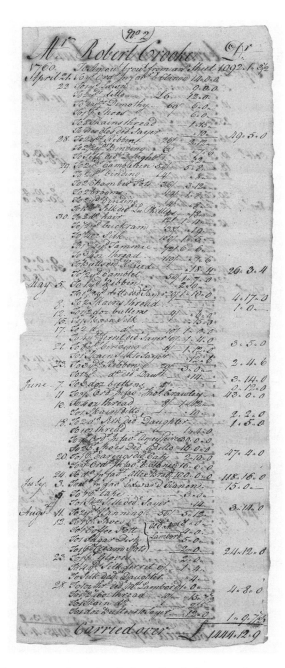

Figure 15. The account is under Robert Crooke's name, but many individuals came to collect goods charged to it. Newport Court of Common Pleas 1763, November term, 193; *Rumreil v. Crooke*. Rhode Island Judicial Archives.

Peer proxies performing "commissions" for relatives and friends had limited financial power but significant economic responsibilities. Sometimes, the request for a commission was accompanied by cash, such as a bill pinned to the letter. Other times, relatives kept running accounts, marking debits and credits to keep the reciprocal requests equal. These were not casual arrangements: their letters record costs precisely. When Ann Simons sent a package of fabric and ribbons back to Mary Singleton, she appended an account detailing that she had spent only $5.37 ½, and explaining her plan to "retain the balance for further commands."[35] Like many women, Singleton and Simons kept ongoing accounts, reconciled to the last half cent.

Women used the skilled work demanded by the business of consumption as an indirect kind of social currency. Because they had to obtain credit from others and enlist the labor of peers, servants, relatives, or mistresses to obtain goods, women's choices were constantly under review. "Mastery" of money was not a private matter, confined to tense reckonings between spouses or an hour spent with the improving literature pouring out of Britain. It was a social skill, honed and sharpened by shopping. One by-product for elite women was ostentatious thrift and a preoccupation with demonstrating financial savvy. Shunning the heedless impulse buying decried by advice writers, literate women prided themselves on obtaining good value and rejecting overpriced items. They championed hard bargaining: "If you think I gave just what they asked you are mistaken," which they viewed as a sign of good sense and determination.[36] They cautioned against hasty decisions: "I thought if we remained in Paris I should get better acquainted with the prices of the articles I wished for, & that my money would go further."[37] As they talked about value, elite women could even joke about the account books in their minds. Mary Pinckney, touring the sights and shops of Europe, told Margaret Manigault that she "felt a little pride in giving you the history of my expences—in the first place, no china, no clocks, no nice little tables, no looking glasses &c. &c.—may I call these my negative expenses?"[38]

Concern over budgeting skills connected shopping with the changing vocabulary of "economy." J. E. Poyas instructed his married daughter "of all thing[s] Observe Oconomy in your domestic concerns this being very necessary."[39] Ann Robinson, who was spending the winter of 1815 "knitting stockings and learning French," asked her aunts for money, fretting, "I have been in difficulty all winter, in *debt,* and *coatless,* although *I'm very economical.*"[40] Literate families used the term "economical" the way advice writers did—to mean restraint in spending. Theirs was a market-based, money-oriented conception of economy. Earlier in the colonial period, "economy" was understood to be a wide-ranging practice of "conserving and enriching" a family's resources, whether this meant cutting up and reusing old clothing or clearing new land for farming. The importance of avoiding waste and putting all of God's bounty to use marked "economy" as a moral imperative for men and women. By the mid-eighteenth century, however, new ideas about economy saw it as an activity that happened away from the home in transactions of cash value. Many traditional housewifery tasks, not easily translated into cash, lost clout.[41] Budgeting and saving, however, were all the more important, and in an urban setting they depended upon careful shopping done by women. Letters of urban families in Newport and Charleston make it clear that they saw women's wise spending practices as the valuable contributions that they were. Women had to know finances and negotiate skillfully within them. Working in tandem, numeracy and commercial consciousness produced vital domestic knowledge, deployed in the streets and markets of port cities.

Free women exulted in their thrifty ways; free men worried about looking cheap. Catherine Read attempted to defend her status as family economist to her skeptical sister-in-law, insisting that her husband "seems to wish me to be extravagant & it seems to contribute to his pleasure to administer to any wants that mony can procure for me." She assured Betsy Ludlow that she "would just as leave be dress'd in a plain clean gown as in ever so fine one," but it would displease "Mr. R."[42] Catherine Read knew that other women judged her by her skills in thrift and saving; her husband felt the family needed to look prosperous. John Ball's advice to his son John at Harvard revealed similar concern: "be not extravagant, because rice does not sell well," he told his son; but "I wish you to avoid being niggardly as much as to avoid extravagance, a certain medium of generosity tempered with prudence ought to be your guide."[43] Both men and women constructed public identities through their purchasing—men with displays of liberality and financial prosperity, women with thriftiness and restraint. Although feckless female shoppers were blamed in the popular culture for "wasting" men's money, these diatribes may have reflected men's lack of confidence in their own ability to keep up appearances with limited resources. In contrast, women confidently prided themselves on this skill.

Middling and poor women's budgeting had less flexibility and higher stakes in terms of survival. Newport and Charleston had almshouses and workhouses in the revolutionary era, but both cities gave assistance to most poor residents via relief payments, doled out to either the individual or a designated caretaker. Since this money came from taxes, overseers pared small allowances to the bone.[44] In 1788 the Newport Town Council granted two poor women, Susannah Sims and Mrs. Hasted, each five shillings per week to support themselves. This was one shilling more than the council paid appointed caretakers for merely boarding the poor. With these small sums, women had to shop for housing, food, clothing, firewood, and other basic necessities; a 1s 4d pocket handkerchief became a luxury.[45] Poor-relief recipients in most port cities could not cover even food costs with their pensions and had to supplement careful budgeting with charity and paid odd jobs.[46] Unable to purchase large quantities, poor women could not take advantage of bulk discounts and instead had to mete out income in small increments. Cut off from generous lines of credit, they had to find sources of ready money. For all of these reasons, the women receiving charitable allowances did not practice the economy of the more well-to-do. They were at such a great disadvantage in the urban economy that "budgeting" is probably an inappropriate way to describe their efforts to gather and marshal meager resources.

The frustration that city fathers and overseers expressed over poor women's inadequate mastery of money failed to account for how these women were situated as consumers. Because they lacked rich consumer networks, shopping was a pinched experience; prices had a different meaning for them. Among the middling and wealthy customers, cost was a matter of long-term budgeting rather than immediate negotiation. These customers usually did not select and pay on the same day; there were trips for choosing and trips for reckoning. Regular patrons in this group could keep an eye out for a specific style or price. Their servants, slaves, and dependents shared some of these benefits, since they, too, could postpone payment or delay purchases with a flexibility rooted in the third-party reimbursement available to them. Poor shoppers without these ties felt the connection between object and price most directly, not only because they had less money to spare but also because they were granted less latitude in paying their bills. These considerations strongly shaped any choices they were able to make as consumers.

The pleasure of finding a bargain was real for women at all levels. Delight in saving space in the budget for a set of spoons that improved her family's daily life and sense of status surely motivated many female economists. Planning for, shopping for, and repairing household goods were skills that men and women valued. But there were limits to how much satisfaction and self-expression shopping brought, given the way that the economies of proxies and third parties channeled consumer choice. Sarah Martain bought thread, pins, and tape from Jabez Carpenter rather than another Newport merchant because Francis Honyman had credits with Carpenter that he was willing to extend to cover Martain's costs.[47] If Carpenter presented her with unacceptable choices in tape, charged too much, or provided lousy service, that was too bad for Martain. Her autonomy and agency in the marketplace were limited by the realities of her credit network. Women like Martain without accounts of their own had to shop where their connections permitted. Their ability to exhibit their own preferences—whether calculated in comparison shopping or honed in discussions with other shoppers—was facilitated but also constrained by the credit economy.

In many ways, though, not even elite free women had unquestioned freedom to spend as they saw fit. In spite of all their efforts to demonstrate financial competence and economic responsibility on behalf of others, women were vulnerable to charges from polemicists and their own families that they were wasting family resources that did not really belong to them. To modern readers, Caroline Ball's lists of purchases and payments made at the shop of Ann Savage appear to be a model of prudent record keeping.[48] A very wealthy woman with the freedom to indulge her tastes, Ball made purchases ranging from 12½ cents for ribbon to $50 for a Morocco dressing case and paid off the account herself about once each year. Ann Savage no doubt appreciated her regular payments; friends surely trusted her with their commissions as a proxy; Hester Chapone, the advice writer and champion of female mastery of money, would have awarded Ball an approving nod. Caroline's heirs were not impressed. After her death they referred to her as "Buzzard Wing," the free-spending wife who had cursed the family with her extravagance.[49]

The Social Functions of Shopping Networks

Looking over the cast of consumers, intermediaries, agents, advisers, proxies, overseers, and confidantes involved, it is easy to identify shopping as a social act. But the quality of social interactions across shopping networks could differ dramatically. All kinds of work in the late eighteenth and early nineteenth centuries depended upon informal relationships that gave labors social meaning. The New England tradition of "changing works," for example, involved neighbors visiting one another to help with the tasks of cloth production. The demands of this kind of work encouraged women to travel frequently among an extensive set of relationships rather than cultivate a narrow group of emotionally intense friendships.[50] Women scraping out a living on the streets and stoops of nineteenth-century New York tenements also leaned on each other for assistance. Because their work was outdoors and under the eyes of every neighbor and passerby, their disagreements frequently escalated into public performances.[51] Shopping's social rituals could either tighten ties between women or cast their differences and distance into sharp relief.

Like their genteel English counterparts, well-to-do Charleston women of the early nineteenth century did shop for pleasure and friendly companionship. Ann Deas wrote that on a fine day "I should like very much to go & walk about the town & procure a few things that I want at the shops, & visit my friends."[52] Similar comments can be found in diaries and letters from Philadelphia, New York, and Boston in the eighteenth century; James Murray complained that his daughter spent her afternoons in Boston "making or receiving visits or going about the shops."[53]

This view of elite women shopping and visiting as leisure is familiar to any reader of Jane Austen novels, but it does not describe the experiences of most American women. In fact, comments about friendly shopping outings are surprisingly rare in letters from Charleston and Newport, especially given the volume of detail about shopping overall and about other kinds of socializing. While port cities like Newport and Charleston certainly had populations with enough wealth, interest, and leisure to adopt shopping as a pleasurable social activity, the practice was not as widespread as in English cities. Wealthy and genteel Margaret Manigault delighted in a leisurely walk through Charleston shops, but some women felt that tramping up and down the streets of Charleston in search of ribbon was not only a chore but resulted in too much public exposure. Catherine Read, in preparing her daughters for their first social appearances, spent much of her time on "that odious business of shopping," since "I thought it better that I should do this drudgery than have the girls be seen so much in the streets."[54] Visiting shops was not understood as a major elite pastime until later in the nineteenth century.

Even if the streets of Newport and Charleston were not filled with gossiping groups of female leisure shoppers, the basic tasks of shopping—selecting goods, reporting on prices, and performing commissions for others—all involved social interaction of various sorts. In the late 1790s, Catherine Simons and her daughters, Sarah and Mary, all shopped at the Charleston store owned by Eleanor Vanrhyn and Ann Savage, but they did not shop together. Sarah, the family's biggest shopper, appeared regularly to select fabric, accessories, dishes, and medicine for the rest of the family. Of her forty-six visits from 1796 to 1798, only twenty-one were in the company of her mother, sister, or other relative; most likely, she consulted with the other recipients before coming to the store alone. Mary, in contrast, seems to have shopped for the company as much as for the goods. Not only were most of her visits in the company of her mother or sister, but she frequently purchased similar items: on the same trip that Sarah bought a crooked comb, Mary bought a fine comb; when Sarah purchased Muslinet and a "Work'd dress," Mary also picked up some Muslinet; both women, in September 1796, left the store with whips. Mary accompanied Sarah, the regular shopper, to share the experience of looking over merchandise, conferring with the well-known shopkeepers, and outfitting herself for other social interactions.[55]

The sociability of shopping could be nurtured over distances as well as in shared excursions. For female participants of long-distance consumer networks, shopping for someone else demonstrated emotional care. Small, mundane items illustrated loving concern as well as extravagant purchases did, because it was the bonds reinforced by this circulation that women valued, independently of the goods. Sisters and daughters from the middle and upper ranks were eager to prove their affection and display their skills by selecting and sending items to distant family members. Recipients recognized the valuable time and effort that went into locating goods. Mary Rotch received blancmange molds as evidence of Ruth Hadwin's affection for her: "two days only in Boston, & a part of that time devoted to the pursuit of moulds—ah! I long to do as much for thee. . . . I shall never possess that kind of *active* good will that so abounds in thee."[56]

In letters, discussion of goods was surrounded by local gossip and detailed reports on the health and spirits of family members, making shopping for lace for a distant mother part of showing care for her happiness. This care was ongoing; women remembered each other's clothing and looked for coordinating material. Clothes themselves traveled back and forth among members of a woman's network, as crepe or cambric was chosen, stitched into a gown, repaired with matching fabric, redyed, reworked, and finished according to the judgments of multiple women. Over years of modifications, these clothes reflected both changing styles and the ongoing interest women had in each other's lives. The work of proxies was emotionally integrated into this sense of shared interest by consumers quick to take credit for their work. A woman such as Eliza Pinckney could send Old Mary to the shops and still see her search for crepe as a mother's skilled, loving care for her daughter.

While their actions demonstrated care and assistance, well-to-do women's words cemented a sense of community among themselves as discerning and practical women. One woman sent her sister a large supply of medicine with the reminder that "*A store is no sore*—our dear grandmother used to say," thereby linking several generations of wise female consumers.[57] Female relatives and friends discussed design and evaluated quality, using comparisons with the possessions of mutual friends to describe the merits of various items. They drew attention to their choices and explained the thought behind skilled management of shopping. Ann Kinloch noted that the chairs she purchased in Lisbon were "very suitable for a hot climate" and "required no plague of rubbing, a little warm water & a brush cleans them."[58] A shared appreciation for the skill needed to locate, select, and care for goods transformed economic activities into social ones. These activities, in turn, helped peers confirm and strengthen their social standing.

The skills that literate women praised in their fellow shoppers—a cultivated sense of taste, financial savvy, the ability to make meaningful comparisons, and the discipline to stick to a budget—found endorsement in the advice literature for white women. Hester Chapone exhorted her readers to "acquire skill in purchasing," which meant "learning the real value of everything, as well as the marks whereby you are to distinguish the good from the bad."[59] Much of this language applied equally to butter as to brocade. Housekeepers were schooled to bring their knives and skepticism to meat and dairy goods, slicing and peering into joints, "trust[ing] not to that which will be given you to taste, but try it in the Middle [of the butter]."[60] Discernment and selection were understood as physical processes as much as esthetic or intellectual choices because daily shopping in cities meant shopping for provisions as well as hats.

Even as they congratulated themselves on discernment, well-to-do women acknowledged that in fact these judgments had to be shared with people from outside of their immediate social circle. In Charleston, where wealthy families maintained households in the city as well as plantations in the neighboring countryside, slaves bearing bundles and letters sustained connections between whites. Owners were dependent on their slaves for carrying goods and information and chose their agents carefully. Some were entrusted with money, others, "not accustomed to carry Letters," had to prove their skills and trustworthiness.[61] Slaves, in turn, shaped these economic and social transactions in the ways that they carried out their duties. An enslaved messenger might convey only part of the information, or combine an errand for her owner with visits of her own.[62] The same dynamics applied to the work of all kinds of proxy shoppers; consumers depended upon them but could not control precisely how they conducted business. Mary Morton's servant Bella was not merely the transparent agent of her employer's desires: Morton depended on her specific expertise to locate suitable goods for a reasonable price.

The activities of proxies, many of whom were dependents and social inferiors, sometimes challenged rather than confirmed the social order (Figure 16). The position of intermediary demanded circulation and conferred transient power, two qualities that fit uneasily with racial and gendered expectations about dependents. In Sarah Rumreil's Newport shop, the slaves Caty and Sayer were the faces of merchant Robert Crooke's family.[63] These women stood at the counter with free whites, looking over the selection, and walked through the streets carrying silk and ribbons. Their activities as proxies tied them closely and publicly to fashionable imports and consumer culture. By their work, they earned trust as experts on material goods and culture. The sheer volume of Caty's and Sayer's shopping trips tells us that the Crooke family delegated choice and decision making to these women.

At the same time, enslaved women's purchases on behalf of their

Figure 16. Enslaved women proxy shopping in Charleston sometimes expressed personal style with head coverings. J. S. Glennie, "Slave Girl Going to Market." De Coppett Collection, C0063, no. 8. Rare Books and Special Collections, Princeton University Library.

owners suggest some of the greatest limitations to the celebrated expansion of "choice" and its liberating role for female shoppers. Urban slaves were encouraged to understand consumer language for the benefit of others—indeed, this knowledge made consumer networks in port cities possible—but were not expected to act on the other kinds of desires satisfied by shopping. "Choice" for them was supposed to be the direct application of training, not the free expression of opinion. This dilemma seems to have been particularly acute in Charleston, where slaves who did purchase clothes or accessories with their own money were immediately suspected of theft. Enslaved women realized the potential for self-fashioning that economic autonomy and consumer knowledge provided, but they acted under severe constraint. When Jane Ball said to "tell Binah send me some Black Ribbon wide & narrow," she did not intend for her slave to trim her own jackets according to current styles. It is likely, though, that regular exposure to the values and judgments of shopping networks influenced enslaved consumers' material lives. Bella ducked out on Frances Pinckney one evening in March 1781 in a gown of a red and white calico and a blue callimancoe striped coat, topping her outfit with a muslin cap adorned with just such a black ribbon.[64]

Increased mobility and migration in the nineteenth century enhanced the power and scope of interstate and transatlantic connections, widening the influence of female shoppers on the practices and economies of distant regions. As families split in search of new economic opportunity in the years of the early republic, women's networks expanded, either directly, in the case of the middling and wealthy women who gained new, far-flung contacts, or indirectly, in the case of poorer and enslaved women who served as proxies. City women repeatedly reconstructed networks of goods, information, and labor. Rural women found it much more difficult to recreate economic networks when the sustained personal contact of regular visits and neighborly assistance with illness and childbirth stopped.[65] Divorced from the supportive atmosphere of shared work and physical closeness, any gifts these women received were treated as isolated talismans of emotional ties. For urban women like those in Newport and Charleston, though, gifts and commissions reflected the ability of individuals to mobilize a collaborative network on their behalf to scout, purchase, finish, and repair goods. Physical proximity was not a prerequisite for the collaborative work of shopping, and reciprocity did not have to be symmetrical to sustain ties between parted kin and friends.

Places of Acquisition

Although most decision making took place in confidences and commands exchanged outside of the marketplace, closing the deal required shoppers to confront a variety of specific market spaces that had their own rules and implied consumer scripts. In the market stall, the retail shop, and the auction house, carefully honed consumer knowledge met with the limitations of the goods themselves and the competing kinds of knowledge championed by sellers intent on moving inventory. In other words, the dynamics of collaboration, which characterized out-of-shop interactions, prevailed in the formal spaces of shopping, as well.

Open-air markets, whose origins reached far back in the histories of Europeans, Africans, and Native Americans, promised fairness and transparency. The legal establishment of public markets in Newport and Charleston in the mid-eighteenth century was intended to promote commerce and rein in unofficial markets where expediency rather than law ruled. In an ideal "well-regulated market," goods of standard quality were openly sold such that every participant had an equal chance to make a purchase. Hoarding and speculation (called engrossing) was forbidden, as was forestalling—the practice of manipulating prices by arranging purchases outside of market hours. Transactions at the produce and livestock markets in coastal cities were supposed to be direct and open, enforced by appointed officials and community oversight.

Foodstuffs dominated market stalls, and Anglo-Americans had a long history of paying "just prices" (set by law or custom) rather than what later came to be called "market prices" (set by demand) for food. Revolution-era crowds regularly confronted merchants and shopkeepers suspected of withholding goods and charging "exorbitant" prices. In many cases of crowd action, mobs seized goods and set sale prices themselves, acting on a popular understanding of economic exchange based in "fairness" that had deep roots in Anglo-American culture. Women, as regular shoppers and marketers, were active participants in public debates over what the "law of the market" should be. Concern over equitable pricing and market regulation was as much women's business as men's, because, as historian Barbara Clark Smith notes, "prices represented relationships between neighbors, a part of community life in which women had long been competent and involved."[66] Shoppers, as members of the community, had a right to set the terms of the buyer-seller relationship under what has been called a "moral economy."[67]

When it was an enslaved black woman who sold goods at market stalls and pushed for her competing right to charge what the traffic would bear, she threatened both the moral economy and the racial order of deference and service. In Charleston, as discussed in Chapter 2, female slaves who purchased country produce and then resold it dominated public marketplaces. Their behavior as enterprising vendors drew frequent complaints from those claiming to stand for a well-regulated market. One observer, expressing indignation over the illegal trading practices of enslaved market women and the attendant high prices that resulted, scolded the white shopping community for not enforcing its own rules: "*they* are *your slaves*."[68] Marketplace regulation reflected not only a desire to restrict slaves' freedoms but a debate over what the law of the market should be. Enslaved women who flouted these ordinances by setting their own prices and striking deals whenever opportunity arose operated under another kind of "law of the market"—the laws of profit, competition, and free trade. In part, female hawkers used this competing understanding of commerce to subvert an economic order that viewed them as commodities. By playing the game of the market as well as any free person, they used laissez-faire economic rules to their own advantage, operating as momentary equals of their free customers.[69]

But of course, no transactions were "pure" market transactions; attitude mattered as well as price. The same observer claimed to "have known those black women [marketeers] to be so insolent as even to *wrest* things out of the hands of white people, pretending they had been bought before."[70] Black women, he argued without any sense of irony, injected violence and defiance into what should have been a fair, orderly economic proceeding. It was these women who failed to understand the rules of "fair play" in a moral economy marketplace; their deceptions marked them as market transgressors rather than market innovators. The critique leveled against enslaved marketeers emerged in part from fears many shoppers had of being taken advantage of in an economic climate where you could be dealing with a stranger out to make a profit rather than your neighbor plying her or his customary trade.

These fears flared up in critical essays and desultory regulation, but, for the most part, the deals were too good and the role of enslaved saleswomen too profitable for powerful whites to put an end to them. In addition, slave marketeers like forty-five-year-old Auber, "well known as a market woman," were familiar rather than threatening figures to most city residents, who had the chance to evaluate Auber's goods as well as her honesty as a trader over the years.[71] Familiarity made whites more tolerant of enterprising black women, but it also reduced the potential freeing anonymity of the marketplace. Each fleeting moment of equality or transgression that enslaved women experienced as sellers or as shoppers in the marketplace existed within a larger context that made shopping socially embedded but not necessarily socially rewarding.

Open-air markets were always noisy and noisome, but they were not always places that turned racial and gender power dynamics on their heads. The problems at Newport's Brick Market confirmed an urban social order where poor white women teetered on the brink of charity dependence. Instead of contending with unruly enslaved women, marketers in the North bought from poor white women more likely to earn sympathy than outrage. Violations of market rules, which sparked racist harangues in Charleston, could be tolerated in Newport in the interest of charity. One writer, for example, suggested that the outlawed practice of forestalling should be permitted to deserving "poor Helpless women and devastated Widows," thereby assisting them in their efforts to support themselves.[72] Similarly, women were permitted to peddle their goods (going door to door) while men were not. A Newporter doing her marketing, like a Newporter providing casual employment to neighbors, might consider charity as well as cost in making her decisions about goods. When the Middleton family left Charleston to convalesce in Newport, they exchanged one market culture for the other. Their new record of weekly marketing expenses in the 1790s included regular payments of a few dollars to poor men and women.[73]

In Newport and in Charleston, ideas about what was "fair" for the community as a whole prevailed in discussions of public markets, focused on the role of the market as a place of employment for enslaved and poor free women. Customary prices and orderly proceedings were read through the lens of appropriate female commercial conduct. Sometimes, female marketeers found themselves aligned with communal ideals; other times, they were on the vanguard of acceptable economic self-interest. Shoppers were the foils in these interactions, cast alternately as innocent victims of devious, self-interested sellers and as benevolent consumers spreading the economy's bounty to those willing to help themselves.

Rules of conduct were negotiated more individually in retail stores, the newest spaces dedicated to shopping. These shops accommodated intensive psychological interactions, since within these "intimate" interiors shoppers could be controlled and watched in a manner impossible in the hurly-burly of fairs and market stalls.[74] English and American writers in the eighteenth century were alive to the new social and emotional possibilities of "shopping" as it differed from the more familiar process of provisioning. In their writings, shopping became an exercise in psychological manipulation as well as an economic transaction, a contest often portrayed as taking place between a masculine businessman, who embodied order and mastery, and a female shopper, emotional and chaotic, who "became the one to be 'seduced' as well as mastered" in the retail setting.[75] Bernard Mandeville claimed that a good shopkeeper "has learn'd unobserv'd to slide into the inmost recesses of the Soul, [and] sound the Capacity of his Customers . . . to make her overvaluc her own Judgment as well as the Commodity she would purchase."[76]

In practice, however, the urban shopping scene of the revolutionary period was less claustrophobic and more ambiguous in terms of gender dynamics than fictional tales of vulnerable females and soul-invading men suggested. City shops and stores, while more formal than open-air markets, ranged from a corners of private homes to specialized spaces designed to store and display goods. The diversity of shopping experiences was further increased by the fact that shops competed with tradesmen and merchants, many of whom retailed goods as well. Thus the degree of formality and the level of mutual scrutiny permissible or possible between buyers and sellers varied considerably. Even the gendered composition of the clientele differed according to location. Most merchants

Figure 17. Many shop interiors and customers were humble. This satiric print pokes fun at one social aspect of shopping. Unknown artist, "The Chandler's Shop Gossips, or Wonderful News." The Colonial Williamsburg Foundation.

who conducted the transatlantic trade had few direct female customers. Their account books rarely document more than a handful of women's names.[77] Smaller retailers, who carried a similarly wide variety of merchandise, were more likely to be and cater to women (Figure 17).[78]

Retailers increasingly tried to set the tone for shopping at their establishments through advertisement. By 1760, Newport advertisers were replacing generic promises of quantity and variety with offers of "choice" goods and "the newest fashion," phrases that appealed to consumers educated in making selections. Both kinds of descriptions sought to set apart a particular stock as having superior characteristics. While many purveyors sold rum, gauze, raisins, or artificial flowers, advertisers appealed to a public interested in discriminating among varieties of imported goods. The idea of "selection," another term connoting discrimination, became more important in Charleston advertisements later, after the Revolution. The firm of Shirtliff and Austin promised that the "elegant assortment of the most fashionable ribbons" they were selling had been "chosen by some ladies of great taste in England."[79] Announcements like these promised not only imported goods, but imported taste. By visiting Shirtliff and Austin, customers could (indirectly) learn fashion from those who set the trends.

Shopkeepers and merchants, connected to the fashionable world of new European goods, promoted themselves as educators who would help customers make choices. Unlike a tutor, however, a salesperson wanted to use his or her superior knowledge to make a profit. In the example that opened this chapter, Mary the slave went shopping with specific instructions for "fine" gauze but was sold fabric that Eliza Pinckney dismissed as "coarse stuff." Mary was surely not alone in failing to receive adequate "education" from a storekeeper. Mobile city populations and the difficulty of sustaining a business in the competitive urban marketplace meant that customers were frequently confronted with new stores and new shopkeepers. As in the case of shoppers who feared the loss of customary controls over prices and sales tactics in open-air markets, visitors to new retail establishments sometimes worried about being intimidated into poor decisions. To reassure insecure shoppers, at least one Newport businesswoman promised that "the most unexperienced in the different Qualities of Goods, shall be charged not a Farthing more than the most knowing."[80]

While they cultivated an air of knowledgeable superiority, shopkeepers also had to be careful to emphasize their desire to serve—they were, after all, one of the cornerstones of the Atlantic service economy. Daniel Defoe's *Complete English Tradesman*, written at the beginning of the eighteenth century but still popular at the end of it, described the self-effacing pose required of a shopkeeper. This businessman was supposed to bear any insult to his goods, patiently wait on ladies who he knew had no intention of buying, and serve his customers as a servant served his master. "'Tis his business to be ill used, and resent nothing," Defoe counseled.[81] Newspaper advertisements throughout the period used the language of service when the advertiser—male or female—sold expensive goods or specialized services. Service, in the sense that they used it, meant orchestrating a refined shopping experience in addition to providing the more prosaic variety and cheapness. Charleston mantuamaker Ann Nichols, for example, enumerated the caps, artificial flowers, and other trimmings she had "to dispose of" but also assured customers that they "may depend on having their Work neatly and well done, and in Taste."[82] Demanding customers could take advantage, of course. Milliner Mrs. Bridges ended her advertisement with the warning: "Mrs. B. however anxious to oblige, finds it necessary to decline, giving any patterns, or sending any articles out in future."[83] A shopkeeper needed to be "obliging" but not truly servile—a collaborator more than master or slave.[84] The shopping experience was a shared endeavor; customers were often referred to as "friends." But Mrs. Bridges's true friends knew the rules of patterns. These were not free samples to be hoarded but tools for the circulation of knowledge and merchandise. Retailers tapped into the language and expectations of the culture of shopping networks, presenting themselves as one more knot in the web of commerce.

Many shop interiors failed to live up to their trade-card images of neatness, open space, and exclusivity (Figure 18). Newporter Sarah Rodman, visiting New York, was so concerned about the health dangers of small, enclosed shops that she instead sought out the greater seclusion of "Look[ing] at a fresh importation of goods" in a warehouse to avoid exposure to "putrid fever."[85] She hoped that settling for the limited offerings of a single shipment would pay health dividends. Sadly, she hoped in vain, succumbing to the fever and dying within days of the trip. Rodman's death by shopping surely served as an argument in favor of using proxy shoppers and may help explain why sociable shopping was not as popular among those who could avoid it as contemporary novels portrayed it to be.[86]

Sharp price negotiations were exchanged alongside the deadly germs. With skills honed in conversations between consumers, women were prepared to bargain in shops as well as at markets and auctions. Although haggling threatened the genteel tone that shopkeepers and even some shoppers preferred, price-minded customers did not stand upon ceremony when striking a deal. Mary Pinckney, looking for luxury items in Paris, admitted that this aspect of shopping was disagreeable, but familiar: "I went to several shops, & then beat down, which I am sorry to say one is generally obliged to do here."[87] While some shoppers may have worried about being taken advantage of by savvy retailers, the prevailing culture of comparison shopping left many shopkeepers themselves feeling abused. They depended upon shopping networks to spread information about goods and circulate the merchandise, but this dependence left them vulnerable and bitter about customers who spread false information, lying about their competitors' prices to win discounts.[88]

Proxies, third-party payments, and a range of social considerations shaped the tone of interactions within shops well into the nineteenth century. In the decades after the American Revolution, advertisements became more targeted, shop spaces grew more specialized, and yet business owners continued to adjust their expectations of customers on a purchase-by-purchase basis rather than uphold the preferred script they presented in print. When a formerly enslaved woman went to Samuel Vinson for her child's coffin in November 1806, he provided it on credit worth twelve shillings. The following month, this woman's former owner, Mrs. Duncan, paid Vinson nine shillings on the poor mother's behalf. Vinson, either in an act of charity or sensing that the nine shillings was the most he was likely to get, granted "an abatement to Mrs. Duncan for

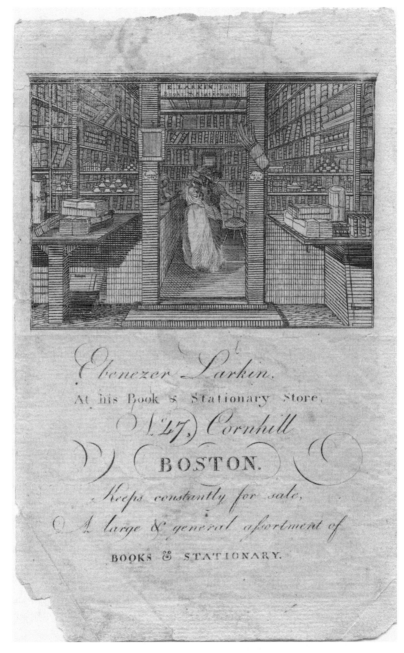

Figure 18. The female shopper enjoys a clean, orderly environment in this Boston store. Ephemera Trade Card 0415, Ebenezer Larkin at his book and stationary store, no. 47, Cornhill, Boston. Courtesy, American Antiquarian Society.

advancing the money for the Black Woman" for the remaining three shillings.[89] Transactions like these show the transitional state of the commercial economy throughout the period, before fixed prices, cash-only sales,
and professional credit bureaus. While Vinson followed modern practices
of double-entry bookkeeping, collected commissions, and used cash and
promissory notes in conducting his business, his interactions with customers also took into account social relationships and obligations.[90]

Jockeying over prices and appropriate commercial behavior was also
a regular feature of auctions. At the same time that shopkeepers were
enticing customers with the promise of choice, auctioneers were repack-
aging people without choices into a source of bargains. The stock of
failed retailers and the estates of deceased city dwellers became discount
treasure troves in the hands of the auction master. When war or national
policy cut off imports, such as during the Embargo of 1807, vendues
(a form of auction) emerged as the liveliest part of the city economy.
Long columns in the local newspapers touted land, houses, and lots of
goods ready for the taking by anyone who still had cash (or needed only
a few weeks of credit). What a seller wanted from an auction was much-
needed cash, even if the goods or property sold below value. A retailer
with unwanted goods might unload them at an auction with the hope
that the low price would entice people unmoved by other qualities of the
goods themselves. Executors under pressure to pay off the debts of the
deceased often auctioned the furniture, tools, books, and clothing the
person had used in life to raise quick funds.

Urban shoppers with an eye for bargains obtained all kinds of goods
at vendue houses, which have been called the "discount stores of early
America."[91] Auctions held in the houses of the recently deceased also
permitted the curious to investigate their neighbors' material lives. Alice
Izard was surprised to discover, upon a neighbor's death, a collection
of silver plate "more than she had any idea of Mrs. B's possessing, &
more than she ever used." Though neither Izard nor her daughter and
son-in-law planned to make a purchase, they tracked with interest the
prices that the silver bread basket sold for (eleven shillings per ounce)
and pondered the fate of a familiar set of "beautiful tea spoons" that
had been sent from England only the year before.[92] All sellers depended
upon the imagination and curiosity of customers, and auctioneers were
no exception. Items of a dead person's property sparked memories of
his or her personality and of shared times in the past. The chance to
pore through those goods one more time served emotional needs as well
as a reliable source of entertainment. In the words of one disgruntled
seller, auctions often drew crowds "more from curiosity than a desire to
acquire."[93] Reports and gossip from auction previews then entered circulation in consumer shopping networks.

Auctions exposed financial failure to public consumption. More tragically, they also exposed enslaved human beings to public appraisal and consumption. In urban ports prior to the Revolution, sales of imported slaves took place on ships, in merchants' homes, on their wharves, and in public streets.[94] Human beings from Africa or the Caribbean were displayed for sale along with other people and goods left from liquidated estates or bankrupt businesses. An enslaved person like "old Mary," Eliza Pinckney's slave who opened this chapter, walked through the streets shopping, purchasing, and bargaining for goods, constantly reminded of her own value.

Slave auctions treated human beings as one more type of commodity. Newspapers and handbills invited the interested public to attend while merchants sent personal invitations to likely purchasers in the countryside (Figure 19). Peleg Thurston promised that potential buyers visiting his Newport wharf could inspect newly imported coal, fabric, hogsheads of sugar and rum, rigging, and "a Parcel of New Negroes, imported directly from the Coast of Africa."[95] In Charleston, where slaves were typically sold in large lots, potential buyers crowded before the auction block, "pulling and hauling who should get the good Slaves."[96] Whites discussed the perceived "merits" of Africans from specific parts of the continent in terms of appearance and utility in the same manner that they evaluated other commodities. Henry Laurens dismissed "Angola's" as "a very small slender People such as our Planters dont at all like"; John Bartram claimed that Koromanti Africans from the Gold Coast were "reckoned the best of slaves."[97] Auction announcements, like all advertisements, capitalized on the fantasies that lay within this consumer language, appealing to visions of potential masters and mistresses.

What distinguished slave auctions from other kinds of shopping venues was that the commodities could talk back. Auctioneers encouraged a perverse kind of collaboration between sellers, shoppers, and slaves by trying to compel the people for sale to highlight their own value. In turn, some slaves pressed the limits of this collaboration to assert their own hopes. Historian Walter Johnson, studying the words of nineteenth-century slaves, found that they described their commodification both from without—noting what the slaveholder saw—and from within. By manipulating how their outer selves were packaged, enslaved people could protect some of their inner desires, occasionally influencing the terms of their sale.[98] Once sold, some of these people reentered shopping networks as agents—the proxies who mediated between free people and imports themselves.

In the years after the Revolution, wharf-side auctions of human beings ceased in Newport, replaced by several decades of furtive negotiations by slaveowners determined to wring the last bit of value out of people

CHARLESTOWN, *April* 27, 1769.

TO BE SOLD,

On WEDNESDAY *the Tenth Day of* MAY *next*,

A CHOICE CARGO OF

Two Hundred & Fifty

NEGROES:

A RRIVED in the Ship
COUNTESS of SUSSEX, THOMAS DAVIES, Mafter, directly from GAMBIA, by

JOHN CHAPMAN, & Co.

** *THIS is the Veſſel that had the Small-Pox on Board at the Time of her Arrival the* 31ſt *of March laſt : Every neceſſary Precaution hath ſince been taken to cleanſe both Ship and Cargo thoroughly, ſo that thoſe who may be inclined to purchaſe need not be under the leaſt Apprehenſion of Danger from In-fection.*

The NEGROES *are allowed to be the likelieſt Parcel that have been imported this Seaſon.*

Figure 19. Slave auction announcements such as this used images of striking physical and cultural difference from European norms, as well as words like "choice" and "likeliest" to entice crowds. BDSDS 1769, Charlestown, April 27, 1769. Courtesy, American Antiquarian Society.

becoming free.[99] South Carolinians also imposed a ban on the importation of new slaves, though auctions of enslaved people living in the state continued. When the ban on imports was lifted, in the years between 1803 and 1808, slave auctions boomed with the arrival of 40,000 imported Africans. After 1808, federal law prohibited foreign slave cargoes, but selling human beings was still so central to daily life in the city that in the nineteenth century, slave traders built dedicated "slave marts" in Chalmers Street and State Street.[100] Auctions along these streets no longer served to link imported people with imported commodities as directly—the human beings for sale were more likely "domestic"—but the commodification of human beings, in the language and architecture of the slave auction, remained a public, formalized part of the city economy.

Of all shopping venues, slave auctions embodied the most unequal power dynamics and the starkest choreography of the struggles among buyers, sellers, and goods. They also represented common urban tensions over shopping such as who would control consumer information and who would determine a "fair" outcome to market transactions. Slaves and would-be masters used the rituals of the auction to test out their identities within consumer culture; so, too, did shoppers at a market stall or milliner's shop test out new consumer identities. No single feature dictated what it meant to be an urban shopper. Collaborations among buyer, seller, and sold were often asymmetrical, shaped by a particular venue's economic niche and range of acceptable behaviors. They also existed in a larger system of law and custom, local and international connections forged far from the place of sale.

In writing the history of eighteenth- and early nineteenth-century shopping, it is tempting to peer through the finest shops' bow windows and imagine a scene of feminine consumption. The psychological battles we envision unfolding between buyer and seller, the pleasurable interactions of friendly shoppers, the fevered desire to obtain the latest trends—all of these dramas, scripted by the implied promises of advertisements, are misleadingly confined by the shop walls. Attention to shop-counter interactions has focused historians on the significance of selection and the power of shopkeepers as guides to the proliferating consumer goods of the eighteenth century. This perspective suggests that free women exercised agency through the fulfillment of consumer desire. Enslaved women in this vision could at best hope to steal their way into a culture of commerce formally closed to them.

Investigating the web of consumer networks makes it clear that the point of purchase—what historian Amanda Vickery has called "a mere snapshot in the life of a commodity"—is also just a corner of the larger portrait of shopping. For residents of cities like Newport and Charleston, shopping depended on backyard directives and epistolary confidences as much as shop-room performances. Consumer decisions were more likely to be made in homes and on the streets than in stores, which strongly influenced the meaning of choice itself. The ubiquity of intermediaries confronts us with the paradox of consumer choice in a world of collaborative shopping. At one level, just as "independence"—political and cultural—for free white men was produced by the labor of white women and slaves, so too was "choice"—economic and cultural—for free white men and wealthy women produced by the shopping labors of the people who made up the web of any consumer's network.[101]

To see the work of shopping as the product of relationships rather than individuals is to see the complex economic and social functions it served. Shopping was a skilled economic practice that brought women into the heart of urban commerce, sometimes on their own behalf and sometimes under the entreaty or command of another. It was also a social undertaking in the broadest sense of the word—a dynamic product of relationships and locations, desires, and constraints.[102] As a social act, it bore the stamp of social inequities and prejudices. Since shopping networks included bonds formed by affection and those formed by violence and compulsion, consumer selections were shaped as much by the limits of choice as by the free exercise of will. At the same time, whether seeking emotional sustenance or a few days of relief from demanding owners, women participating in these shopping networks became social lynchpins in the economic business of buying and selling.

Shopping networks allocated power unequally; they also dispersed a working language of consumption across divisions of race and class. Independence and empowerment were only a small part of this language, which focused more closely on value, utility, and the nitty-gritty of payment. The culture of commerce, constantly invigorated by port cities' ties to Atlantic shipping patterns, extended from the wharf to the table through the discourse and practice of shopping, shaping the way free widows looked at old silver and the way slaves learned to look at themselves.

Chapter 6

The Republic of Goods

The work of shopping networks—circulating information, looking for bargains, arranging credit payments—spurred business, cemented social connections, and offered moments of autonomy and authority to subordinates. The process was emphatically not self-sufficient, which was what made shopping so economically and socially powerful in eighteenth-century commercial life. But its collaborative and even cosmopolitan nature posed a problem for politics that increasingly troubled the writers, lawyers, and rabble-rousers who wanted to harness commercial culture for political ends. The tension at the heart of shopping between frivolous indulgence and thrifty practicality became a glaring rebuke of America's "first consumer economy" during the vulnerable years of revolution and nation building.[1]

Patriots initially saw consumer citizenship as a potent new weapon. In the 1760s and 1770s, a series of political contests over import taxes and trade regulation by Britain prompted colonists in North America to join in Stamp Act protests, nonimportation agreements, and tea boycotts. These consumer protests were the first of their kind, employing a language of goods centered on contrasts between imported wares and those made at home. Patriots exhorted colonists to shun imports like East Indian cloth, leather goods, and black tea and replace them with locally produced wares to bolster American self-reliance. A similar impulse emerged in the early nineteenth century in response to French and British blockades of American trade. Rather than relying on Americans to voluntarily substitute domestic manufactures for troublesome imports, President Thomas Jefferson signed the Embargo Act in 1807 that prohibited American exports to Europe. Supporters hoped that this radical economic and political measure would win free trade concessions from Britain and France while encouraging domestic manufactures. Across the revolutionary and early republic eras, consumer politics made rejecting imported goods and fashioning domestic replacements two sides of the same coin.

A female face was on both sides of that coin. As producers, maintainers, and consumers of material goods, free and enslaved women were at the center of the emerging political economy. The goods under their particular control—cloth, housewares, tea—were the same ones that political rhetoric zeroed in on as emblems of national identity, an identity perched precariously between virtuous self-sufficiency and decadent foreign dependence. The work of free women could tip the balance: "Your Modes of Dress and Tinsel Garbs forsake; / And useful Cloathing for your Country make," urged a typical patriotic couplet.[2] At one level, this was an economic argument that recognized different forms of female work: forsake shopping for sewing in the interests of national self-sufficiency.

A phrase like "Tinsel Garbs," however, comes from a cultural critic, as much as an economic nationalist. The goods under siege were not just economic commodities—cloth, groceries, plates—but expressions of style—fashionable dresses, sociable tea-drinking ceremonies, and elegant furnishings. And matters of style were at the heart of participatory political culture in the revolutionary and early national periods, with its parades and pamphlet wars.[3] William Tennent could therefore not ignore the grave danger posed by the free women of Charleston, who persisted with "their darling tea-dish ceremony," in the early years of the revolutionary struggle. Their behavior, he warned, suggested a willingness for "this empire to be enslaved and your husbands throats to be cut."[4] Imported goods—ubiquitous and enjoyable—provided a rich field for political hyperbole.

Some women took up the charge with gusto, staging competitive spinning bees and clothing drives that were explicitly political. They made patriotic goods and embraced patriotic styles. In response to shortages of imported millinery, two Charleston sisters, Mrs. Cochran and Miss Torrans, designed a "Chesapeake hat" that they promoted with the discerning, budget-minded language familiar to any consumer. The hat, profiled in the news section of the local paper, was made of "canes, cotton and paper, which, for beauty and elegance, will bear a comparison with many similar articles imported from Europe, though [the imported hats] costing five times as much."[5] In such enterprises, free women claimed a patriotic place in the public sphere, using domestic material life, both the goods and the work, as their stake.

All the attention proved short-lived, however. After the revolutionary era's flurry of interest in free women as shoppers and producers, political culture by the second decade of the nineteenth century came to depoliticize female productive work and contain the potentially disruptive features of consumption by domesticating it as leisure. A cockade of red, white, and blue pinned to a free woman's gown might still win acclaim but its value was symbolic rather than economic. Some elite urban women used participation in boycotts and spinning bees to propel themselves into political activities in new institutions such as salons and theaters, but success as playwrights and influence brokers came at the expense of recognized economic clout.[6]

The story of the fizzling of female consumer citizenship is a reminder that people held many contradictory and ambivalent feelings about commerce and the marketplace in the late eighteenth and early nineteenth centuries. Commerce could be freeing, independent, expansive; it was also contingent, dependent, and closely tied to networks of work, credit, and culture. The first group of attributes was successfully mined for political rhetoric, but to do so, politicians had to purge the other elements of commerce from their associations. Credit became a dangerous snare rather than a voluntary, mutual relationship. Shopping, the most dependent and integrated part of consumer culture, was reimagined as pure female leisure. As historians of revolutionary-era religion, politics, and labor have shown, creating a new, independent American citizen meant reassigning all forms of dependence into a category of "femininity" reserved for white women, children, and people of color.[7] This sorting of public life continued down to the very objects that men and women used in their daily lives.

The consumer movements of the revolutionary and early national periods dramatized the fact that "the seemingly private life of households" and "the public worlds of commerce and politics" were bridged every day through material goods.[8] But the language of goods spoken by city women and the one promulgated by political leaders articulated different versions of the place of commerce in people's lives. While political writers formulated a narrow, tightly controlled vision of commercial life, in their crimes, their purchases, and their letters, women of all ranks exhibited an understanding of the flowering material life that embraced its financial, aesthetic, practical, and emotional meanings. There was a broader politics of material life that stretched around and beyond the hardening official line.

Meaning and Material Life

The Boston Tea Party has become the most famous dramatization of the political, cultural, and economic power that a single commodity could simultaneously embody, but daily life was filled with such objects. A patchwork bag could be a utilitarian pouch, a thrifty use for spare remnants, a colorful showpiece of imported fabrics, and the physical reminder of dead loved ones who once wore the garments now turned to rags. A watermelon could refresh a family, impress the neighbors, burden the recipient with obligation, and remind the diner of the enslaved worker who tended the fruit. The eighteenth-century proliferation of goods in urban ports presented people with new opportunities for self-support, self-fashioning, and constructing and preserving relationships.

Legal and cultural influences made women significant beneficiaries of the new possibilities of material life. Throughout the period, free and enslaved women were more likely to possess goods than other forms of property. Free women inherited goods more often than land, and free mothers frequently passed these same goods on to their daughters to form the "core" of their inheritance.[9] In city marketplaces, enslaved women parleyed marketeering profits into access to material goods. Because they worked with them every day in their houses, shops, and alleyways, women were more attuned to the value and specific characteristics of the goods they shared with men. After the Revolution, for example, when Loyalist families submitted claims for compensation, women documented a detailed knowledge of household goods and their value. Male Loyalists, although able to present precise claims for land and money, tended to lump personal property together with an estimate for "a single undifferentiated sum."[10] In enslaved families, too, the division of labor placed material life in women's hands. When Henry Laurens directed his plantation manager to select which slaves to move to a distant farm, he recommended choosing married men, because their wives "will give an Eye to their respective goods" in the move.[11]

Moving from houseful to houseful with only their material goods as permanent possessions, urban women exhibited a commercial consciousness that was well suited to their mobile lives.[12] This meant, for instance, that urban women viewed all kinds of goods, whether produce, imported wares, or home manufactures, as having cash values. In the early nineteenth century, in anticipation of moving from Charleston to be with her mother in Philadelphia, Margaret Manigault sent up a box of "orange sweet meats," which she described as "One of green orange peel, & one large & one small of marmelade for you. . . . All of your was made by old Rachel, & cost about seven dollars & half. My large jar was made by one of the successors of Peg Daniel, & cost eighteen dollers . . . I have not tasted the last—& hope that it may be good."[13] Highlighting the dollar value of goods handmade by slaves and poor women conveyed to recipients information about the quality and quantity of the item. It also suggested what the recipient could get for the marmalade if she decided to sell it herself.

Material goods acquired and shed these cash values as they circulated. Women regularly converted earnings to prices to goods in their own minds as they thought about money, as discussed in Chapter 4. Making these conversions tangible depended upon the alchemy of local merchants and shopkeepers who changed raw materials to credit to imports in their exchanges with female customers. A woman like Mary Crandall, who spun cotton for Newport merchant Aaron Lopez in the 1760s and 1770s, knew for every pound of homespun thread (twenty-eight shillings) she brought to his store she could take two pounds of sugar back home. The per-pound value of thread, sugar, or tea was carefully recorded in shopkeepers' books but also was a visible reality to the women who used work and goods to buy more goods.[14] Homespun, the quintessentially "domestic" product that gained such emotional and political weight in the revolutionary and early national periods, was almost as good as cash in hand for many of the women who produced it. Many of the free women who made homespun cloth had no plans to wear it themselves—coarse, homemade fabrics were appropriate for slaves or for limited household use. Instead, they sold this homespun in order to purchase imported cloth to wear, because for them, the value of the thread or cloth was monetary, not sentimental. It was politicians and patriot writers who advocated turning this form of money into clothing when they urged free Americans to make and wear homespun fabrics.[15]

The investment and connections required to transform one kind of goods into another were beyond the reach of the very poor, unless they performed this transmutation by theft. In June 1775, Mary Moody and Susannah Lamb, two Newport spinsters, stole thirty pairs of women's shoes, a quarter pound of thread, one paper of needles, ten papers of pins, and nineteen pairs of scissors from shopkeeper Robert Bagnal and his partner Paul Mumford and hid them with female relatives. When the women were caught, they were sentenced to return the goods and pay double the goods' value to the victims, then be publicly whipped or pay a fine.[16] The objects that they stole and undoubtedly hoped to sell were associated with female retailing and clothing production, mainstays of the Atlantic service economy. In the hands of a middling woman, the shoes would have represented the stitching skills of daughters; the thread, needles, and pins the stock of a saleswoman's shop. In the hands of a domestic servant or slave, needles and thread would have signified the tools of her livelihood. Moody and Lamb, lacking the resources to buy, produce, or employ these goods in their own support, stole them for their cash value.

Moody and Lamb were able to conceive of their plan because the expanded consumer world of the late eighteenth century provided the goods and the commercial context to make it feasible. Trade brought portable, valuable objects into the city, where there was an eager population waiting to buy. Middling shopkeepers and tavernkeepers with capital resources employed these objects in service work, and they, along with the well-to-do, employed them as tools in social rituals. Poor women like Moody and Lamb might have been able to afford small tokens of imported culture for their own pleasure, but mainly, they saw in the shoes, pins, and scissors cash for rent or for food. Their utilitarian engagement in material culture signaled their economic marginality, as well as the interchangeable nature of goods, cash, and work. Their punishment sealed the connection. According to their sentence, if either woman lacked "the goods and chattels to pay, she [would] be sold by the sheriff for a term not exceeding 3 years"; the value of the goods could be translated back into three years' worth of female labor.[17]

Whether the exchange was legal or criminal, the transformation of goods into cash depended upon a willing market and an imagination that could look at a pair of shoes and see £2. Both were accessible to women across the social spectrum of city life. In 1810, as gradual emancipation laws were freeing Rhode Island slaves, Suka, an enslaved woman still belonging to Ann Oliphant, used her mistress's weakness and her own access to household goods to carve out some financial and social independence. Oliphant saw herself as the victim of her slave's aspirations, petitioning the civil court that she was "a lone crippled woman unable to see to things herself that her said slave takes advantage of her situation & perloins every thing in her power. That she is continually depredating upon her provisions her meat her flour her vegetables, upon her fire wood, her ashes, upon her cloathing and furniture. That she adds to all this the utmost insolence and defiance."[18] For Suka as for Moody and Lamb, theft provided access to saleable goods. Suka valued the ashes, food, furniture and clothing for the money they could bring her in the marketplace, a form of initiative that Oliphant labeled "insolence."

Material objects selected for their beauty or fashionableness were also useful sources of cash when the sheriff or the bill collector came knocking. For many decades, Newport sheriffs accepted pewter spoons as bail from urban wives to guarantee their husbands' appearance at civil court.[19] The presence of pewter spoons in these households was a product of the expanding availability of higher-quality tableware and the desire and ability of Americans to improve their daily material lives. If the family continued to do well, they might trade up for silver spoons, as Benjamin Franklin's wife, Deborah, famously did, declaring that "*her* Husband deserv'd a Silver Spoon and China Bowl as well as any of his Neighbours."[20] The good opinion of neighbors helped motivate the purchase of the spoon but did not define its uses. Alice Izard called her son's purchase of some silver plate "a prudent, & a proper measure. . . . A piece of silver carries its worth in its weight, & in times of distress will always be useful." Writing in 1808, she was particularly aware of the value of owning something like silver: "I have looked upon the little I am in possession of as much more valuable since the Embargo than it ever was before."[21] In good times, silver announced Izard's status and style; in bad ones, it offered financial reserves.

Silver was the rare safety net of the elite; for the balance of women, free and enslaved, cloth was the most valuable, portable possession. Clothing was bequeathed in wills, included in the payment of servants, and carefully tended to by its owners. Historian Christine Stansell, examining the survival strategies of early nineteenth-century New Yorkers calls a "substantial wardrobe" "one hedge against adversity." Urban families traded and redeemed goods in a constant "pawning cycle," depending on income fluctuations.[22] Small wonder that runaway slaves and servants took as many clothes as they could carry. When Abigail Lewis, a Native American servant of Rhode Islander Samuel Gardner, ran away, she took with her not only the skirt, robe, and hat she wore but "carried away with her all her other wearing Apparel," probably to sell it. Jenny carried away a total of six suits of clothing, ranging in quality from osnabrug to callimanco to linen.[23]

Although owners like Samuel Gardner saw their servants' contraband as simple theft, runaway servants and slaves likely saw clothing as their rightful work product as well as a pawnable item. Men who ran away were frequently reported as taking their tools with them, in the hopes that they could ply their trade as if free. Women rarely took tools, but they often carried cloth with them. Betty, for example, had been bought "for a seamstress," and so when she left Thomas Evance's plantation "she carried all her cloaths with her, some of them very good."[24] Clothing was women's work made visible, bearing the value of the raw material and the labor together sewn together in shirts and petticoats that could be transformed again into cash, food, or a room to sleep in.

Sometimes the work made visible in material objects was emotional work. Shopping, of course, could be viewed as emotional investment, but goods themselves were also rich with possibilities for expressing social and emotional connections. Handmade gifts incorporated materials and caring labor to stand in for the physical presence of parted family and friends (Figure 20). In 1808 Ann Hart had moved away from Charleston but took pains to send back to her niece and granddaughter pin cushions of her own work, telling one that although it was a "trifle," it "will serve as a remembrance of her, you may never behold."[25] Abigail Robinson constructed an even more emotionally laden memento for her sister around the time of their mother's death: "In the parcel is a little bag to keep in thy work-basket, to receive the daily clippings & shreds of thy work. It is made of *Aunt Jacob's cloaths bag*, The *cord* . . . I took off of *mother's wedding stays* & Ann Newberry's floss.—plaited with my dear Esthers bobbins."[26] This work bag, intended for daily use, was constructed with materials that would be a constant reminder of friends and family. The value of the bag came both from its material sources and from the work put into it by a sister.

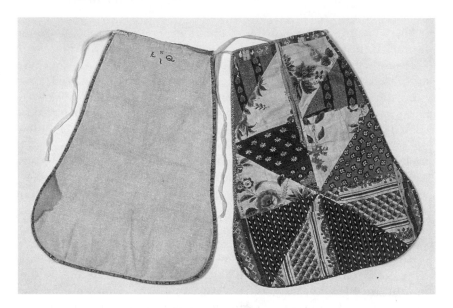

Figure 20. This pair of pockets (front and back shown) was made of scraps of material from other garments that could have retained emotional meaning for the owner. Pocket 60.1013.001, 1780–1840, cotton and linen. Courtesy, Winterthur Museum, bequest of Henry Francis du Pont.

Naturally, objects could mean different things to the sender and receiver. While consumer networks developed a common language of appraisal and economy, they could not coerce uniformity in the feelings people had for goods. Separated from her husband for more than a year, a melancholy Anne Hart sent Oliver in Pennsylvania a letter "beg[ging] your Acceptance of four stocks, four handkerchiefs, I have sent you also ten Bands and a few of your old Stocks. . . . I feared you might want some of these Articles as such things may be scarce with you."[27] Anne viewed these linens as intimate testimony of her tender care. Although Oliver expressed fervent thanks, other men took such supplies as their due. Thomas Pinckney complained to his sister that the night caps she had sent "are rather too big, and the Strings do not draw easily by which means I tear them"; furthermore, the "under small cloaths" needed buttons.[28]

Just as they claimed credit for their slaves' shopping savvy, wealthy owners frequently attached personal sentimental meanings to the products of their slaves' labor. Rice, for example, a staple crop grown by slaves under brutal conditions in the swampy South Carolina lowcountry, was so essential to the economy that it served as a form of money; it was also a valued sentimental gift for wealthy Charlestonians far from home. Eliza Lucas Pinckney repeatedly tried to send a large barrel of "the best" rice to the headmaster of her sons' English school. Since, she wrote, "the children love it boiled dry to eat with their meat instead of bread," she perhaps hoped it might soften the news of their father's death.[29] Rice offered more than a taste of home to traveling South Carolinians. Part of the nostalgia that the dish evoked was inseparable from the people who had grown it. Georgina Smith was so happy to receive regular shipments of rice and corn from South Carolina that she had her mother arrange for her slaves back home to receive pipes, tobacco, and handkerchiefs as gifts of thanks.[30]

Smith was unusual in expressing her thanks but typical in treating slave-produced goods as labors of love. Patriots and philanthropists counted on such associations. During the War of 1812, the *Charleston Investigator* solicited participants for a clothing drive for soldiers. "Camilla," the organizer, asked women to "purchase three yards of Homespun or Humhums, which will cost not more than seventy-five cents or a dollar, and make it herself, (or cause it to be made) into a shirt or pantaloons." She promised that the soldiers who received the results would have the "pleasure of knowing they own a shirt or pantaloons made by the fair hands of their country-women."[31] Although Camilla allowed that many of her readers would take the cloth and "cause it to be made" into shirts, very likely by enslaved women, she still asserted that the soldiers who wore these slave-made shirts and pantaloons could feel cared for by the "fair hands" of white women. Purchasing an object with someone else in mind, or transporting it in spite of the inconvenience, was enough to invest the item with emotional meaning that both the giver and receiver could read clearly.

To say that material objects served emotional needs does not mean that most women whiled away the hours collecting, caring for, and thinking about the history and meanings of their possessions. Scholars have argued that one of the things that motivated female consumerism in the eighteenth century was a yearning for the tools to cultivate sensibility, a refined sensitivity to emotional life. Enlightenment philosophers believed that this receptivity to the emotions of others and of oneself was a necessary foundation for a moral life. Material objects such as books, lace, or mirrors offered women a focus for this "luxury of feeling," whether they were engaged in self-contemplation or pondering memories of grandmothers and sisters.[32] Yet this intimate, contemplative relationship with material life was undoubtedly a "luxury" only fleetingly available to the bulk of urban women.

Emotional life in a broader, social sense was lived through objects precisely because of their portability and alienability. Just as hoarding spoons would never pay the rent, hoarding handkerchiefs was a recipe for social isolation. The social and emotional value of many objects could be realized only through sharing and circulation. Regional foods, such as Pinckney's rice, had a local value, but sending them along to homesick children endowed them with additional emotional value. Catherine Reed used watermelons to similar effect in 1791, telling the New York recipient, Charles Ludlow, that she hoped "they will prove a rarity to you." She asked him to distribute them according to her orders among their relatives and friends "with her love & Compliments."[33] Sophia Penn was disappointed in the design and execution of a British tea caddy she sent along to a friend but persevered, since it was "a specimen of a work very much the fashion here," which would be instructive for those living in Charleston; furthermore, she hoped it would serve "as a small proof of the regard I have for [you]."[34] Imported furniture, handmade undershirts, and New England cranberries all sustained social, emotional connections in gift exchanges.

Clothing was one of the clearest examples of material culture gaining social value through circulation. In his Revolutionary War letters to his sister Harriott Horry, Thomas Pinckney enlisted her help in provisioning himself for war. He suggested that not only would she have the emotional satisfaction of helping him, but, in locating a "Paste Board and Cloth Cap" for him, she would "have a fine Opportunity of displaying your Taste."[35] Clothing and accessories were a way for women to say something publicly about their knowledge, connections to international changes, and good sense. They also served as a form of self-expression as well as a selected "mask of personality" with which to face the community.[36]

It was this "mask," in the sense of a calculated presentation of identity, that made clothing one of the most contentious forms of material culture, as well. Those who wore fashionable clothing, critics argued, had not acquired material goods to better their souls or help out their brothers, but to impress the neighbors. One contributor to Charleston's *Columbian Herald* commented, "So prone are the greatest part of the fair sex to vanity, their reigning passion, that there is scarce any thought so ravishing, as the hopes of appearing with a brilliancy surpassing the rest of their neighbors."[37] Competition worked hand-in-hand with emulation; politicians and cartoonists portrayed weak-willed women emulating British fashions to the point of "absurd mimicry" (Figure 21).[38] In a poem addressed "to the fair" in March 1770, the *Newport Mercury* decried "folly and fashions" by hailing their opposites, "freedom and truth."[39]

It is true that women paid attention to the clothing and property of others and used others' choices to guide their own. Newporter Hetty Earl ruefully commented to her cousin about a recently received article of clothing, "I wore it abroad the afternoon I received it, & it was so much

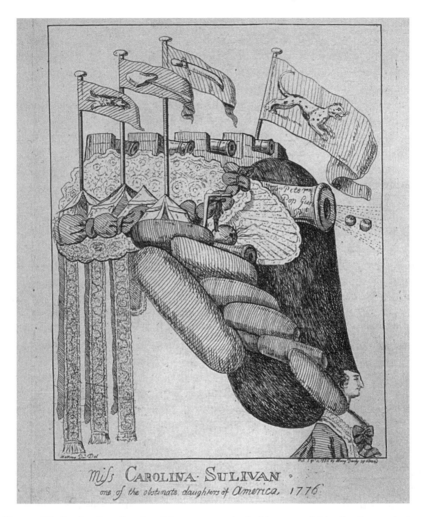

Figure 21. In the hands of satirists, women's fashions could be both emulative and patriotic. Matthew Darly (attributed), "Miss Carolina Sullivan—one of the obstinate daughters of America, 1776." Library of Congress.

admir'd, that I fear it will not be the only one long."[40] Such observations were the stock in trade of consumer networks. Part of what free women sought, however, was participation in a shared culture, rather than anxious one-upmanship. Catherine Read recalled a visit to a milliner's shop in Philadelphia in which Mrs. Champlin "tried on a frightful mob Cap & looked so handsome that I said if she could detain Mrs. Champlin's head she would soon sell all her caps."[41] Elite urban women used fashion to form a communal feminine identity reinforced in letters and polite conversation.[42] Many writing at the time assumed that fashion coerced uniformity from women anxious to be a part of this community, but the reality was far less rigid. Sharing tea with her friend Alice Izard one evening in 1802, Mrs. Pinckney so admired her hostess's cap that she sent a slave the following day to borrow it, so she could use it as a pattern to make a copy. "Since it pleases her, it will have an additional charm for me," Izard commented in a letter to her daughter.[43] Pinckney's desire to copy her friend's cap validated Izard's sense of style but also her ingenuity, since it was edged with valenciennes lace reclaimed from a cap Izard's daughter had given her several years before.

The public nature of fashion provided the means for an expanded public and civic life for late eighteenth-century white women. Elite women's attention to and interest in fashion was part of their full participation in public rituals of sociability, which included dancing, dining, and conversation. Fashionable goods provided the props for expressing sociability, as well as signaling the user's membership in polite society. Viewed from this angle, even widely criticized emulation in fashionable clothing and furnishings looks different. Rather than being a powerless act of following the herd, it could instead, as Richard Bushman argues, represent an empowering impulse "to partake—of power and of the glory, strength, and beauty that were believed to inhere in those who stood at the peak of society and government."[44]

Availability of new material goods and the impulse to emulate had some democratic effects, but consumer culture of the revolutionary and early national period was far from homogeneous; people were choosy and constrained in how they emulated.[45] Subcultures formed around the circulation of goods and information. In the decades after the American Revolution, interest in style and culture sent Charleston elites across the continent of Europe. When Ann Kinloch planned to move back to Charleston from England in 1787, she informed her son that she would be purchasing her own new furniture rather than using his old-fashioned items, as he had suggested: "you may make a vendue of it or a bonfire I care not which, for I tell you positively Ill have none of it." Instead, she had found in Lisbon the ideal "very pretty, neat cane chairs."[46] Knowledge of European styles and goods was valuable among wealthy women, because they were seen as the newest, and often the best, of available goods, but the same women acknowledged that what was suitable in Europe might not be appropriate in America, and vice versa. Mary Pinckney reported that a fellow American's furniture was "handsome, but as he bought it with a view to take it to America, the chairs are not gilt, & do not suit the [French] rooms."[47]

Charleston elites had one fashion culture; Newport Quakers formed another, explicitly struggling with the snare of fashion as a "Cross" presented by God as a spiritual test.[48] Quaker meetings policed themselves, encouraged each other to resist inappropriate styles, and assisted each other with locating appropriate fashions. Hannah Rodman noted in her journal when one of the elders spoke powerfully about following Christ's example of simplicity and "particularly advising against *Silk gowns* & *spotted Calico's.*"[49] When Hetty Robinson showed signs of embracing sober styles at last, Abigail Robinson wrote to her own sister for help in preventing Hetty "going back in *this—she* desires that there should not be any *bloom* in the colour, and I request that thou wilt give particular directions to the maker of it, that it may not be such as thou would think unsuitable—anything like that sent for Hetty Thomas would be equally disagreeable to her and to me."[50] Even though Abigail Robinson and Margaret Manigault looked different walking down the streets of Newport and Charleston, for both of them, fashion was a topic for specific, knowledgeable debate, a marker of group identity, and a form of self-expression.

The poor and enslaved had far less control over their own self-presentation through goods, but their clothing was no less a contest of identity. In fact, it was the fear that the undeserving were dressing in disguise to overturn the social order that lay behind endless tracts against "luxury" and the precise language of runaway slave advertisements. While plays and literature could joke about the difficulty of telling mistress from maid, control over clothing was of vital interest in a slaveholding society. Southern plantation owners hoped to cloak their slaves in an undifferentiated servile identity by handing out poorly constructed "uniforms" by the hundreds. No one but slaves wore the ill-fitting jacket and petticoat or breeches. The coarse fabric that arrived in bulk from overseas to make these clothes was even called "negro cloth," named for the people who were supposed to be dressed in it.[51] The identification between material object and human being was intended to be complete, reinforcing the notion that the enslaved person was less than fully human and certainly not unique.

With these tactics to hand, the southern master class zeroed in on slave clothing as the signal marker of identity; slaves who changed clothing were dressing to deceive. As they meticulously recorded what each runaway slave was wearing when he or she "went off," many, like Charlestonian Anne McKernan, cautioned that a slave like Hannah "may however change her dress, as she has many acquaintances in the city who would no doubt lend her clothes."[52] So invested were these masters and mistresses in the ability of clothing to announce identity, they even described the "blue jacket and peticoat" worn by Nancy, a woman surely more identifiable as a runaway slave by the "iron hoop about her neck."[53]

While undoubtedly, slaves traded or changed their clothing as one of several strategies to disguise their identities, the numbing sameness of runaway slave descriptions suggests that anonymity rather than a secret identity was the way to elude capture. Elizabeth Brewer announced that her slave, Jane, "had on when she went away a yellow striped homespun wrapper and blue coat," but since Jane was "well known in the city as a seller of milk and vegetables," shedding her colorful clothing might not do much to conceal her.[54]

Enslaved people resisted their identification as wearers of "slave uniforms" with modifications and ornamentation of their own. City slaves who made extra money by "hiring out" frequently bought clothing. Their goal was not disguise but a proclamation of belonging to a fashionable urban subculture created out of scraps of independence. Even before she ran from Thomas Farr's house, Isabella, identified as a mustee, had taken to wearing mourning clothes "for the death of her mother"—using part of the profits she had made as a hired out seamstress to honor the death of her parent. Displaying goods, rather than concealing them, also helped slaves—always under suspicion of theft—shore up their claims to ownership.[55]

In a city like Newport, where many fewer slaves lived with a majority white population, both anonymity and disguise were hard to come by. Before postwar emancipation laws created a modestly sized free black community, the line between free and enslaved was less ambiguous, and less open to negotiation by material goods than in the South. As a result, the clothing of enslaved Newporters did not unsettle the white population enough to complain about it in court or in newspaper editorials. Whatever measures enslaved people took in Newport to express their individuality through clothing were not seen as a threat to the social order in the way they were in the southern city. Nor was clothing likely to be the ticket to escape. Enslaved women in Newport were far less likely to run away not only because their options were fewer, but their presence was more conspicuous due to their smaller numbers. Changing clothes would not sufficiently conceal them.

The power of clothing for self-fashioning is evident in the volume and consistency of criticism it drew, in spite of wide variation in the particulars of the styles themselves. Black women in colorful skirts and white teenagers in low-cut gowns faced whispers and sneers; even Quakers in bonnets and shawls drew scorn for the "*conceit* and *pride*" of their "prodigious, *overacted* plainness."[56] Advice books sniped at women who chose goods they deemed inappropriate. Sniffed one: "Those who obtain for four pounds that which is worth five, are neither to be praised nor envied, if two were as much as they ought to have spent" on an item that "ill accords with the rank in life, or confined income, of the purchaser."[57]

But the opinions of others were not the last word on a woman's possessions. An object's meaning took shape not only in its display but also in its construction and use. Even items destined for public exhibition, such as clothing or accessories, could be as highly prized for their economic value or ability to foster personal relationships. Circulation fundamentally shaped the meanings of material life, by fostering group identities and linking consumption to production, even in the case of blossoming imports.

Material Patriotism

The campaigns against imported goods that began in the 1760s and re-emerged at various points through to the early national period imagined an American audience made up of individual consumers with choices. Released from the obligations compelled under the old system of British mercantilism, Americans were encouraged to embrace competitive markets in which decisions about goods depended on quality, price, and availability. But consumer politics was filled with contradictions that reveal the ambivalence people felt about consumer society. After decades of ambiguous and sometimes conflicting messages, political writing by the early nineteenth century tamed the dangerous tendencies of consumption by reaffirming gender differences and separating production from consumption in national discourse.

Neither Newport nor Charleston was among the first commercial communities to sign the nonimportation agreements of 1768–69; in both cities, self-interest prevailed over patriotism as merchants, artisans, and planters debated among themselves how best to protect their livelihoods and avoid additional import taxes.[58] Eventually, though, residents in both cities adopted the two-front nonimportation agreements that countered reliance on British imports by refusing to import specified commodities and by increasing intercolonial trade and domestic manufactures. Free women in both communities supported nonimportation and their patriotic efforts were acknowledged in print. But while Newporters celebrated public exhibitions by Daughters of Liberty, Charlestonians found virtuous restraint to be the most noble female contribution.

Patriotic enthusiasm for domestic manufacture of cloth ran high in the northern city, and public reports on the output of local spinners and weavers became a regular feature in the *Newport Mercury*. Women called attention to their productive work and patriotism through public spinning bees. At these demonstrations, which were held throughout New England, women gathered together to spin large quantities of thread. Reports in the *Newport Mercury* highlighted the amounts spun, the lengths of material that could be woven, and the cost savings involved. A giddy atmosphere surrounded the demonstrations, as people scrambled to praise or capitalize on the efforts of patriotic-minded women. One man wrote to the *Mercury*'s editor vowing to marry the fastest spinner, "provided her other Accomplishments be agreeable (provided likewise, she will have me)." At least one Newporter saw a business, rather than a matrimonial opportunity, and opened a spinning school for "young Misses" at Mary Wing's house, "as such a one seems to be much wanted." Female industry compared favorably to young men's indifference: "alas! we hear nothing of their working matches."[59]

Merely wearing patriotic clothing that could be doffed for an elegant party was a much weaker sign of true patriotism. There was something in the effort of construction that signified a commitment to the cause, which gave women the advantage under the prevailing sexual division of labor. In an essay published throughout the colonies, the pseudonymous "Margery Distaff" contrasted men who wore clothing with women who made it, commenting that "to wear a *Homespun Coat* only, will never pass, with *Women*, for a Mark of *thorough Amendment*, unless they [men] give us *better Proofs* thereof than this paltry *outside Shew* of it."[60] "Distaff" believed that to display patriotism through clothing was inadequate when the men in question had not performed the labor that gave meaning to the fabric; in fact, these men's activities were the opposite of the industrious (and patriotic) female spinner.

Christopher Gadsden's 1769 campaign to enlist the assistance of white Charleston wives in nonimportation agreements targeted the women as family shoppers, not producers: "For where is the hard-hearted mother or wife to be found, when properly warned, that every farthing she lays out, even *unavoidably* and *necessarily*, for herself and family, in European goods, tends only to encrease a power, that is, at that very time, distressing herself, her family, her dearest friends and relations."[61] Although his manner was condescending and he addressed husbands and fathers rather than the free women themselves, Gadsden's message was radical. He advocated an explicitly political role for white women that depended on their economic work as consumers. Female self-sacrifice was a common theme in wartime appeals, but this had traditionally focused on reminding mothers and wives to cheerfully send men into battle. Gadsden told female consumers to see themselves as economic and cultural warriors on the larger front. Shopping trips, like spinning bees, were potent and practical gestures because they represented economic work as much as any merchant keeping accounts.

If there was patriotic glory in the hard work of homespun for free northern women, enslaved women were extended no such recognition, which posed a problem for southern strategists. Free Charleston women did not participate in anything equivalent to the Newport spinning bees, in part because spinning and cloth production in the southern city was associated with slaves. The difference between the northern and southern campaigns did not stem from the facts of cloth production on the ground; female slaves in and around both communities spun. Samuel Brenton advertised in the *Newport Mercury* that his thirty-five-year-old female slave was "a remarkable fine Spinner of Worsted" in addition to being a skilled dairymaid. Charleston stocking weaver P. Giroud had room in 1770 for two new "negro girls" apprentices to learn carding, spinning, and weaving. But for late eighteenth-century southerners, home spinning was a fairly new enterprise. While spinning and cloth making in New England was deemed to be general women's work, in the plantation communities surrounding Charleston, this was work for slaves, not patriots.[62] The close link between enslaved women and cloth production limited the scope of consumer politics in plantation-based economies. Patriotic discourse in Charleston, like patriotic displays, rarely acknowledged enslaved or free women as valuable producers, reserving praise for acts of consumer restraint.

Enslaved women could not win plaudits as "daughters of liberty" turning out "domestic manufactures" in part because of their race and servile rank, which rendered their work the product of coercion, not free will. Equally troubling was their status as imported commodities themselves, whose purchase removed scarce specie from the local economy. Charleston nonconsumption agreements included slaves as one of the group of "goods" that were to be rejected. "A Planter" argued that "purchasing Negroes is, in fact, purchasing their [England's] manufactures."[63] Enslaved women, therefore, were not only the consumers of foreign luxuries but the dangerous commodity itself. "Manufactured" by a commercial system that linked communities across the Atlantic, enslaved people were, the Planter argued, an imported problem. As female workers in the late eighteenth-century labor force, slave women were also the solution to the import problem. If South Carolinians were to replace the imported canvas, linens, and other cloth that they could not produce, the enslaved members of the community were crucial to their efforts. Individuals recognized the productive niche that enslaved women could fill. Alice Izard talked of putting Beck to work in cloth production and "see what she is capable of doing."[64] Her comments, however, were part of personal rather than regional strategy. In the prewar years, supporters of nonimportation solved the dilemma of Beck's status as both a commodity and a productive member of society by rendering her participation invisible.

In gathering together to spin, Newport women were able to publicly link their work as producers and consumers in the name of supporting the Revolution, and the rest of the community took this link seriously. Public discourse ignored the role of enslaved women as spinners or shoppers, but the public spinning displays were open acknowledgment of the fact that cloth was the product of collaborative work, performed by women, sometimes for money and sometimes for charity. Charlestonians, at least in their public rhetoric, focused on free female consumption. As a result, free women in the South did not have a tradition of useful public work to draw upon in the years of the new republic. The sixty-seven seamstresses who petitioned the South Carolina legislature in 1789, discussed in Chapter 2 as casualties of the import economy, were one example. These women, who asked for increased tariffs on imported ready-made clothing, did not claim attention as patriots but as working mothers suffering from the loss of male relatives during the Revolution.[65] After the war, the seamstresses had no legacy of virtuous public manufacture to draw on in making their request for economic assistance; all they had was the argument that they needed to support themselves. The Assembly turned down the seamstresses, favoring instead the consumers who would have been forced to pay more for imported clothing under the proposed tariff.

The Assembly's decision portended changes in the North and South that would depoliticize women's productive work. In their public declarations and private confidences, some Americans began to wonder whether domestic work or labor not remunerated in money was "economic" at all. Spinning for home use, shopping for meat, or bargaining for buttons didn't "earn" cash; could the women who engaged in these activities be considered (or consider themselves) as a part of the economy? Initially, the answer was "yes." Consumption of homemade and imported goods was economic. Buying tea, Christopher Gadsden had warned, filled the coffers of an increasingly hostile opponent. Women, ubiquitous in the urban marketplace, had an economic role to play in the future of their communities.

During the later consumer campaigns that targeted women, the symbolic, rather than economic, meanings of commodities prevailed. When patriots initiated tea boycotts in 1773–75, they launched a "watershed" in consumer politics in America precisely because of the rich, multiple meanings the leaf had.[66] Tea was not just an imported grocery; it symbolized prosperity and comfort and it orchestrated social gatherings. Though enjoyed by the majority of the population, it was also, symbolically, feminine. In Britain and North America, women's hands directed tea drinking; men bonded with one another over coffee.[67] Literature and material culture strengthened the gendered social associations, with the result that tea became, in the minds of revolutionaries, an effeminate luxury. Effeminacy was a slur with a long history in Anglo-American culture, but its deployment in the political rhetoric of the Revolution reinforced white female exclusion from the new polity and denigrated many imported goods as artifacts of a weak, corrupting culture. While tea boycotts recognized female sacrifice as patriotic, it was a patriotism that relied on renouncing the feminine power of sociability and that denounced the favored beverage of Americans as both "feminine" and "poison."

Shunning tea as weak and effeminate was part of a larger attack on fashionable consumer goods taking place on both sides of the Atlantic. Anglo-American political power in the late eighteenth and early nineteenth centuries bolstered its legitimacy on a "masculine renunciation" of all things luxurious and fashion-minded. Brocaded coats and pink vests, formerly emblems of masculine splendor, were put aside or cut up to make clothes for children. Spartan simplicity and brown suits came to signify masculinity and power. If political legitimacy meant plain, dark attire, women could be shut out of political institutions for their clothes and the vanity and luxury those frothy gowns implied.[68] In fact, faced with competing ideas about what forms of renunciation were masculine enough, republican political culture found the presence of "naturally" luxury-loving, fashion-minded women to be a valuable foil.[69]

Campaigns of the later revolutionary period also took a more pessimistic look at free women's potential as consumer-citizens. Popular humor charged that women failed to see the economic implications of consumption. In one magazine, the fictional "Arabella" asked why she should give up material pleasures: "I know your zealous patriots, like my husband, will cry out *the public cause!* and *the liberties of America!*–but, Lord bless us! what have we women to do with these matters? If we are to be taxed must not our fathers, and husbands, and uncles, and brothers pay these taxes? must *we* be deprived of all the comforts of life for *the public cause* and *the liberties of America?* It is quite unreasonable."[70] By claiming that women were not responsible for economic burdens, and indeed did not connect their daily lives to matters of money, the author of Arabella's complaint hoped to dismiss reluctant boycotters as thoughtless girls. Given the shrewd financial eye with which women from enslaved runaways to elite wives viewed their possessions, it is hard to imagine such a person in real life. Arabella's words, suggesting that "the liberties of America" were of no interest or relevance to "we women," instead articulated a genuine political problem. Those who did not benefit from political participation and "the liberties of America" might not see it in their interest to support these economic measures. Milliners, for example, who imported British goods and were almost exclusively female, were common business casualties of the nonimportation movements. In 1770, Anne Mathewes, a long-established Charleston milliner and shopkeeper, was denounced for selling imported goods in spite of having signed the resolutions against imports.[71]

Arabella's complaint points to the disconnect between women's experience of commercial life and politicians' words. For free women in the late eighteenth century, knowledge of European styles and prices was a form of business competence, yet displaying this knowledge during national crises opened them up to accusations of frivolity at best, and lack of patriotism at worst. Appeals to female patriotism acknowledged the social and economic fact that women did much of the regular, daily shopping. But such appeals dismissed the shared networks of knowledge, skills of evaluation, and judgments about price that were a central part of women's shopping and provisioning. Women might have been avid participants in consumer boycotts, but the politics of boycotting were ambivalent about the power they received in return, since virtuous participation mainly meant resisting what were styled as "effeminate" luxuries from abroad.[72] Compliance with these measures might win white women credit as patriotic household economists, but it deprived them of their central forum for displaying expertise and maintaining social ties. These campaigns tried to control the public manifestation of consumer discourse by replacing an informal network of knowledge and judgment with new, political criteria for choice. They mobilized a world of consumption that women were central to but discounted the values that enlivened female participation.

As the nation confronted the question of what a republic should be, free women were encouraged by writers to see the patriotic potential of their work. But while these women in their letters shared information about construction, quality, style, and use of goods among a network of like-minded individuals, newspaper coverage featured thread yardage and shrill exhortation. Friends and family developed integrated networks through years of investigating and using goods; newspaper writers followed trends, highlighting female domestic work when the topic of nonimportation heated up and ignoring it when the political issue cooled. Mary Robinson regarded these exhortations, like all patriotic enthusiasms, with skepticism. Her pledge to a friend to take up the cause of domestic manufactures smacks more of knowing tolerance than sincere passion, vowing "one of these days, when I get time, I intend to learn to spin for the good of my Country, & shall please my self, as I sit at my task, with thinking that for every thread I draw, a thread less will be imported from Britain. Is not this Patriotic?"[73] Until she "got time" to learn spinning, however, she intended to purchase her thread in Newport shops or from the poor women who spun for money rather than accolades.

Others rejected the model of republican simplicity that was integral to calls for austerity and homespun. The letters of Charleston elites in the years of the early republic testify to a world of European-led fashion, sociable pastimes, and female cultural authority exhibited through imported and handmade goods. Their cultural style was out of sync with the posture of national political culture, which constituted itself around a rejection of consumption and the feminine. And yet, their words reveal that they were not oblivious to the political implications of consumption. In late 1811, Alice Izard complained to her daughter that "The shops are almost exhausted of European goods, & they are excessively dear. I hear that the Merchants in Charleston are suffering exceedingly. We feel the want of the Bank of the U.S. There is no medium for monied intercourse. Oh what wise Rulers we have!"[74] Unlike the fictional Arabella, Izard chose her material life fully aware of its symbolic and economic context, and expected the government to come around to her view.

Perhaps in part responding to the uncertainties of voluntary consumer movements, the American government in the early nineteenth century turned to legally enforceable forms such as the Embargo of 1807 to shore up American economic and cultural autonomy. Familiar themes of self-sacrifice in material goods and the importance of domestic manufactures remained part of the landscape in the decades between the end of the Revolution and the War of 1812. Commerce with England had rebounded, and cultural ties continued to join the two countries, leaving a troubling legacy of dependence and, some thought, the persistent taint of European degeneracy. Alarmed after witnessing a public exhibition of young women performing military formations on horseback, Margaret Manigault wrote, "It is well that our Government in its wisdom decrec'd a non-intercourse—for we make much alarming progress in civilisation—we are so imitative—so emulative."[75] Manigault was referring to the Non-Intercourse Act, which replaced the blanket trade prohibitions of Jefferson's Embargo with a more targeted exclusion of trade with Britain and France. Although these acts responded to a specific diplomatic trade problem—Britain and France were each trying to deny American trade with the enemy—in a larger sense, the goal was economic and cultural independence for the United States.

To counteract the losses from trade, entrepreneurs and politicians in Newport and Charleston called for state pride and new industries rather than individual sacrifice and family production. New England communities continued to celebrate "feats of household manufacture" by industrious female spinners, but these women were holdovers in a climate of ever-increasing spinning mills and new forms of textile production.[76] Even in agricultural South Carolina, one Charlestonian collected subscriptions for "The Carolina Homespun Company," which would, like similar companies in other states, boost South Carolina's independence from foreign imports and provide manufacturing work for the worthy poor.[77] Although home manufactures continued to be significant in fact—southern women likely produced more homespun in the early republic than in the revolutionary era—political attention shifted to larger manufacturing initiatives. Newspapers counted and reported on the establishment of new factories that would show England "that we cannot only do without her fabrics, but that we shall find greater profit in our manufacturing establishments than in the trade that enables us to part with our surplus agriculture."[78]

Spinning bees and subscription lists gave way to charity clothing drives. Mary Rotch and her Quaker friends formed a society to help clothe the Newport poor, "since the pressure of this wicked war has been so much felt in our town." The women gathered together to make much of the clothing themselves, with the financial assistance of other Newporters who "have been liberal according to their ability & always offer us the language of encouragement."[79] Rotch did not attach any larger political significance to the women's work; these clothes were comfort for the poor, not standards in the battle against tyranny. By staging their own clothing drive for soldiers and sailors, free Charleston women did claim some public attention as patriots, though the degree of commitment was minimal: women were asked to provide one shirt, in contrast to the competitive efforts of the Newport spinners thirty years earlier. The historical credit they received in exchange was sentimental rather than strictly accurate. One toast to the "Fair of America" reprinted in Charleston proclaimed optimistically, "They who so patriotically wrought the dresses of our Revolutionary Soldiers, will once more ply the Loom and Needle to cloathe the *Seamen* of our country."[80]

Overall, public discourse ignored the sectors where women were most likely to contribute economically. Instead, newspapers concentrated on a new element of specifically free male identity—political party affiliation. As during the Revolution, merchants and farmers, planters and laborers, milliners and seamstresses all had different views on commerce, and bore its penalties and benefits in different ways. In the early decades of the nineteenth century, however, these differences were linked to national party affiliation. Instead of hailing consumers who complied with federally directed non-importations, writers harped on the political machinations that led to the Embargo and war in the first place. In downplaying consumer choice, they downplayed female agency and the potential for a consumer-based female political voice. Although in fact women continued to buy or resist imported goods, spin thread, and make shirts, whether at home or in one of the new factories, their public role was curtailed.[81]

As serious attempts to engage female consumers as patriots faded, homespun politics lost power, as well. During the congressional debates of the Embargo period, Congressman Eppes proposed to require all representatives to appear in homespun and expressed the desire for "the ladies" to do the same. A North Carolina congressman complained that such a policy was unfair to "those who like him, had no wives at home to make them coats." Furthermore, he argued, "Had I a wife, I should be willing to see her dressed to her own satisfaction. The ladies have a right to dress as they please."[82] The exchange, described as a "pleasant statement of political trifling," did not take up women's clothing as a topic of national concern. In public discourse, shopping was the indulgence of vanity, and women's labor a family obligation rather than an activity of national importance. Party men rejected both the style and the content of eighteenth-century consumer politics; they ended boycotts, arrested rioters, and forgot about the Boston Tea Party. The radical potential of making every shopping trip a venture in political self-discovery and participation fell, in favor of a political power proclaimed at the polls.[83] Consumption remained politicized, but the politics of imports was no longer a story in which women could be heroines.

The failed revolution of participatory female consumer politics by the early nineteenth century was not a forgone conclusion. Across the Atlantic, British Quakers launched an anti-sugar campaign that was successful in bringing men and women into politics. By urging members to abstain from using slave-grown sugar, Quakers made "consumer choice a matter for self-examination." New commodity relationships provided the means to influence public policy: "Only as consumers, a category of economic agent given new preeminence in the free-market capitalism of the later eighteenth century, could these campaigners proclaim their political power."[84] Participation in these boycotts gave women the opportunity to make consumption choices that reflected fundamental values and consequently marked them as political and moral beings. The American consumer movements of the late colonial and early national period, in contrast, were organized around national economic and political goals, not questions of morality. A woman who rejected imported calico struck a blow against the theoretical "enslavement" of her community, not the actual enslavement of the person who had produced the item. Her choices reflected her degree of compliance with a national campaign more than a desire to bring ethics to the international market.

The Gender Politics of Objects

Running through the multiple messages of consumer politics of the late eighteenth and early nineteenth centuries was a larger issue troubling American society; namely, the worry that the fixed order of patrician privilege and plebeian deference would be replaced by a confusing collection of people defined by what they owned. The democratic promise of the marketplace—that pleasure, status, refined feeling, taste were available to all—was also its danger, since in the marketplace, there were no reliable measures of character or status, just attributes to be purchased and assembled. Identity itself seemed uncertain and mutable. When critics railed against the heedless purchase of luxuries, they expressed concern with what historian Dror Wahrman calls "the mutability and transience of forms," especially "those forms that affected people's signs of identity, now available for anyone willing to pay the price."[85]

Patriots who masterminded consumer boycotts or politicians who favored embargoes hoped to convince people that the objects they owned did declare their identities as political beings. Political culture of the revolutionary and early national periods therefore seemed to make a virtue out of the troubling idea that identity was as changeable as a homespun shirt. Choice rescued the subjectivity of the shopper. Political rhetoric, by framing consumption decisions as the products of individual choice, insisted that goods were props for the individual, not vice versa. The mutually dependent manner in which men and women actually acquired goods had no place in this formulation. Instead, commercial practices and commercial language offered writers a way to mine the relationship between subject and object to define public life.

Focusing on the materiality of consumer goods, advice writers addressing free women encouraged them to "objectify" themselves in a manner that also significantly narrowed the meanings to be found in material life. Miss More's essays in the *Ladies Pocket Library* used an analogy of ladies to porcelain as the starting point for her own speculations on the differences between men and women. She asked her readers, "if we do not put the finest vases, and the costliest images in places of the greatest security, and most remote from any probability of accident or destruction? By being so situated, they find their protection in their weakness, and their safety in their delicacy." Men were different, More asserted, "Like the stronger and more substantial wares, they derive no injury, and lose no polish, by being always exposed, and engaged in the constant commerce of the world.[86] In writing for a young female audience, More drew upon a familiarity with the widely marketed yet genteel ceramics of the eighteenth century to make her points about gender and class. The feminine object was imbued with fragility as well as beauty, and the author suggested that femininity, when exposed to the "constant commerce of the world," risked losing its "polish." Men, like "more substantial wares" could easily withstand commerce. Alluding to distinctions between "best" and "common" wares to advocate feminine withdrawal from "public exhibitions," More was also drawing class boundaries around her advice.[87] A young woman who washed clothing for her own support would not recognize herself in the guise of a fine vase.

Nor would urban residents uniformly agree that vases were "female." The growth and specialization of retail shops at the turn of the century intensified the association of each gender with specific goods, but with mixed results. Advertisements in Charleston, for example, began to imagine a clientele divided by gender-specific interests, calling out from the pages with news "IMPORTANT TO THE LADIES!" and promising that discerning Englishwomen, not the male proprietors, had overseen the selection of fashionable goods.[88] The division of interests was repeated in the letters of wealthy Charleston families, where a sense of gender specialization began to appear along with the pragmatic deployment of proxies without regard to gender. From his Jamaican plantation, Oliver Hering regularly exchanged seed rice and plants with his sister Mary Middleton in Charleston, but when she wrote to him in England for boots and shoes, he reported, "Your commissions . . . is forwarded through my Mother to Kitty."[89] Newporters, by contrast, tended to expect men and women to be ready to use their best judgment on a wide variety of imported goods. If a sister could not fill a commission for purple gloves, a male cousin could be pressed into service. As with tea, the "gender" of goods was reimagined in different contexts.

By urging well-to-do free women to let storage be their domestic ethos, rather than circulation and publicity, writers like Miss More drew not on the multiple characteristics of goods that people valued, such as utility and the ability to circulate and exchange, but on the fact that objects, once placed, could stay put. It was a reading of gender and material life that was often played for humor. Newspaper readers were treated to the anecdote of "Lady Elizabeth Dryden," who suggested to her husband, the Restoration poet, that if she were a book, she would receive more attention from him. Her husband responded, "when you do become a book, pray let it be an almanac; for then at the end of a year I shall lay you quietly on the shelf, and shall be able to pursue my studies without interruption."[90] For this imaginary Dryden as for More, free women who circulated were a problem. Far better to cast a curatorial rather than a social eye on women and the objects in their homes. This new attitude toward goods (and ladies) was surely a hard sell. The circulation of information and goods was currency in the emotional economy of eighteenth- and early nineteenth-century Americans. To isolate oneself from this kind of exchange was to be shut out of basic social interactions.

Proxies stepped into the breach to help assure the proper "disposal" of goods and free women. Abraham Greenwood, who came to Charleston in the late 1780s to collect the business debts of his uncle, an exiled loyalist, teased his cousin Betsey back in England with an extended play on the trope of women as goods and himself as proxy agent. "Tell the Ladies at Hickmondwike that there are few or no old Maids here," he told her, "if they are afraid of Yorkshire being overstocked with that article I would advise a cargo to be sent out & I will get them disposed of at Vendue I am of the opinion thay will go readily if well chosen, & sent out in proper order."[91] The appearance of fine versus common wares as metaphor, or the familiarity of the vendue as a disposer of overstock, reveals the depth to which commercial language penetrated early republic society. Old jokes about unmarried women were reframed around the auction of imports in an economy hungry for them. As an agent for his uncle, Greenwood likely used the services of the vendue masters of Charleston himself. He also expected his female cousin in England to appreciate the references to cargo being "well chosen & sent out in proper order" in order to ensure quick disposal.[92]

The real women who were "disposed of" as objects at vendues were enslaved, and their value to their owners was rooted in their mobility. In the legal language of commerce, these women were "moveables" with an explicit exchange value. Their bodies were treated like other types of property and as such were subject to dower claims, creditor demands, and estate divisions. Enslaved men and women were seized by the courts to pay debts as any other property would be. When Charlestonian James Miller's Federal Street tenant John Ker was two years late in paying the rent, Miller got a warrant to take "goods and chattels" worth the missing payments out of the house. Sheriffs removed Sally, an enslaved woman valued at $150, along with $100 worth of furniture and tableware.[93] Even as they depended on the individual subjectivity of enslaved people to hustle bargains in the marketplace or evaluate commercial goods, masters and mistresses built their economic strategies around the commodification of those same individuals. As "moveables," enslaved workers circulated among the various Izard houses and plantations, but owners kept careful track of whose property was whose. "You mention that the youngest of Beck's Children is given to Ralph in the division of her family between him & Georgina," Alice Izard wrote, "You must recollect that the youngest belongs to me, as it has been born since Beck has been my property."[94] Elite white family members might be willing to loan or rent the labor of their slaves to each other on credit terms, but each enslaved person represented a market value that was jealously monitored.

Even an enslaved person's relationship with her own family members was filtered through her status as an object. Beck's youngest daughter was allowed to stay with her mother not because of the tie between them, but because she, unlike her siblings, was the property of her mother's current owner. Relatives with means had to buy their kin to free them. Even manumissions could be couched in terms of a sale. In 1799 Charlotte, a free black Charlestonian, purchased her granddaughter Jenny from Eleanor and Francis Bonneau for the nominal sum of five shillings.[95]

The sum Charlotte paid was not the market price of Jenny's labor; it was a token offered to seal the legal transfer of a human object.

After the Revolution, freedpeople faced a culture eager to keep them in object status. In Charleston in 1800, the sheriff "levied" a judgment against the estate of Edgar Wells by placing Dinah and Hannah in jail. A few months later, Dinah was discharged because "having been previously emancipated by Mr. Wells" she was "not liable to this execution."[96] In Newport, Mary Womsley had to go to court to establish her own free status and that of her daughter Susannah, who had been seized and sold to cover the debts of her insolvent former owner.[97] In cases like these, the courts had to determine the degree to which a person would be treated like an object of another's financial machinations or the subject of her own life. By examining evidence and hearing testimony, the court helped define legal and economic identities. Still, many whites could not imagine that formerly enslaved people, many of whom were forced by economic necessity to continue to live with former masters (now as part of an urban houseful rather than patriarchal household), were no longer objects under their control. They persisted in attempts to list them in inventories and command their presence.[98]

Objects, as entities acted upon, gave shape to the new political culture. Free women were subjects under the law but linked with "useless" objects by authors who ignored their productive work. Enslaved women's useful work, and therefore subjectivity, was harder to deny, but their legal status as objects, along with their racial status as "others," justified their political marginalization.[99] Objects forged vital links between individuals and communities because they could circulate and acquire new meanings. People could move along similar pathways. Enslaved women, at the command of owners, changed locations, owners, and names. Historian Laurel Thatcher Ulrich has even suggested that free women in eighteenth-century families were a kind of "moveable," because they might change names and alliances several times over the course of their lives, while men and real estate were the stable base of the social and economic order.[100] In a sense, then, free and enslaved women were creatures of "commerce," circulating from home to home. Just as objects acquired meaning through creation, circulation, and use, female identities were relational rather than fixed, able to adapt to the setting they found themselves in.

While rhetorically, the linking of free women with objects diminished them as individuals, in practice, women themselves used goods to communicate their sense of self, to foster friendships and alliances, and to provide material and financial comfort. Objects helped to define social affiliation, personal beliefs, and economic status not only by negative contrast but through positive appropriation. Even enslaved women, treated by law as objects, found ways to claim their own subjectivity with goods. Some women used clothing to express cultural identity, like the wraparound skirts that echoed African styles.[101] Others employed their skills with material culture to improve their circumstances. The slave Beck saw her children assessed for value and divided with the Izard estate, but she also used her expertise with turning cotton fiber into woven cloth to earn status as a specialized worker. An expanding material life provided not only diverting or disturbing analogies but also the tools for women to shape identities and relationships to some degree as they saw fit.

A consumer society, historian Leora Auslander writes, is one "in which subjectivities, identities, and solidarities are created by commodities."[102] The consumer movements of the late eighteenth and early nineteenth centuries appealed to people on these terms, since refusing to drink tea or to wear British cottons indicated membership in a certain kind of community. But in privileging political communities, these campaigns marginalized others formed through the acquisition and use of material goods. Material life was at the heart of female differences in rank: gentility was expressed in tea equipage and silk floss, poverty in bare feet and pawned spoons. It could also foster cross-class alliances, as between elites and the female retailers and artisans who furnished the props of genteel living. Material goods created subcommunities among those who stole and pawned them for their financial value and among those who adopted particular styles of clothing and furniture to pronounce their membership to the world.

The story of women and material life highlights the gender trouble at the heart of republican rhetoric regarding luxury and corruption. The links between production and consumption were central to the political problem, and women—white and black—were at the nexus of the two. Despite efforts to contrast the vicious female shopper with the virtuous female spinner, these were, in practice, the same person. By naturalizing luxury as female and tarring imports with the brush of effeminacy, the rhetoric of political economy in the early republic turned away from the troubling implications of citizens as consumers. Urban women's work, too, which depended upon the goods and people of Atlantic commerce, could have no political standing in a labor culture trumpeting the independent producer.

American women were unable to translate their roles as producers and consumers of goods into explicit political power in the new United States. But an expanding material life did offer important social, emotional, and economic benefits, as women used goods of all kinds to sustain and nurture themselves and their families. By drawing upon the increasing availability of goods, female shoppers linked local provisioning with international commerce. Women of all ranks used material goods to create credit reserves and launch new businesses. Sending gifts, commissions, or provisions to friends enabled many to extend their influence in a time of economic and geographic expansion. In these social and material dimensions, commercial culture had a profound effect on urban women's lives that politics could not suppress.

Conclusion

"All the World is becoming commercial," Thomas Jefferson wrote to George Washington after the Revolution, though he would not say "whether commerce contributed to the Happiness of mankind."[1] Ambivalence over commerce, which brought great wealth and sudden disaster, was at the heart of heated transatlantic debate over human nature, authority, and economy. Commerce, as everyone could see, was social and interdependent. In the minds of some philosophers, these qualities made it the basis of civil society, because the conduct of commerce instilled trust and friendship.[2] Adam Smith believed that for the majority of people, "the road to virtue and that to fortune . . . are very nearly the same," because their success "almost always depends upon the favour and good opinion of their neighbors and equals; and without a tolerably regular conduct these can very seldom be obtained."[3] For Americans of the early republic, who had just declared their freedom from relations of dependence, commerce looked less benign. Jefferson's doubts about whether commerce fostered "Happiness" referred to a familiar construct in American political thought and culture in the early republic. Should the United States be a nation of farmers, whose independence lay in their ownership of land? Or would it be a commercial nation, whose influence came from wealth and trade? Political rhetoric hinged on stark contrasts between the two options, masking interaction among property, commerce, and constructions of dependence that already pervaded American lives. This oppositional way of framing the problems of a newly independent nation contributed to the attenuated patriotic consumer campaigns in the early republic as well. Writers found it increasingly difficult to conceptualize a voluntarily virtuous consumer and so fashioned a solo, stalwart producer to fit their political needs.

This producer was a man. Even as the number of paid female laborers increased, political writing established a gendered opposition of the feminized consumer and masculine producer. Some forms of this rhetoric had circulated for decades in Anglo-American writing, in which commerce was frequently feminine, given its seeming irrational changeability and its ties to fashion and desire. "Lady Credit" presided over transactions between countries and between neighbors. "Effeminate luxury" tempted consumers to buy things they did not need with money they did not have. These concepts filtered into the consciousness of Americans in the late eighteenth century so that, for example, Philadelphia merchants, fearing that an aura of feminine servile dependency clung to their commercial relationships, struggled to insist that such ties were instead "manly mutual service and connections."[4] At every turn in revolutionary America, then, the perils of commerce were linked to dependence, moral weakness, and femininity. But commerce, like femininity, also had improving tendencies in the minds of those who wielded gender metaphors. Commerce had potential to calm and civilize raw masculine aggression. Luxury, according to some, would "soften and humanize our manners."[5] A home well appointed with material goods could both soothe a tired laborer in the evening and motivate him to work harder the next day to save for more purchases. Commerce and productive labor, for that matter, supported each other.

This concept of mutual support between gendered production and consumption found its most sentimental allegory in the idealized middle-class home depicted in advice books and romantic tales. The literature of domesticity did not really describe a world where free women knew nothing about money but rather one where free, middle-class women domesticated commerce, muted its reliance upon competition, and bolstered its potential for civilizing men and promoting cooperation. American conduct books for women suggested that women's commercial savvy was particularly important in a nation without fixed ranks. Enos Hitchcock, for example, told his female readers: "In a free country, under a republican form of government, industry is the only sure road to wealth; and economy the only sure means of preserving it. . . . It is an old adage, 'A man must ask his wife, whether he may be rich.' He gets the estate by his industry; she preserves it by her economy. If she has no economy, he labors in vain."[6] Female economy, Hitchcock believed, was the complement of male industry. He worked hard for the money; she was its steward, through well-informed purchasing and saving decisions. And yet, under law and in common perception, it was his estate. His work was productive, hers visible only when she failed to do it well. By the early decades of the nineteenth century economic autonomy, and the market economy itself, were increasingly discussed as fundamentally masculine. Historians have argued that this language of domesticity and separation between middle-class men and women salved some of the wounds inflicted by a rapidly changing, industrializing world.[7] It also served to justify the many changes that did not take place in the American polity after the Revolution, such as the expansion of the vote to women and black men, the extension of property rights to free married women, or the abolishment of slavery.[8]

But other languages, relevant to a larger segment of urban society, emerged in the eighteenth century to compete with, complement, or supplant domesticity. Commercial language provided the metaphors for literate women's social exchanges. Talk of thrift and frugality in an explicitly commercial sense bolstered the reputations of a wide range of women among their peers. Numeracy and accounting practices gave shape and limits to relationships among men and women sharing rooms but not kin ties. This language of commerce was supple. Some writers deployed the metaphors of commercial circulation to urge well-to-do women to reform their lives of shopping and socializing. Others frankly calculated the movement of enslaved women around various homes and plantations as if they were mere objects. Aggrieved husbands and indignant mistresses warned their fellow residents not to "credit" the words or transactions of women who ran away. Runaways who could talk back reminded their communities that credit was built by collective transactions, not the amorphous reputation of an individual. Commercial language presumed a world of people and objects on the move, unconfined by spheres of influence or customary codes.

Political economists and fiction writers of the eighteenth century focused on the ability of money to circulate and change hands freely, without the stabilizing—or suffocating—bonds of obligation and deference that accompanied credit exchanges.[9] Historians, too, have tended to read the language of the market as the liberal language of individualism and self-interest. In port cities like Newport and Charleston, however, commerce was shot through with other concerns, including affection, family obligation, and ideas about appropriate "masculine" or "feminine" interests. Shopkeepers and artisans gave discounts to the poor. Sisters sent medicine and cranberries to each other as signs of affection, then recorded the prices in account books. Aunts provided food and shelter on the strength of a promissory note. Free men in Newport looked for lavender gloves but those in Charleston deferred such requests to their female kin. If a market ethos permeated social and emotional lives, so, too, did social and emotional concerns influence commercial decisions.

Real women's roles in the transformation of the American economy were complex and contradictory, but no less central, through their labor, connections, and mobilization of money and credit. The attributes of female paid work—its lower wages, intermittent pace, and material and ideological flexibility—made it especially deployable in a changing economy.[10] Women's knowledge of exchange and material goods likewise proved invaluable for housefuls scraping through periods of inflation, instability, and the losses of familiar business connections or for escaped and freed slaves trying to establish new lives. These forms of knowledge and patterns of work did not just help men navigate the urban economy; they were the economy.[11]

Throughout *The Ties That Buy*, women's activities have emerged as using and constituting the commercial economy of American port cities. Theirs was not the "economy" that advice writers like Hitchcock spoke of but rather a productive, active, money-oriented series of activities and practices. They created and sustained an Atlantic service economy by looking for ways to turn "women's work" into paid labor and by intensifying existing economic relationships to include more services. Commercial growth offered new opportunities for female employment and economic participation as well as new vulnerabilities. Strong ties with European suppliers brought goods and business to urban female shopkeepers but threatened seamstresses with low-priced competition. The expanding service economy in Charleston provided more opportunities for landladies in 1820 than in 1750, but the physical devastation of postwar Newport and loss of the transient seagoing population meant constrictions for enterprising female Newporters.

Market culture, it is now clear, extended women's use of money and credit in spite of legal restrictions and popular skepticism. An increasing sophistication in financial matters sent more women to court over debt after the Revolution than before. Up and down the coast, trade became more pervasive and more specialized over the course of the revolutionary and early national periods, making the process of obtaining and judging goods more central to women's lives.[12] Commercial transactions excluded some women, but others used formal, legalistic instruments to strengthen their traditional exchanges of goods and services. A Newport saleswoman armed with a promissory note had a stronger legal case to make than one who exchanged goods on the grounds of neighborliness. An enslaved Charlestonian with cash earnings could range farther over the city than one without. Women of all ranks drew upon ideas about money and commerce as they settled estates, negotiated cash wages, or loaned and borrowed money at interest, depending on their circumstances. A combination of class, occupation, and gender determined the form that economic participation took. Poor women and businesswomen lived by the quick turnover of cash into goods. Wealthier women could see money as a tool of investment over the long term. While differences of wealth and rank were exacerbated by the market, neither gender nor rank isolated any group from commercial concerns.

Even with the emergence of new commercial forms and financial connections, however, economic life remained a tangle of expectations, prejudices, cooperation, and competitive behavior. Despite the stubborn stereotypes of giddy female shoppers, obtaining goods remained an often protracted process involving men and women. In 1804, Newport Quaker Hetty Earl received a commission from her Philadelphia cousin for dried apples, a local specialty. Her first thought was to head for Thames Street to bargain with a local "market woman," but her aunt convinced her to wait "till we could see some of friend Motts family as she could warrant theirs certain to be *clean* and free from sweet ones." Market women tended to be poor; Earl's aunt felt that their produce probably was as well. While Earl prized low prices and convenience, her aunt pressed for high quality and a known supplier. They decided to deal with fellow Quakers, but neither woman felt the need to negotiate personally. As Earl later reported, her uncle got involved in the search by deploying a male servant as proxy, which, Earl noted, "I would have done before if I had known it would have met with his approbation but our male domesticks are such choice peaces that we never dare employ them without leave, unless we do it slily." Horizontal and vertical ties, family connections and urban labor calculations, men and women all came together in this errand. And still, the job was not done. Hannah Mott had no apples; instead, she sent the male servant on to Peter Lawton. Once again, personal connections failed. Hetty Earl was disgusted to discover that Lawton, "who tho *my Cousin* took advantage of our necessity and ask'd just double the market price." Earl spent the afternoon visiting with friends and complaining about her cousin's business practices. She claimed to be "very sorry since that I did not send it immediately back"—not because she could not afford the apples, not because she was unaware of the market price for them, but rather "for I think it wrong to indulge such jewish dispositions." The social conversation paid handsome dividends; that very evening her friend sent seven and a half pounds of apples to her and told her to treat them as a gift.[13] Commercial life was a messy, contingent process in which men and women pushed their own agendas, clung irrationally to customary methods, and judged economic actions by social codes.

The prevalence of proxy shoppers, family credit, socially coded cash, urban housefuls, and the other practices of city women point us toward a collaborative model of economic and material life in these transitional years. Looking at women's economic networks, for example, reveals a system of credit—only partly governed by gender—that was dominated by mediated access for urban residents. Attention to "family credit" and the pooling of houseful resources reminds us that men's interactions with commercial organizations depended on familial and social relationships as much as women's did. Many of these patterns continued beyond the period discussed here. In the nineteenth century personal ties, especially between kin, continued to structure commercial relationships and institutions. When capital was scarce, new organizations like banks drew from a group of well-known associates who could be depended upon for investment—and who then would expect special consideration.[14] Countless so-called rugged individuals relied upon the pull of informal networks for success. Just like "self-made" Benjamin Franklin, they might tout hard work and thrift, but lean on mothers' friends and wives' money.[15]

In this book, I have used the metaphor of the network to analyze female participation in economic life because it captures both the idea of connection and the importance of what exists "in between." Recent work on women in the eighteenth and early nineteenth centuries has opened our eyes to the fact that women's centrality to labor systems and political culture in this period can be understood only by taking their actions as intermediaries as seriously as people in the long eighteenth century did.[16] The fact that enslaved women gave birth to the next generation of slaves meant that their reproductive capacities were foremost in the minds of slave owners as they planned their operations and managed their households. The ability of elite political hostesses to bring together political friends and adversaries in quasi-public parlors made them vital players in the creation of a national style of politics in the early republic. Intermediaries, proxies, and go-betweens are central to political, economic, and social life. Until we give these "in-between" institutions and individuals the serious notice that they deserve we will never see the whole.

The same eighteenth-century developments that fostered proxy shopping, family credit, and the other adaptations used by women in port cities raised new questions about trust and identity in the marketplace. Free single women maintained reputations for personal credit that relied on newer financial calculations rather than the older (and persistent) standards of sexual restraint. Community policing of these reputations meant the threat of debtors' prison rather than the stocks. For enslaved people, who were themselves commodities with a price, economic autonomy seemed a fundamental contradiction to many whites, who resorted to a system combining surveillance with significant latitude to circulate for urban slaves. In 1822, this tenuous hybrid was to snap in the trial and execution of former Charleston slave Denmark Vesey and his followers, many of whom had been intermediaries in the stores and workshops of Charleston. The mobility and autonomy of urban slaves had, according to many whites, presented them with the perfect conditions to mount an insurrection. More woundingly to the master class, the practical attitude of trust and discretion that created the proxy system was clearly being used by proxies for their own, independent ends. In family letters, mistresses lamented that "all confidence is lost in our house servants."[17] Whites demanded not only the death of the alleged conspirators but also a crackdown that included new restrictions on enslaved people's mobility and stepped-up official patrols through the city. Dependency in the marketplace was fodder for jokes and moralizing when the subjects were well-to-do white girls, but, as the Vesey case highlights, more important principles were at stake.

Neither harsh slave codes nor shrill domesticity literature could ultimately resolve the tensions created by commercial life. By the late nineteenth century, institutions took on many of the functions pioneered by consumer networks. Large, diversified department stores flourished by catering to the social and material needs of middle-class customers and offering spaces to relax and talk as well as a staggering variety of stock. Mail-order businesses delivered goods to disparate communities. Loan companies and large stores offered consumer credit to a wide range of shoppers. Advertisements in newspapers and the new catalogues included detailed pictures and consumer testimony.[18]

The vocabulary of commerce that colonial women helped shape with their economic networks became the familiar argot of Americans in the nineteenth century. As talk of cash and competition replaced older ways of conceptualizing personal relationships, Americans faced disturbing questions about their affectionate ties. If a free white woman discussed correspondence with her sister in terms of credits and debits, what did that suggest about sisterly bonds? If a husband joked that the best wife was like an almanac—cheap and quickly shelved—what did that say about the source and strength of his authority? Such questions, always ambiguous in a society where human beings were bought and sold on city streets, only became more troubling as the nineteenth century progressed.

Notes

The following abbreviations appear in the notes.

Charleston CCP	Charleston Court of Common Pleas (Judgment Rolls and Petitions and Decrees in Summary Process)
NCH	Newport Court House, Newport, Rhode Island
NHS	Newport Historical Society, Newport, Rhode Island
NPCCP	Newport Court of Common Pleas
RIHS	Rhode Island Historical Society, Providence, Rhode Island
RISA	Rhode Island State Archives, Providence, Rhode Island
SCCCP	South Carolina Court of Common Pleas (Judgment Rolls)
SCDAH	South Carolina Department of Archives and History, Columbia, South Carolina
SCHM	*South Carolina Historical Magazine*
SCHS	South Carolina Historical Society, Charleston, South Carolina
SCL	South Caroliniana Library, Columbia, South Carolina

Introduction

1. NPCCP 1770, November term, #97.

2. For an introduction to the social scientific literature on embeddedness, see the introduction to Sharon Zukin and Paul DiMaggio, eds., *Structures of Capital: The Social Organization of the Economy* (New York: Cambridge University Press, 1990), 1–36. Toby Ditz, in "Shipwrecked; or Masculinity Imperiled: Mercantile Representations of Failure and the Gendered Self in Eighteenth-Century Philadelphia," *Journal of American History* 81 (June 1994): 51–80; and David Hancock, in *Citizens of the World: London Merchants and the Integration of the British Atlantic*

Community, 1735–1785 (New York: Cambridge University Press, 1995), among others, have explored what embeddedness meant for men's commercial relationships in the colonial period. Deborah Valenze provides a valuable exploration of the embeddedness of money itself in early modern England in *The Social Life of Money in the English Past* (New York: Cambridge University Press, 2006).

3. Jean-Christophe Agnew, *Worlds Apart: The Market and the Theater in Anglo-American Thought, 1550–1750* (New York: Cambridge University Press, 1986), chapter 1; Robert Olwell, *Masters, Slaves, and Subjects: The Culture of Power in the South Carolina Low Country, 1740–1790* (Ithaca, N.Y.: Cornell University Press, 1998), chapter 4. Joyce Appleby, *Capitalism and a New Social Order: The Republican Vision of the 1790s* (New York: New York University Press, 1984), 30–38, has a useful summary of the intellectual history of market thought.

4. Studies of business and finance have for some time urged us to think in terms of networks, not individuals, and to see financial transactions embedded within social connections and cultural practices. See Grahaeme Thompson et al., *Markets, Hierarchies, and Networks: The Coordination of Social Life* (London: Sage, 1991); Toshio Yamagishi et al., "Network Connections and the Distribution of Power in Exchange Networks," *American Journal of Sociology* 93, no. 4 (January 1988): 833–51; Mustafa Emirbayer and Jeff Goodwin, "Network Analysis, Culture, and the Problem of Agency," *American Journal of Sociology* 99, no. 6 (May 1994): 1411–54; Brian Uzzi, "The Sources and Consequences of Embeddedness for the Economic Performance of Organizations: The Network Effect," *American Sociological Review* 61, no. 4 (August 1996): 674–98. English historians have begun to explore the importance of intermediaries. See Margot Finn, *The Character of Credit: Personal Debt in English Culture, 1740–1914* (New York: Cambridge University Press, 2003), and Craig Muldrew, *The Economy of Obligation: The Culture of Credit and Social Relations in Early Modern England* (New York: St. Martin's Press, 1998). Karin Wulf deploys the concept of networks to analyze women in colonial Philadelphia in *Not All Wives: Women of Colonial Philadelphia* (Ithaca, N.Y.: Cornell University Press, 2000).

5. Adam Smith, *The Wealth of Nations*, reprinted in Robert L. Heilbroner, ed., *The Essential Adam Smith* (New York: Norton, 1986), 241. Smith acknowledged the interdependence of men upon each other in a commercial society, particularly as regards the division of labor. The interdependence, he argued, was negotiated through one man's self-interest appealing to another man's self-interest in forging exchanges.

6. An extensive literature explores the concept of separate male and female "spheres" of life in the late eighteenth and nineteenth centuries. See Linda Kerber, "Separate Spheres, Female Worlds, Woman's Place: The Rhetoric of Women's History," *Journal of American History* 75, no. 1 (1988): 9–39. For a recent reconsideration of the analytical utility of the public/private binary in women's history, and how it intersects with and differs from the idea of "spheres," see the articles in *Journal of Women's History* 15, nos. 1 and 2 (2003).

7. Joan Jensen, *Loosening the Bonds: Mid-Atlantic Farm Women, 1750–1850* (New Haven: Yale University Press, 1986).

8. Christine Stansell, *City of Women: Sex and Class in New York, 1789–1860* (1982; Urbana: University of Illinois Press, 1986), 52. See also Jeanne Boydston, "The Woman Who Wasn't There: Women's Market Labor and the Transition to Capitalism in the United States," *Journal of the Early Republic* 16 (Summer 1996): 183–206; Thomas Dublin, *Transforming Women's Work: New England Lives in the Industrial Revolution* (Ithaca, N.Y.: Cornell University Press, 1994); and Lisa Nor-

ling, *Captain Ahab Had a Wife: New England Women and the Whalefishery, 1720–1870* (Chapel Hill: University of North Carolina Press, 2000). Several works on women in early cities make a similar point, often implicitly. See Serena Zabin, "Women's Trading Networks and Dangerous Economies in Eighteenth-Century New York City," *Early American Studies* 4 (Fall 2006): 291–321; Seth Rockman, "Women's Labor, Gender Ideology, and Working-Class Households in Early Republic Baltimore," *Pennsylvania History* 66 (1999): 174–200; Billy G. Smith, *The "Lower Sort": Philadelphia's Laboring People, 1750–1800* (Ithaca, N.Y.: Cornell University Press, 1990) 111–12; Wulf, *Not All Wives*; Patricia Cleary, *Elizabeth Murray: A Woman's Pursuit of Independence in Eighteenth-Century America* (Amherst: University of Massachusetts Press, 2000).

9. Cynthia Kierner, *Beyond the Household: Women's Place in the Early South, 1700–1835* (Ithaca, N.Y.: Cornell University Press, 1998), 13. See also Cornelia Hughes Dayton, *Women Before the Bar: Gender, Law, and Society in Connecticut, 1639–1789* (Chapel Hill: University of North Carolina Press, 1995); Deborah Rosen, *Courts and Commerce: Gender, Law, and the Market Economy in Colonial New York* (Columbus: Ohio State University Press, 1997); Elaine Forman Crane, *Ebb Tide in New England: Women, Seaports, and Social Change, 1630–1800* (Boston: Northeastern University Press, 1998); Susan Branson, "Women and the Family Economy in the Early Republic: The Case of Elizabeth Meredith," *Journal of the Early Republic* 16 (spring 1996): 47–71.

10. Finn, *Character of Credit*, 11; John Styles, "Custom or Consumption? Plebeian Fashion in Eighteenth-Century England," in Maxine Berg and Elizabeth Eger, eds., *Luxury in the Eighteenth Century: Debates, Desires and Delectable Goods* (London: Palgrave, 2003), 103–15.

11. The literature on consumption is booming, led by work on eighteenth-century Britain. Beginning with the classic works, see Neil McKendrick, John Brewer, and J. H. Plumb, *The Birth of a Consumer Society: The Commercialization of Eighteenth-Century England* (Bloomington: Indiana University Press, 1982); John Brewer and Roy Porter, eds., *Consumption and the World of Goods* (London: Routledge, 1993); Carole Shammas, *The Pre-Industrial Consumer in England and America* (Oxford: Clarendon Press, 1990); Lorna Weatherill, *Consumer Behavior and Material Culture in Britain, 1660–1760* (London: Routledge, 1988); Amanda Vickery, *The Gentleman's Daughter: Women's Lives in Georgian England* (New Haven: Yale University Press, 1998). Historians of America have expanded this research, as well, beginning with Cary Carson, Ronald Hoffman, and Peter J. Albert, eds., *Of Consuming Interests: The Style of Life in the Eighteenth Century* (Charlottesville: University Press of Virginia, 1994); and Richard Bushman, *The Refinement of America: Persons, Houses, Cities* (New York: Vintage Books, 1992). For recent useful summaries and critical reviews of the literature of consumption, see Paul G. E. Clemens, "The Consumer Culture of the Middle Atlantic, 1760–1820," *William and Mary Quarterly*, 3rd ser., 62, no. 4 (Ocober 2005): 578–624; and Sara Pennell, "Consumption and Consumerism in Early Modern England," *Historical Journal* 42, no. 2 (1999): 549–64.

12. John Styles, "Lodging at the Old Bailey: Lodgings and Their Furnishing in Eighteenth-Century London," in John Styles and Amanda Vickery, eds., *Gender, Taste, and Material Culture in Britain and North America, 1700–1830* (New Haven: Yale University Press, 2006): 61–80. See also Ann Smart Martin, *Buying into the World of Goods: Early Consumers in Backcountry Virginia* (Baltimore: Johns Hopkins University Press, 2008).

13. Finn, *Character of Credit*, 9–10.

14. Gary B. Nash, "Urban Wealth and Poverty in Pre-Revolutionary America," *Journal of Interdisciplinary History* 6, no. 4 (Spring 1976): 545–84; Smith, *The "Lower Sort,"* 84–91; Peter Coclanis, *The Shadow of a Dream: Economic Life and Death in the South Carolina Low Country, 1670–1920* (New York: Oxford University Press, 1989), 79–91; and Alice Hanson Jones, *Wealth of a Nation to Be: The American Colonies on the Eve of the Revolution* (New York: Columbia University Press, 1980).

15. Charleston was originally named Charles Town; when the city was incorporated in 1783, the name was officially changed to Charleston. The port's name had been pronounced and known as "Charlestown" from the 1760s, however. I have therefore used the "Charleston" spelling, its current name, throughout the book.

16. Recent important studies that use the theme of theme of liberal free choice and the problem of dependency as a context for understanding economic life in the revolutionary era include Bruce Mann's *Republic of Debtors: Bankruptcy in the Age of American Independence* (Cambridge, Mass.: Harvard University Press, 2003) and T. H. Breen's *The Marketplace of Revolution: How Consumer Politics Shaped American Independence* (New York: Oxford University Press, 2005). Both discuss women briefly but do not make gender a significant part of their analyses. Likewise, the debates between "moral economy" historians and "market economy" historians, which concern the economic mentalités of eighteenth-century Americans, touch only tangentially on the influence of gender. For a summary of these debates, see Naomi Lamoreaux, "Rethinking the Transition to Capitalism in the Early American Northeast," *Journal of American History* 90, no. 2 (September 2003): 437–61.

17. "A Midnight Soliloquy in the Market House of Philadelphia," quoted in Steven Watts, *The Republic Reborn: War and the Making of Liberal America, 1790–1820* (Baltimore: Johns Hopkins University Press, 1987), 81.

18. See Jacob M. Price, "Economic Function and the Growth of American Port Towns in the Eighteenth Century," *Perspectives in American History* 8 (1974): 173; and Carl Bridenbaugh, *Cities in Revolt: Urban Life in America, 1743–1776* (New York: Oxford University Press, 1955).

19. For a recent review essay that highlights some of these similar trends in the study of early American port cities, see Seth Rockman, "Work in the Cities of Colonial British North America," *Journal of Urban History* 33, no. 6 (September 2007): 1021–32.

20. 9 mo. 7, 1796, letter from S. Robinson in Newport to her daughter Molly [in Philadelphia], Robinson Family Papers, New England Women and Their Families in the 18th and 19th Centuries: Personal Papers, Letters, and Diaries, series b: selections from the Newport Historical Society (Bethesda, Md.: Lexis-Nexis Academic & Library Solutions, 2000), reel 2, box 2 (hereafter Robinson Papers). For all quotations from manuscript sources, I have retained original spellings and wordings, without adding [*sic*].

21. Bryan Rommel-Ruiz, "Atlantic Revolutions: Slavery and Freedom in Newport, Rhode Island, and Halifax, Nova Scotia, in the Era of the American Revolution" (Ph.D. diss., University of Michigan, 1999), 57; Peter J. Coleman, *The Transformation of Rhode Island, 1790–1860* (Providence: Brown University Press, 1969), 54.

22. Letter from Moses Lopez in Charleston to Aaron Lopez in Newport, May 8, 1764, translated with notes by Thomas J. Tobias, "Charles Town in 1764," *South Carolina Historical Magazine* 67, no. 2 (April 1966): 67. See also Stanley F. Chyet, *Lopez of Newport: Colonial American Merchant Prince* (Detroit: Wayne State University Press, 1970), 42–44, 80–83.

23. 3 mo. 25, 1820, letter from Mary Robinson Morton at Philadelphia to her sister Abigail Robinson in Newport, Robinson Papers, microfilm, reel 14.

24. C. Read to Mrs. Charles Ludlow, May 9, [1787], Read Family Papers, folder 2, SCL.

25. Quoted in Carl Bridenbaugh, "Colonial Newport as a Summer Resort," *Rhode Island Historical Society Collections* 26, no. 1 (January 1933): 1.

26. For urban populations, see P. J. Corfield, *The Impact of English Towns, 1700–1800* (New York: Oxford University Press, 1982), 8; Bureau of the Census, *A Century of Population Growth: From the First Census of the United States to the Twelfth, 1790–1900* (Washington, D.C.: Government Printing Office, 1909), 11–14. Paul Langford surveys many of the new cultural institutions and practices that grew up with commercial development in England in *A Polite and Commercial People: England, 1727–1783* (New York: Oxford University Press, 1989).

27. May 22, 1801, letter from John Ball to John Ball, Jr., Ball Family Papers, 11/516/13, SCHS; July 1, 1802, letter from same to same, Ball Family Papers, 11/516/14a, SCHS.

28. See 1774 letters from Gabriel Manigault in Newport to Mrs. Anne Manigault in Charleston. Manigault Family Papers, box 1, folder 5, SCL.

29. Mark Granovetter, "The Strength of Weak Ties: A Network Theory Revisited," *Sociological Theory* 1 (1983): 215. For Granovetter's original formulation of weak ties, see "The Strength of Weak Ties," *American Journal of Sociology* 78, no. 6 (May 1973): 1360–80.

Chapter 1. Urban Housefuls

1. Quoted in Daniel Scott Smith, "The Meanings of Family and Household: Change and Continuity in the Mirror of the American Census," *Population and Development Review* 18 (1992): 421.

2. For use of the term "family economy" as a unit of production, see Julie A. Matthaei, *An Economic History of Women in America: Women's Work, the Sexual Division of Labor, and the Development of Capitalism* (New York: Shocken Books, 1982), 15–35; and Laurel Thatcher Ulrich, *A Midwife's Tale: The Life of Martha Ballard, Based on Her Diary, 1785–1812* (New York: Vintage Books, 1990), 75–84. Patricia Cleary, in "'She Will be in the Shop': Women's Sphere of Trade in Eighteenth-Century Philadelphia and New York," *Pennsylvania Magazine of History and Biography* 119, no. 3 (July 1995): 184; and Susan Branson, "Women and the Family Economy in the Early Republic: The Case of Elizabeth Meredith," *Journal of the Early Republic* 16 (Spring 1996): 47–71, use the term more generally. Louise Tilly and Joan Scott use the term to discuss the family as a "strategic unit" in England and France in *Women, Work, and Family* (New York: Methuen, 1987), 9, chapter 2, and chapter 3, while Sarah Mendelson and Patricia Crawford highlight its limitations in the same period, *Women in Early Modern England, 1550–1720* (Oxford: Clarendon, 1998), chapters 5 and 6.

3. Elaine Forman Crane, *Ebb Tide in New England: Women, Seaports, and Social Change, 1630–1800* (Boston: Northeastern University Press, 1998), 125; Christine Stansell, *City of Women: Sex and Class in New York, 1789–1860* (Urbana: University of Illinois Press, 1986), 52–53; Thomas Dublin, *Transforming Women's Work: New England Lives in the Industrial Revolution* (Ithaca, N.Y.: Cornell University Press, 1994), introduction.

4. U.S. Bureau of the Census, *Heads of Families at the First Census of the United*

States, Taken in the Year 1790—South Carolina (Baltimore: Genealogical Publishing Co., 1992), 43; Jacob Milligan, *The Charleston Directory and Revenue System by Jacob C. Milligan, of the Intelligence Office, September 1790* (Charleston, S.C.: T. B. Bowen, 1790), 1, 20, 36.

5. See E. A. Hammel and Peter Laslett, "Comparing Household Social Structure over Time and Between Cultures," *Comparative Studies in Society and History* 16, no. 1 (January 1974): 78, 88. Subsequent scholars have used the term to highlight potential economic ties between households and resident cottagers or slaves in a rural setting. See Lucy Simler and Paul G. E. Clemens, "The 'Best Poor Man's Country' in 1783: The Population Structure of Rural Society in Late-Eighteenth-Century Southeastern Pennsylvania," *Proceedings of the American Philosophical Society* 133, no. 2, Symposium on the Demographic History of the Philadelphia Region, 1600–1860 (June 1989): 237; Smith, "The Meanings of Family and Household," 435.

6. See Carl Bridenbaugh, *Cities in Revolt: Urban Life in America, 1743–1776* (New York: Oxford University Press, 1955); Antoinette F. Dowling and Vincent J. Scully, Jr., *The Architectural Heritage of Newport Rhode Island, 1640–1915* (New York: Clarkson N. Potter, 1967); Elaine Forman Crane, *A Dependent People: Newport, Rhode Island in the Revolutionary Era* (New York: Fordham University Press, 1992); Lynne Withey, *Urban Growth in Colonial Rhode Island: Newport and Providence in the Eighteenth Century* (Albany: State University of New York Press, 1984).

7. See Bridenbaugh, *Cities in Revolt*; Peter A. Coclanis, *The Shadow of a Dream: Economic Life and Death in the South Carolina Low Country, 1670–1920* (New York: Oxford University Press, 1989); Walter Edgar, *South Carolina: A History* (Columbia: University of South Carolina Press, 1998); Walter J. Fraser, Jr., *Charleston! Charleston! The History of a Southern City* (Columbia: University of South Carolina Press, 1989); Jonathan H. Poston, *The Buildings of Charleston: A Guide to the City's Architecture* (Columbia: University of South Carolina Press, 1997); Jeanne Calhoun, Elizabeth Paysinger, and Martha Zierden, *A Survey of Economic Activity in Charleston, 1732–1770, Charleston Museum Archaeological Contributions* 2 (October 1982): 34–39.

8. U.S. Bureau of the Census, *Historical Statistics of the United States, Colonial Times to 1970*, part 2 (1975; White Plains, N.Y.: Kraus International, 1989), 1180–81.

9. Crane, *A Dependent People*, 20.

10. Philip J. Greven Jr., "The Average Size of Families and Households in the Province of Massachusetts in 1764 and in the United States in 1790: An Overview," in Peter Laslett, ed., *Household and Family in Past Time* (Cambridge: Cambridge University Press, 1972), 558; Lynne E. Withey, "Household Structure in Urban and Rural Areas: The Case of Rhode Island, 1774–1800," *Journal of Family History* 3, no. 1 (Spring 1978): 38–39, 41.

11. Withey, "Household Structure," 41, 43. On wives and widows of mariners, see Ruth Wallis Herndon, "The Domestic Cost of Seafaring: Town Leaders and Seamen's Families in Eighteenth-Century Rhode Island," in Margaret Creighton and Lisa Norling, eds., *Iron Men, Wooden Women: Gender and Seafaring in the Atlantic World, 1700–1920* (Baltimore: Johns Hopkins University Press, 1996), 55–69.

12. Daniel Scott Smith, "Female Householding in Late Eighteenth-Century America and the Problem of Poverty," *Journal of Social History* 28, no. 1 (Fall 1994): Karin Wulf, *Not All Wives: Women of Colonial Philadelphia* (Ithaca, N.Y.: Cornell University Press, 2000), 90–102; Crane, *Ebb Tide*, 16–18, 50–51; and Withey, "Household Structure," 43.

13. In Newport, women headed only 6 percent of free black households, prob-

ably because free black households were small nuclear families rather than the larger groupings of free and enslaved blacks typical in Charleston.

14. The average female-headed household size in Newport was 4.4 people, but double that number in Charleston. For this analysis, I identified those household heads who had female first names where the household makeup supported a female head. As there were a few cases of ambiguous names, these figures are approximate. The average size of the group made up of the first twenty and last twenty female names on the Charleston city census was 9.3 people; if the largest household, Mary Middleton's forty-two-person household, is removed, the average size is 8.5. For Newport and Charleston household-size averages for 1790, see Greven, "The Average Size of Families and Households," 558–58; and Lynne Withey, "Population Change, Economic Development, and the Revolution: Newport, Rhode Island, as a Case Study, 1760–1800" (Ph.D. diss., University of California at Berkeley, 1976), 43–44.

15. Smith, "Female Householding," 93–95.

16. In the 1760s, 42 percent of Newport taxpayers owned at least one slave; in the same period, 77 percent of Charleston residents died as slave owners. Withey, *Urban Growth*, 130–31. Richard Waterhouse, *A New World Gentry: The Making of a Merchant and Planter Class in South Carolina, 1670–1770* (New York: Garland, 1989), 67; Robert Olwell, *Masters, Slaves, and Subjects: The Culture of Power in the South Carolina Low Country, 1740–1790* (Ithaca, N.Y.: Cornell University Press, 1998), 45.

17. Rhode Island Governor, "An Account of the People in the Colony . . . December 24, 1755" (1755; Rhode Island: [reprint publisher unknown], 18—); Rhode Island General Assembly, "The Following is an Account of the Number of Inhabitants . . . " (Newport: Solomon Southwick, 1774); Jay Mack Holbrook, *Rhode Island 1782 Census* (Oxford, Mass.: Holbrook Research Institute, 1782), vi; U.S. Bureau of the Census, *Heads of Families at the First Census of the United States, Taken in the Year 1790—Rhode Island* (Baltimore: Genealogical Publishing, 1992), 9. According to subsequent censuses, the proportion in Newport was 9 percent in 1800 and 8 percent in 1810 and 1820. U.S. Bureau of the Census, *Second Census of the United States, 1800*, vol. 2 (New York: Norman Ross Publishing, 1990), 26; U.S. Bureau of the Census, *Third Census of the United States, 1810*, vol. 3 (New York: Norman Ross Publishing, 1990), 23; U.S. Bureau of the Census, *Fourth Census of the United States, 1820*, vol. 5 (1821; New York: Norman Ross Publishing, 1990), n.p. New York City and County's population was 14 percent black in 1771 and 10 percent black in 1790. See Evarts Greene and Virginia Harrington, *American Population Before the Federal Census of 1790* (New York: Columbia University Press, 1932), 102, 105. Philadelphia in 1790 had 4.5 percent of the population listed as slaves or "other [nonwhite] free persons." For information on New York, Philadelphia, and Boston, see U.S. Bureau of the Census, *Heads of Families at the First Census of the United States, Taken in the Year 1790—New York* (Baltimore: Genealogical Publishing, 2004); U.S. Bureau of the Census, *Heads of Families at the First Census of the United States, Taken in the Year 1790—Pennsylvania* (Baltimore: Genealogical Publishing, 2002); U.S. Bureau of the Census, *Heads of Families at the First Census of the United States, Taken in the Year 1790—Massachusetts* (Baltimore: Genealogical Publishing, 1998); and Greene and Harrington, *American Population*, 22.

18. Philip D. Morgan, *Slave Counterpoint: Black Culture in the Eighteenth-Century Chesapeake and Lowcountry* (Chapel Hill: University of North Carolina Press, 1998), 96–97.

19. William Davis Miller, "The Narragansett Planters," *Proceedings of the American Antiquarian Society*, n.s., 43 (April–October 1933): 49–115; and chapter 2, "A

Clustered Minority," in William D. Piersen, *Black Yankees: The Development of an Afro-American Subculture in Eighteenth-Century New England* (Amherst: University of Massachusetts Press, 1988), 14–22.

20. Cynthia Kennedy, *Braided Relations, Entwined Lives: The Women of Charleston's Urban Slave Society* (Bloomington: Indiana University Press, 2005), 150–53.

21. *South Carolina Gazette and Country Journal*, December 8, 1767.

22. NPCCP, 1770 November term, #7. Sarah S. Hughes notes that single and widowed women in Elizabeth County, Virginia, commonly hired out their slaves and depended on the income that they earned to support themselves. "Slaves for Hire: The Allocation of Black Labor in Elizabeth City County, Virginia, 1782 to 1810," *William and Mary Quarterly*, 3rd ser., 35, no. 2 (April 1978): 271–73.

23. For a comparison of male and female patterns of "exchanging works" in New England, see Daniel Vickers, *Farmers and Fishermen: Two Centuries of Work in Essex County, Massachusetts, 1630–1850* (Chapel Hill: University of North Carolina Press, 1994), 52–64; and Ulrich, *A Midwife's Tale*, 81–90.

24. Withey, "Population Change," 19–23. For an extensive discussion of the causes and consequences of mobility in revolutionary Philadelphia, see Billy G. Smith, *The "Lower Sort": Philadelphia's Laboring People, 1750–1800* (Ithaca, N.Y.: Cornell University Press, 1990), chapter 6.

25. *Newport Mercury*, January 9, 1775.

26. Capt. Martin, "A Description of Charles Town in 1769," reprinted in H. Roy Merrens, ed., *The South Carolina Scene: Contemporary Views, 1679–1774* (Columbia: University of South Carolina Press, 1977), 231. The editor notes that the origins of this verse are unknown.

27. John Maylem, "Description of the Town of Newport, Rhode Island" [1768], quoted in "Notes on Newport in 1768," *Rhode Island Historical Society Collections* 12 (1919): 51.

28. For an extended historical exploration of the relationship between the theater and the market, see Jean-Christophe Agnew, *Worlds Apart: The Market and the Theater in Anglo-American Thought, 1550–1750* (New York: Cambridge University Press, 1986).

29. Robert Wells's study of colonial census data found that in most counties, there were 1.11 to 1.38 families per household. *The Population of the British Colonies in America Before 1776* (Princeton, N.J.: Princeton University Press, 1975), quoted in Creighton and Norling, *Iron Men, Wooden Women*, 296, n. 84.

30. For this analysis, I identified those household heads with female first names where the household makeup supported a female head. As there were a few cases of ambiguous names, these figures are approximate. The average size of the group made up of the first twenty and last twenty female names on the Charleston city census was 9.3 people; if the largest household, Mary Middleton's forty-two-person household, is removed, the average size is 8.5. For Newport and Charleston household-size averages for 1790, see Greven, "The Average Size of Families and Households," 558–58; and Withey, "Population Change," 43–44. I used a city directory to determine the occupation (when available) and address of these female heads of household. See Milligan, *The Charleston Directory*.

31. U.S. Bureau of the Census, *Heads of Families . . . South Carolina*, 38, 40; Milligan, *The Charleston Directory*, 25, 30, 37. By cross-referencing the census listing and the city directory for this year (1790), it is possible to determine several cases where individuals with the same last name did or did not live and/or work together. For these purposes, it is helpful that the census lists names not alphabetically but apparently by neighborhood or ward. I have presumed that the "free

white females" living with McNabb (one woman/girl) and Pierce (two women/ girls) included their wives.

32. In addition to city directories, U.S. Census reports for Newport and Charleston, 1790, seem to show some grouping of female householders.

33. Wulf, *Not All Wives*, 125–30. Similar patterns existed in Boston in the second half of the eighteenth century. Crane, *Ebb Tide*, 17–18.

34. U.S. Bureau of the Census, *Heads of Families*, 23. The census in this year was printed not alphabetically, but house-by-house, so it is possible to presume neighbors in a general sense.

35. Schenck and Turner, *The Directory and Stranger's Guide for the City of Charleston: Also A Directory for Charleston Neck, Between Boundary Street and the lines, for the Year 1819* (Charleston, S.C.: A. E. Miller, 1819). Two of the women were listed with no specific address.

36. Gary Nash posits a staged withdrawal from owners' houses into nuclear family units, based on his study of census figures for New York, Philadelphia, and Boston. See "Forging Freedom: The Emancipation Experience in Northern Seaport Cities, 1775–1820," in Ira Berlin and Ronald Hoffman, eds., *Slavery and Freedom in the Age of the American Revolution* (Urbana: University of Illinois Press, 1893), 33–39.

37. Calhoun et al., *A Survey of Economic Activity in Charleston*, 58.

38. Bernard L. Herman, "Slave and Servant Housing in Charleston, 1770–1820," *Historical Archaeology* 33, no. 3 (1999): 97.

39. Henry Izard in Charleston to Mrs. Manigault in Pennsylvania, September 30, 1808, Manigault Family Papers, box 3, folder 55, SCL. See also Ann Izard in Charleston to Margaret Manigault, October 6, 1802, Manigault Family Papers, box 2, folder 38, SCL.

40. NPCCP, 1750 May term, #252, 1750 November term, #270.

41. This prompted Loveland to sue him in order to recover for damages to her investment, resulting in the court cases named above.

42. January 6, 1799[?], letter from Sarah Rutledge at Newport to her husband, John Rutledge, in Philadelphia. John Rutledge Jr. Papers, 948, box 1, folder 8, Southern Historical Collection, University of North Carolina Library.

43. Charles William Janson, *The Stranger in America, 1793–1806*, reprinted, with an introduction and notes by Carl S. Driver (1807; New York: Press of the Pioneers, 1935), 369; *Newport Mercury*, February 11, 1804; *Newport Mercury*, February 18, 1804.

44. The Middleton family account book records an end-of-summer payment of $9.50 to Mrs. Rogers for the "hire of beds" in 1796; a newspaper advertisement from four years later suggests that Mrs. Rogers regularly hosted southern families. In 1800, when ten visitors wanted passage to Virginia they asked interested parties to apply at "Mrs. Rogers's." Middleton Account Book for Newport, R.I., 1795–1796, 12/177/1. Middleton Family Papers, 1795–1887, 1168.02.05.01, SCHS.

45. July 1, 1802, letter from John Ball to John Ball Jr., Ball Family Papers, 11/516/14a, SCHS.

46. Edward Ball, *Slaves in the Family* (New York: Ballantine Books, 1999), 255.

47. August 23, 1798, letter from John Rutledge, Jr., at Newport to Bishop Smith [his father-in-law] in Charleston. John Rutledge, Jr., Papers #948, box 1, folder 7, Southern Historical Collection, University of North Carolina Library.

48. See entries in Middleton Account Book for Newport, R.I., 1795–1796, 12/177/1. Middleton Family Papers, 1795–1887, 1168.02.05.01, SCHS.

49. Newport Supreme Court Record Book, March term, 1776, vol. f, p. 128.

50. John Hammond Moore, ed., "The Abiel Abbot Journals: A Yankee Preacher in Charleston Society, 1818–1827," *South Carolina Historical Magazine* 68, no. 2 (April 1967): 68.

51. NPCCP, 1760 November term, #123. The court sided with Mary and John but rewarded them only a nominal sum above their court costs.

52. Claire Lyons, *Sex Among the Rabble: An Intimate History of Gender and Power in the Age of Revolution, Philadelphia, 1730–1830* (Chapel Hill: University of North Carolina Press, 2006), 97.

53. Stephanie Grauman Wolf, *As Various as Their Land: The Everyday Lives of Eighteenth-Century Americans* (New York: Harper Collins, 1993), 47.

54. Historian Bernard Herman has noted that the architecture and furnishings of an eighteenth-century merchant's house enacted multiple personalities. The "local exterior" of the home, with its substantial brick walls, grand scale, and up-to-date ornamentation loomed over neighbors and reinforced competitive distinctions of status among city dwellers. The "transatlantic interior" of the home, furnished in imports and occupied by people well schooled in transplanted elite codes of behavior, competed in Atlantic cosmopolitanism. Bernard Herman, *Town House: Architecture and Material Life in the Early American City, 1780–1830* (Chapel Hill: University of North Carolina Press, 2005), 39.

55. *South Carolina Gazette*, November 1, 1770.

56. *South Carolina Gazette*, March 16–23, 1765.

57. Herman, *Town House*, chapter 4; for the nineteenth century in particular, see Maurie McInnis, *The Politics of Taste in Antebellum Charleston* (Chapel Hill: University of North Carolina Press, 2005).

58. *(Charleston) City Gazette and Daily Advertiser*, January 9, 1809, and January 11, 1809.

59. NPCCP, 1780 November term, #6.

60. [Ann] Taylor, *Practical Hints to Young Females, on the Duties of a Wife, a Mother, and a Mistress of a Family* (Boston: Wells and Lilly, 1816), 49.

61. William Ellery Account Book, 1780–1805, p. 26, RIHS.

62. Thomas M. Doerflinger, *A Vigorous Spirit of Enterprise: Merchants and Economic Development in Revolutionary Philadelphia* (Chapel Hill: University of North Carolina Press, 1986), chapters 1–3.

63. Poston, *The Buildings of Charleston*, 335 and chapter 5, passim.

64. Coclanis, *The Shadow of a Dream*, 111–17; Poston, *The Buildings of Charleston*, 197–98, 335–39.

65. J. P. Brissot de Warville, *New Travels in the United States of America, 1788*, trans. Mara Soceanu Vamos and Durand Echeverria (Cambridge, Mass.: Harvard University Press, 1964), 128.

66. *Newport Mercury*, January 1, 1820; Downing and Scully, *Architectural Heritage*, 106–9, pl. 128.

67. August 29, 1806, letter from Charles Fraser in Boston to Mrs. Mary Fraser in Charleston, S.C. Mary DeSaussure Fraser Papers, box 1, folder 1, Rare Book, Manuscript, and Special Collections Library, Duke University.

68. Minutes of the African Benevolent Society, Union Congregational Church records 1807–1824. Newport Historical Society. See also Bernard E. Powers Jr., *Black Charlestonians: A Social History, 1822–1855* (Fayetteville: University of Arkansas Press, 1994), 51.

69. See Gary B. Nash, "The Social Evolution of Preindustrial American Cities," 130–32; Paul Gilge, *The Road to Mobocracy: Popular Disorder in New York City, 1763–1834* (Chapel Hill: University of North Carolina Press, 1987), 127–28.

70. Peter Coclanis describes the lowcountry's relative decline to northern areas in *Shadow of a Dream*, chapter 4; see also Fraser, *Charleston! Charleston!* 192, 197–98. For factors contributing to the decline of Newport in the nineteenth century, see Peter J. Coleman, *The Transformation of Rhode Island, 1790–1860* (Providence, R.I.: Brown University Press, 1969), 67–69.

71. *South Carolina Gazette*, January 6, 1757.

72. Carole Shammas, *A History of Household Government in America* (Charlottesville: University Press of Virginia, 2002).

Chapter 2. Work in the Atlantic Service Economy

1. Karin Wulf, *Not All Wives: Women of Colonial Philadelphia* (Ithaca, N.Y.: Cornell University Press, 2000), chapter 4, analyzes how women's work created connections locally within a city.

2. For the gendered concept of "skill," see Ava Baron, ed., *Work Engendered: Toward a New History of American Labor* (Ithaca, N.Y.: Cornell University Press, 1991), 14.

3. Margaret Rose Hunt, *The Middling Sort: Commerce, Gender, and the Family in England, 1680–1780* (Berkeley: University of California Press, 1996), 137. Jeanne Boydston, "The Woman Who Wasn't There: Women's Market Labor and the Transition to Capitalism in the United States," *Journal of the Early Republic* 16 (Summer 1996): 186, 190–94; Gloria Main, "Gender, Work, and Wages in Colonial New England," *William and Mary Quarterly*, 3rd ser., 51, no. 1 (January 1994): 40.

4. This depiction of the transformation of the British Atlantic draws from David Hancock, *Citizens of the World: London Merchants and the Integration of the British Atlantic Community, 1735–1785* (New York: Cambridge University Press, 1995), 36–39.

5. In the 1803 Charleston directory, for example, women represented more than half of the boardinghouse keepers and likely performed the bulk of the work at the other establishments. Eleazer Elizer, *A Directory for 1803: Containing the Names of all the House-keepers and Traders in the City of Charleston, Alphabetically Arranged, their Particular Professions, and their Residence* (Charleston: W. P. Young, 1803). Forty one women were listed running boarding houses, out of seventy-one people total. An additional four hotels were listed; one was run by a man, the other three did not indicate the proprietor's first name. The occasional provision of boarding and lodging was undoubtedly far more widespread than remaining documents indicate.

6. NPCCP, 1790 November term, #118; U.S. Bureau of the Census, *Heads of Families at the First Census of the United States, Taken in the Year 1790—Rhode Island* [1790 census] (Baltimore: Genealogical Publishing, 1992), 20.

7. Newport Town Council Minutes, 1784–1794, #2013, May 29, 1786; July 24, 1786, NHS. More commonly in the 1790s, the Overseers paid direct pensions to the poor or aged of the town. Later, an institution was built to house them.

8. Simon Newman, *Embodied History: The Lives of the Poor in Early Philadelphia* (Philadelphia: University of Pennsylvania Press, 2003), 76–81.

9. Lisa Norling finds this pattern among Nantucket seafaring families of the late eighteenth century, and attributes some of the interest and willingness to forgo privacy for company to Quaker culture's community-oriented "tribalism." Lisa Norling, *Captain Ahab Had a Wife: New England Women and the Whalefishery, 1720–1870* (Chapel Hill: University of North Carolina Press, 2000), 73–77.

10. When Sheffield died, Christie boarded with Sarah Tucker, the executrix of Sheffield's estate, for eighty-five weeks under similar arrangements. NPCCP, 1770 May term #479; 1770 May term, #478; 1770 November term, #69.

11. Charleston CCP, Summary Process Rolls, 1805 50a.

12. For the links among consumption, female self-employment, and the service industry in the nineteenth and twentieth centuries, see Angel Kwolek-Folland, "Gender, the Service Sector, and U. S. Business History," *Business History Review* 81, no. 3 (Autumn 2007): 429.

13. Charleston CCP, 1810 344a.

14. NPCCP, 1771 May term #294.

15. U.S. Bureau of the Census, *Heads of Families . . . South Carolina*; Jacob Milligan, *The Charleston Directory and Revenue System by Jacob C. Milligan, of the Intelligence Office, September 1790* (Charleston, S.C.: T. B. Bowen, 1790). In 1790, the directory listed a total of twenty-two boardinghouse keepers and six innholders. The one female innholder listed in 1790, Margaret Stewart, had ten slaves.

16. Joanne Pope Melish, *Disowning Slavery: Gradual Emancipation and "Race" in New England, 1780–1860* (Ithaca, N.Y.: Cornell University Press, 1998), 20.

17. U.S. Bureau of the Census, *Heads of Families . . . South Carolina*; Milligan, *The Charleston Directory . . 1790.*

18. *Newport Mercury*, August 4, 1795.

19. Milligan, *The Charleston Directory . . . 1790*; *The Charleston Directory, by Jacob Milligan, Harbour Master, September 1794* (Charleston: W. P. Young, 1794); John Dixon Nelson, *Nelson's Charleston Directory, and Strangers Guide, for the Year of our Lord, 1801. Being the Twenty Fifth Year of the Independence of the United States of America, Until July Fourth* (Charleston: John Dixon Nelson, 1801); Elizer, *A Directory for 1803.* It is possible that this last move was not a relocation, since street numbers could change yearly.

20. NPCCP, 1820 term, #158.

21. Jeanne Boydston, *Home and Work: Housework, Wages, and the Ideology of Labor in the Early Republic* (New York: Oxford University Press, 1990), 51.

22. *The Directory and Stranger's Guide for the City of Charleston . . . for the Year 1819 . . .* (Charleston: Schenck & Turner, 1819).

23. [23] *Gazette of the State of South Carolina*, August 5, 1778. Philip Morgan found that by the mid-eighteenth century "perhaps as many as a quarter of them [female slaves in Charleston] served in specialized roles as house servants, seamstresses, cooks, or washerwomen." See Morgan, "Black Life in Eighteenth-Century Charleston," *Perspectives in American History*, n.s. 1 (1984): 200–201.

24. (*Charleston*) *City Gazette and Commercial Daily Advertiser*, May 30, 1816.

25. *South Carolina Gazette*, October 13, 1757, in Lathan A. Windley, ed., *Runaway Slave Advertisements: A Documentary History from the 1730s to 1790*, vol. 3 (Westport, Conn.: Greenwood Press, 1983), 158.

26. *The Directory and Stranger's Guide for the City of Charleston . . . for the Year 1819.* As was typical for city dwellers, many of these women crowded together in small homes and apartments. Two of the women were listed with no specific address.

27. Marla Miller, "The Last Mantuamaker: Craft Tradition and Commercial Change in Boston, 1760–1840," *Early American Studies* (Fall 2006): 377.

28. Charleston CCP, 1820 339a. On female expertise and occupational identity in eighteenth-century Europe, see Deborah Simonton, "Gendering Work in Eighteenth-Century Towns," in Margaret Walsh, ed., *Working Out Gender: Perspectives from Labour History* (Brookfield, Vt.: Ashgate, 1999), 29–47.

29. Presentments of the Grand Jury for the District of Charleston at a Court

of General Sessions on May 16, 1775, Journal of the South Carolina Court of General Sessions, 1769–1776. Microfilm copy, South Carolina Department of Archives and History.

30. Undoubtedly this was in part a function of numbers: pre-Revolutionary War Newport had a population of 15 percent to 18 percent people of color, including slaves; Charleston's was around 50 percent. By the early nineteenth century, Newport was phasing out slavery (and the population of people of color reflected this change, dropping well below 10 percent), while Charleston was as dominated as ever by the presence of enslaved people.

31. Wendy Gamber, "Tarnished Labor: The Home, the Market, and the Boardinghouse in Antebellum America," *Journal of the Early Republic* 22, no. 2 (Summer 2002): 193. For a discussion of women as the "central agents" in the rental housing market in late eighteenth-century New York, see Elizabeth Blackmar, *Manhattan for Rent, 1785–1850* (Ithaca, N.Y.: Cornell University Press, 1989), 60–68. Blackmar includes an extended discussion of Thomas Paine's complaints about the services provided by the wife of the man he boarded with. Jeanne Boydston also discusses the social dynamics of boarding in "The Woman Who Wasn't There," 193 n.18. For a vivid description of tensions between male customers and female servers, see NPCCP, May term 1770, #26.

32. Boydston, *Home and Work*, 146.

33. Charleston's average shipping tonnage cleared outward was 31,551, which was ahead of New York's 23,566 tons. Other pre-Revolutionary War cities had nowhere near Charleston's close association with the imperial center. New York's shipping was the next most tied to Great Britain, which accounted for 22 percent of the exported and 33 percent of the imported tonnage. Rhode Island's exports to Europe as a whole amounted to only about 5 percent of its shipping. See U.S. Bureau of the Census, *Historical Statistics of the United States, Colonial Times to 1970*, part 2 (1975; White Plains, N.Y.: Kraus International, 1989), 1180–81; Lynne Withey, *Urban Growth in Colonial Rhode Island: Newport and Providence in the Eighteenth Century* (Albany: State University of New York Press, 1984), 122.

34. In the five years 1768–72, Rhode Island saw an average of 1,171 ships per year enter and clear its ports; Newport's shipping accounted for approximately two-thirds of this traffic (about 780 vessels). For the same time period, an average of 913 vessels per year entered and cleared the port of Charleston. Withey, *Urban Growth*, 117–19; U.S. Bureau of the Census, *Historical Statistics*, 1181. Both figures are based on the records at the British Public Records Office; the two-thirds estimate of Newport's share of the Rhode Island shipping is Withey's. For per capita calculations, see U.S. Bureau of the Census, *Historical Statistics*, 1168, 1179. Rhode Island's rate was 0.36, South Carolina's 0.26, New Hampshire's 0.32, and Massachusetts's 0.30. Other figures were lower.

35. Studies of Boston, Philadelphia, and New York suggest that the two decades prior to the Revolution saw a large expansion in the number of shopkeepers overall, and female shopkeepers in particular, opening businesses to meet a growing demand for imported consumer goods. Cleary, "'She Merchants' of Colonial America: Women and Commerce on the Eve of the Revolution" (Ph.D. diss., Northwestern University, 1989), 91–94. For women retailers in Philadelphia, see Wulf, *Not All Wives*, 142–47.

36. Sharon Salinger, *Taverns and Drinking in Early America* (Baltimore: Johns Hopkins University Press, 2002), 51; David Hancock, "Commerce and Conversation in the Eighteenth-Century Atlantic: The Invention of Madeira Wine," *Journal of Interdisciplinary History* 29, no. 2 (Autumn 1998): 219.

37. Account of William Huggins for Ann Cross. Paul Cross Papers, folder 4, SCL.

38. *Newport Mercury,* June 5, 1769.

39. Account, NPCCP, 1771 May Term, #40.

40. Nathaniel Coggeshall Ledger Book, 1764–1767 (Ledger #2), NHS.

41. Charleston CCP, Judgment Rolls, 1820 term, #475a. Some retailers of alcohol accumulated larger stocks than the small purchases of tavern keepers would suggest. Elizabeth Miller, who purchased retail licenses in the 1780s and 1790s in Newport, died with an estate appraised at $6,153.84, which included twelve gross empty bottles, more than eighty-five gallons of Madeira wine, and more than one hundred gallons of brandy, in addition to the large amounts of sugar, playing cards, tea, coffee, whitewash brushes, and thread that she also had in her shop. Inventory of Elizabeth Miller, Newport Probate Records, vol. 4, p. 274, NCH.

42. For the relationship among British imports, American consumption, and shopping, see T. H. Breen, "'Baubles of Britain': The American and Consumer Revolutions of the Eighteenth Century," *Past and Present* 119 (1988): 73–104; T. H. Breen, "An Empire of Goods: The Anglicization of Colonial America, 1690–1776," *Journal of British Studies* 25 (October 1986): 467–99; Bushman, "Shopping and Advertising," 233–51; Cleary, "'She Will Be in the Shop,'" 181–202.

43. *South Carolina Gazette,* September 6–September 13, 1760; *South Carolina Gazette,* September 13–September 20, 1760; *South Carolina Gazette,* September 20–September 27, 1760. Six years later the captain supplied Anne Mathews, Agnes Lind, and Frances Swallow in the same shipment. *South Carolina Gazette and Country Journal,* June 10, 1766; *South Carolina Gazette and Country Journal,* June 17, 1766.

44. Jabez Carpenter Ledger, 1750–1754, and Journal, 1750–1753, NHS.

45. Charleston CCP, 1800 term, #499a, #525a, #526a; Charleston CCP, 1801 term, 646a.

46. For a thorough discussion of the succeeding prohibitions and practices, see Robert Olwell, *Masters, Slaves, and Subjects: The Culture of Power in the South Carolina Low Country, 1740–1790* (Ithaca, N.Y.: Cornell University Press, 1998), 166–80. See also Philip D. Morgan, *Slave Counterpoint: Black Culture in the Eighteenth-Century Chesapeake and Lowcountry* (Chapel Hill: University of North Carolina Press, 1998), 250–53.

47. *South Carolina Gazette,* September 24, 1772, quoted in Olwell, *Masters, Slaves, and Subjects,* 170.

48. Cynthia Kierner, *Southern Women in Revolution, 1776–1800: Personal and Political Narratives* (Columbia: University of South Carolina Press, 1998), 64–65. There is no clear pattern to these widows' households. In 1790, four of them appear in census records as heads of households, presiding over more than seven members, but the age, gender, and status of free or slave of individuals within the household varied considerably. See U.S. Census, *Heads of Families . . . South Carolina,* 39, 42.

49. Kierner, *Southern Women in Revolution,* 70–71.

50. Presentments of the Grand Jury for the District of Charleston at a Court of General Sessions on May 16, 1775, Journal of the South Carolina Court of General Sessions, 1769–1776. Microfilm copy, SCDAH.

51. *South Carolina and American General Gazette,* 1774.

52. *South Carolina Gazette,* May 31, 1770.

53. *South Carolina Gazette,* June 7, 1770. Alex Lichtenstein has noted that although the majority of slave theft was of food, and therefore operated within

what he describes as a "moral economy," "the bolder step of stealing in order to participate in market transactions rested on a stronger consciousness of counter-morality and an inherent right to economic autonomy, and thus represented a greater threat to the slave system." Lichtenstein, "'That Disposition to Theft, With Which they Have Been Branded': Moral Economy, Slave Management, and the Law," *Journal of Social History* 21, no. 3 (Spring 1988): 416.

54. (*Charleston*) *City Gazette and Commercial Daily Advertiser*, September 19, 1816; see also (*Charleston*) *City Gazette and Commercial Daily Advertiser*, May 1, 1816; (*Charleston*) *City Gazette and Commercial Daily Advertiser*, July 10, 1815; (*Charleston*) *City Gazette and Daily Advertiser*, July 11, 1809.

55. J. P. Brissot de Warville, *New Travels in the United States of America, 1788*, trans. Mara Soceanu Vamos and Durand Echeverria (Cambridge, Mass.: Harvard University Press, 1964), 128.

56. For a thorough discussion of the literature estimating female shopkeeper, see Patricia Cleary, "'She Merchants,'" 91–96. In her analysis of the difficulties of enumerating female shopkeepers in colonial cities she particularly cites the limitations of relying upon newspaper and other advertisements. By incorporating merchant records and tax assessments, she found much higher numbers of female retailers than were advertised prior to the Revolution in New York, Boston, and Philadelphia. Jacob Milligan, in *The Charleston Directory . . . 1790*, recorded 10 percent of shopkeepers in that year as female. For city directories as a genre, see Hunt, *The Middling Sort*, 131.

57. Jabez Carpenter Ledger, 1750–1754, and Journal, 1750–1753; Jabez Carpenter Ledger, 1755–72, 200, NHS. These kinds of payments in kind or in work continued in Newport after the Revolution and were not restricted to merchants or sellers of dry goods. James Taylor, a cabinetmaker who also sold groceries from the 1760s to the first decade of the nineteenth century, received payments from his female customers in the form of tailoring and clothing repair, as well as teaching his children and unspecified "work." Some he paid by the day, others by the piece. James Taylor, cabinet maker, Ledger Book, 1767–1802, #498, NHS.

58. Jan de Vries, "The Industrial Revolution and the Industrious Revolution," *Journal of Economic History* 54, no. 2 (June 1994): 249–70.

59. For a discussion of candle making in Newport and Providence, see Elaine Forman Cranc, *Ebb Tide in New England: Women, Seaports, and Social Change, 1630–1800* (Boston: Northeastern University Press, 1998), 105.

60. Stanley Cheyet, *Lopez of Newport: Colonial Merchant Prince* (Detroit: Wayne State University Press, 1970), chapters 4–11; Aaron Lopez, "Taylors and Spinners" book, 1769–1774, # 767, p. 9, NHS.

61. Lopez, "Taylors and Spinners," 13, 14, 16, 18, 31–34.

62. Kierner, *Southern Women in Revolution*, 70–71.

63. Milligan, *The Charleston Directory . . . 1790*; U.S. Census, *Heads of Families . . . South Carolina; South Carolina Gazette*, November 1, 1773. See Linda Kerber's discussion of the petition in *Women of the Republic: Intellect and Ideology in Revolutionary America* (Chapel Hill: University of North Carolina Press, 1980), 98–99. Cynthia Kierner notes that the petition was rejected in *Southern Women in Revolution*, 70.

64. *Newport Mercury*, July 16, 1785.

65. Laurel Thatcher Ulrich, *The Age of Homespun: Objects and Stories in the Creation of an American Myth* (New York: Alfred A. Knopf, 2001), chapter 8.

66. See Boydston, *Home and Work*, 128; Rockman, "Women's Labor, Gender Ideology, and Working-Class Households in Early Republic Baltimore," *Pennsylvania History* 66 (1999): 174–200; Smith, *The "Lower Sort*,*"* 111–12.

67. For a useful summary of the literature on artisan republicanism, see the introduction to Howard B. Rock, Paul A. Gilje, and Robert Asher, *American Artisans: Crafting Social Identity, 1750–1850* (Baltimore: Johns Hopkins University Press, 1995).

68. April 19, 1808, letter from Alice Izard in New York to her son Henry Izard in Charleston, box 2, folder 30, Ralph Izard Family Papers, SCL; October 16, 1808, Letter from Alice Izard at Clifton to Henry Izard at Charleston, box 2, folder 32, Ralph Izard Family Papers, SCL.

69. *Gazette of the State of South Carolina*, November 25, 1777. See also Philip Morgan, "Black Life in Eighteenth-Century Charleston," *Perspectives in American History*, n.s. 1 (1984): 214–15.

70. Ira Berlin, *Many Thousands Gone: The First Two Centuries of Slavery in North America* (Cambridge, Mass.: Harvard University Press, 1998), 157. See also Betty Wood, *Women's Work, Men's Work: The Informal Slave Economies of Lowcountry Georgia* (Athens: University of Georgia Press), chapter 4; and Olwell, *Masters, Slaves, and Subjects*, 154–55.

71. Among the works that discuss the role of family ties in urban business, see Hunt, *The Middling Sort*, and Peter Mathias, "Risk, Credit and Kinship in Early Modern Enterprise," in John J. McCusker and Kenneth Morgan, eds., *The Early Modern Atlantic Economy* (Cambridge: Cambridge University Press, 2000), 15–35.

72. Each son signed his attestation at various times to the copies she submitted for evidence. The earliest accounts were signed by Sarah, later Ebenezer, then Thomas, and finally Simon took over this task. For Sukey's contributions, see NPCCP, 1774 May term, #140. Out of the seventeen parties that Sarah engaged in court in 1744 and 1755 over her husband's debts and credits, eight went on to have individual court suits with her as the owner of the shop. Customers and suppliers clearly identified the shop as Sarah's, as Jonathan Boyd noted on his account of "Other small articals that I Deliverd to Mrs. Rumreal My Self at her Shoop," NPCCP, 1759 November term, #56.

73. For example, in 1767, one of the debts on Sarah's account with Naphtali and Isaac Hart was for a discount of £173.6.2 old tenor with Thomas Rumreil. NPCCP, 1770 May term, #469.

74. February 23, 1767, letter to "Dear Brother" Thomas Robinson, Robinson Family Papers, New England Women and Their Families in the 18th and 19th Centuries: Personal Papers, Letters, and Diaries, series b: selections from the Newport Historical Society (Bethesda, Md.: LexisNexis Academic & Library Solutions, 2000), reel 19, frame 223–24.

75. Susan Branson, "Women and the Family Economy in the Early Republic: The Case of Elizabeth Meredith," *Journal of the Early Republic* 16, no. 1 (Spring 1996): 53–54.

76. *Newport Mercury*, January 9, 1775.

77. *South Carolina Gazette*, March 16–23, 1765.

78. Wednesday, March 2, 1785, *Journals of the House of Representatives, 1785–1786*, ed. Lark Emerson Adams (Columbia: University of South Carolina Press, 1979), 179.

79. *South Carolina Gazette*, August 3–10, 1767.

80. The classic work on women's legal status in the colonial period is Marylynn Salmon, *Women and the Law of Property in Early America* (Chapel Hill: University of North Carolina Press, 1986). Many of the essays in Linda Kerber, *Toward an Intellectual History of Women* (Chapel Hill: University of North Carolina Press, 1997),

address the implications of coverture for free women in the revolutionary era and beyond.

81. Salmon, *Women and the Law of Property*, 44–53.

82. Mary Roberts Parramore, "'For Her Sole and Separate Use': Feme Sole Trader Status in Early South Carolina" (master's thesis, University of South Carolina, 1991), 39–40, 55–56. In Pennsylvania, the only other colony to provide for feme sole traders prior to the Revolution, the status was only granted when a husband failed to support his wife. See Salmon, *Women and the Law of Property*, 48–49. Cynthia Kierner found that the majority of women announcing their feme sole trader status in the *South Carolina Gazette* advertised that they were taking in boarders or otherwise running a public house. Cynthia Kierner, *Beyond the Household: Women's Place in the Early South, 1700–1835* (Ithaca, N.Y.: Cornell University Press, 1998), 24.

83. One was the "law of necessaries." See Margot Finn, "Women, Consumption, and Coverture in England, c. 1760–1860," *Historical Journal* 39, no. 3 (September 1996): 709. See also Craig Muldrew, "'A Mutual Assent of Her Mind'? Women, Debt Litigation, and Contract in Early Modern England," *History Workshop Journal* 55 (2003): 47–71.

84. Samuel Vinson Ledger Book, 1797–1813, #514, (pages unnumbered), NHS; South Carolina Secretary of State Bills of Sale, 1814, #04i 218; Ball Family Papers, box 1, folder 22, SCL. December 13, 1802, letter from Jane Ball to Isaac Ball, Ball Family Papers, SCL.

85. Laurel Thatcher Ulrich, "Martha Ballard and Her Girls: Women's Work in Eighteenth-Century Maine," in Stephen Innes, ed., *Work and Labor in Early America* (Chapel Hill: University of North Carolina Press, 1988), 85. Ulrich notes that neither men's nor women's activities were necessarily part of a "fully integrated family economy." See *A Midwife's Tale*, 80. Linda Sturtz explores the uses of "chicken and egg money" in *Within Her Power: Propertied Women in Colonial Virginia* (New York: Routledge, 2002), chapter 5.

86. April 11, 1803, letter from Jane Ball to Isaac Ball, Ball Family Papers, box 1, folder 23, SCL.

87. *Newport Mercury*, September 5, 1774.

88. Jeanne Boydston explains the changing understanding of "economy" from a word used to describe household activities conducted by men and women to a word describing extra-household activities solely the domain of men in *Home and Work*, chapter 1.

89. John R. Bartlett, *Census of the Inhabitants of Rhode Island and Providence Plantations 1774* (1858; repr. Baltimore: Genealogical Publishing Co., 1969), 31.

90. Many scholars have discussed this transition. Susan Branson presents a generational reading in Branson, "Women and the Family Economy."

91. Jeanne Boydston, Christine Daniels, and Richard Stott, among others, have all shown that the influence of industrialization on artisan practices varied considerably according to geography and craft. See Boydston, "The Woman Who Wasn't There"; Daniels, "'WANTED: A Blacksmith who Understands Plantation Work': Artisans in Maryland, 1700–1810," *William and Mary Quarterly*, 3rd ser., 50, no. 4 (October 1993): 743–67; Stott, "Artisans and Capitalist Development," *Journal of the Early Republic* 16, no. 2 (Summer 1996): 257–71.

92. Clare Lyons, *Sex Among the Rabble: An Intimate History of Gender and Power in the Age of Revolution, Philadelphia, 1730–1830* (Chapel Hill: University of North Carolina Press, 2006), 30–32.

Chapter 3: Family Credit and Shared Debts

1. *South Carolina and American General Gazette*, March 27–April 3, 1776.

2. Bruce Mann discusses a commercial "community of the marketplace" in eighteenth-century New England in which long-standing accounts rested on international supply chains and regular infusions of cash. See Mann, *Neighbors and Strangers: Law and Community in Early Connecticut* (Chapel Hill: University of North Carolina Press, 1987), 61.

3. Paula R. Backscheider, "Defoe's Lady Credit," *Huntington Library Quarterly* 44, no. 2 (Spring 1981): 94–95.

4. For an introduction to the literature on economic networks and the social "embeddedness" of market activity, see the introduction to the second edition of Mark Granovetter and Richard Swedberg, *The Sociology of Economic Life* (Cambridge, Mass.: Westview Press, 2001), 1–28.

5. Historians who have discussed the shifting uses and meanings of credit as they appear in court records include Mann in *Neighbors and Strangers*, Cornelia Hughes Dayton in *Women Before the Bar: Gender, Law, and Society in Connecticut, 1639–1789* (Chapel Hill: University of North Carolina Press, 1995), Deborah A. Rosen in *Courts and Commerce: Gender, Law, and the Market Economy in Colonial New York* (Columbus: Ohio State University Press, 1997), Margot Finn in *The Character of Credit: Personal Debt in English Culture, 1740–1914* (New York: Cambridge University Press, 2003), and Craig Muldrew in *The Economy of Obligation: The Culture of Credit and Social Relations in Early Modern England* (New York: St. Martin's Press, 1998). Muldrew in particular discusses the shift from "relationship" to "contract" and the implications for trust in the conclusion of *The Economy of Obligation*.

6. Dayton, *Women Before the Bar*, 72. Deborah Rosen presents a similar story of women's "peripheralization from the expanding market" in *Courts and Commerce*, 110.

7. Cornelia Hughes Dayton found that as many as 90 percent of civil cases were uncontested by mid-decade in New Haven County. Dayton, *Women Before the Bar*, 91. Bruce Mann found a similar decline in contested cases in Hartford County. See Mann, *Neighbors and Strangers*, 39–40, 172. The trend may have begun earlier in England. In late seventeenth-century King's Lynn, Craig Muldrew found that only 4 percent of cases resulted in judgment; he argues that this is evidence that the early stages of litigation were a "common part of the credit arrangement." See Muldrew, "Credit and the Courts: Debt Litigation in a Seventeenth-Century Urban Community," *Economic History Review* 46, no. 1 (1993): 27. For a discussion of the intersecting legal, political, and social factors that influence the proportion of contested debt cases, see Robert A. Kagan, "The Routinization of Debt Collection: An Essay on Social Change and Conflict in the Courts," *Law and Society Review* 18 (1984): 323–71.

8. Michael Woods, "The Culture of Credit in Colonial Charleston," *SCHM* 99, no. 4 (October 1998): 360.

9. For the economic activity of enslaved people, see Philip Morgan, *Slave Counterpoint Black Culture in the Eighteenth-Century Chesapeake and Lowcountry* (Chapel Hill: University of North Carolina Press, 1998), chapter 6; and Robert Olwell, *Masters, Slaves, and Subjects: The Culture of Power in the South Carolina Low Country, 1740–1790* (Ithaca, N.Y.: Cornell University Press, 1998), chapter 4.

10. Mann, *Neighbors and Strangers*, 22. The distinctions were not absolute. At times, women postponed book debt payment by signing a promissory note, and some bonds were guaranteed with mortgages of property. There are also a number of cases in Newport and Charleston in which the courts applied deductions

to judgments based on promissory notes. See the case of Sarah Bliss, NPCCP, 1810 May term, #4, and the case of Elizabeth Mitchell, Charleston CCP, 1810 0243.

11. NPCCP, 1772 May term, #302. All of the information in the paragraph is taken from this court file.

12. The following table reflects the number of women involved in court cases overall and the number and proportion of those women involved in book debt cases in the Newport Court of Common Pleas.

Year	Total # Women Named	Women in Book Debt Cases (% of total women named in court cases)
1750	105	39 (37%)
1760	48	21 (44%)
1770	147	54 (37%)
1780	45	6 (13%)
1790	93	35 (38%)
1800	61	3 (5%)
1810	40	5 (13%)
1820	63	11 (17%)

For a detailed discussion of these figures, see Ellen Hartigan-O'Connor, "The Measure of the Market: Women's Economic Lives in Charleston, SC, and Newport, RI, 1750–1820" (Ph.D. diss., University of Michigan, 2003), 148.

13. NPCCP, 1750 May term, #333; NPCCP, 1750 May term, #335.

14. The following table reflects the number of women involved in court cases overall and the number and proportion of those women involved in book debt cases in the Charleston Court of Common Pleas.

Year	Total # Women Named	Women in Book Debt Cases (% of total women named in court cases)
1755	38	11 (29%)
1760	44	16 (36%)
1770	30	6 (20%)
1775	29	5 (17%)
1780	3	0 (0)
1790	156	23 (15%)
1800	164	61 (37%)
1810	72	27 (38%)
1820	145	37 (26%)

For a detailed discussion of these figures, see Hartigan-O'Connor, "The Measure of the Market," 148.

15. The population appearing in court was also likely more urban. Prior to the Revolution, cases from the whole colony could be brought to the court in Charleston, and so while the city always had close ties to the surrounding farm and plantation population, the geographical scope of the courts narrowed.

16. NPCCP, 1760 November term, #40.

17. SCCCP, 1755, 40a 134a.

18. NPCCP, 1770 May term, #478 and # 479.

19. SCCCP, 1760, 49b 025a.

20. Rosen, *Courts and Commerce,* 40–41.

21. To arrive at these percentages, I counted all cases involving bonds in which a woman was the plaintiff, defendant, or interested third party (for example, if a woman's new husband was appearing in court on behalf of a bond she had signed while single). I also counted all cases involving women for each year examined, and used those two figures to determine the percentage of women's cases that involved bonds each year. Cases were drawn from the South Carolina Courts of Common Pleas, Summary Process Rolls and Petitions and Decrees in Summary Process, SCDAH.

22. Peter A. Coclanis, *The Shadow of a Dream: Economic Life and Death in the South Carolina Low Country, 1670–1920* (New York: Oxford University Press, 1989), 104. Russell R. Menard discusses the role of widows' mortgages (which were often joined with bonds) in funding the expansion of small and large South Carolina planters' operations in "Financing the Lowcountry Export Boom: Capital and Growth in Early South Carolina," *William and Mary Quarterly,* 3rd ser., 51, no. 4 (October 1994): 659–76.

23. For widows as a source of capital, see Dayton, *Women Before the Bar;* Lisa Wilson, *Life After Death: Widows in Pennsylvania, 1750–1850* (Philadelphia: Temple University Press, 1992); Rosen, *Courts and Commerce,* 46–47; William Chester Jordan, *Women and Credit in Pre-Industrial and Developing Societies* (Philadelphia: University of Pennsylvania Press, 1993); Julian Hoppit, *Risk and Failure in English Business, 1700–1800* (Cambridge: Cambridge University Press, 1987), 147–48, 153; Jacob M. Price, *Capital and Credit in British Overseas Trade: The View from the Chesapeake, 1700–1776* (Cambridge, Mass.: Harvard University Press, 1980), 47, 53; and Daniel Scott Smith, "Female Householding in Late Eighteenth-Century America and the Problem of Poverty," *Journal of Social History* 28, no. 1 (fall 1994): 98.

24. SCCCP, 1755, 39b 053a; 1762, 55b 005a; 1766, 65a 090a; 1769, 83a 160a; *South Carolina Gazette and Country Journal,* April 22, 1766. Paty Holmes also sold Carne three slaves in 1784.

25. Walter Edgar, *South Carolina: A History* (Columbia: University of South Carolina Press, 1998), 247.

26. Elizabeth Marie Pruden, "Family, Community, Economy: Women's Activity in South Carolina, 1670–1770" (Ph.D. diss., University of Minnesota, 1996), 259, 268–69.

27. I group notes and bills together, following the practice of Bruce Mann, who argues that "the similarities among them are far more important than the differences" for the purpose of contrasting the different forms of credit available to early Americans. Mann, *Neighbors and Strangers,* 29.

28. NPCCP, 1750 May term, Record Book C, p. 514.

29. Sarah Smith was named as defendant in the following cases involving promissory notes from Roger Smith: Charleston CCP 1800 490a; 1800 491a; 1800 492a; 1800 515a; 1800 542a; 1800 543a; 1800 546a; 1800 561a; 1800 566a.

30. Sarah Smith's personal debts included an account with Lauderdale and Dowthwaite for bulk purchases of sugar, molasses, butter, and spermaceti oil. Charleston CCP, 1800 544a. See also rental notice in the *(Charleston) City Gazette and Daily Advertiser,* March 22, 1800.

31. NPCCP, 1770 November term, #178.

32. Legal interest in South Carolina was 8 percent in 1750, 7 percent in 1777.

Peter Coclanis found that the length of time allowed for repayment of bonds and notes increased over the early decades of the eighteenth century in South Carolina; this trend seems to have continued in the second half of the century, though promissory notes usually had shorter terms than bonds. See Coclanis, *The Shadow of a Dream*, 105.

33. Margaret Rose Hunt, *The Middling Sort: Commerce, Gender, and the Family in England, 1680–1780* (Berkeley: University of California Press, 1996), 145–46.

34. [Pelatiah Webster], *An Essay on Credit, in which the Doctrine of Banks is Considered* (Philadelphia: Eleazer Oswald, 1786), 3–4.

35. January 3, 1808, letter from Alice Izard in New York to her son Henry Izard in Charleston, Ralph Izard Family Papers, box 2, folder 29, SCL.

36. For the importance of personal connections in commercial relationships, see David Hancock, *Citizens of the World: London Merchants and the Integration of the British Atlantic Community, 1735–1785* (New York: Cambridge University Press, 1995), 139–42; Thomas M. Doerflinger, *A Vigorous Spirit of Enterprise: Merchants and Economic Development in Revolutionary Philadelphia* (Chapel Hill: University of North Carolina Press, 1986); John J. McCusker and Russell R. Menard, *The Economy of British North America, 1607–1789* (Chapel Hill: University of North Carolina Press, 1991), 334–36; and two chapters in John J. McCusker and Kenneth Morgan's *The Early Modern Atlantic Economy* (Cambridge: Cambridge University Press, 2000): Peter Mathias, "Risk, Credit and Kinship in Early Modern Enterprise," 15–35; and Kenneth Morgan, "Business Networks in the British Export Trade to North America, 1750–1820," 36–62. For alliances among women, in particular, see Karin Wulf, *Not All Wives: Women of Colonial Philadelphia* (Ithaca, N.Y.: Cornell University Press, 2000), chapter 4; Susan Frye and Karen Robertson, eds., *Maids and Mistresses, Cousins and Queens: Women's Alliances in Early Modern England* (New York: Oxford University Press, 1999); and Leonore Davidoff and Catherine Hall, *Family Fortunes: Men and Women of the English Middle Class, 1780–1850* (Chicago: University of Chicago Press, 1787), chapter 6.

37. NPCCP, 1774 May term, Record Book I, p. 552; 1774 November term, #258; and Record Book I, p. 257.

38. Peter Mathias, "Risk, Credit and Kinship," in McCusker and Morgan, *The Early Modern Atlantic Economy*, 15–35. Naomi Lamoreaux discusses the resulting unwritten rules that governed contracts among members of an urban mercantile community in "Rethinking the Transition to Capitalism in the Early American Northeast," *Journal of American History* 90, no. 2 (September 2003): 437–61.

39. December [January] 21, 1806, letter from Joseph Manigault to Gabriel Manigault, Manigault Family Papers, box 3, folder 45, SCL.

40. NPCCP, 1754 November term, #495.

41. In the early 1760s, Mary sued her customer mariner John Scanlain twice—once for a book account and once for a £182.7.0 old tenor promissory note. NPCCP, 1761 May term, #105; 1762 November term, #296. Rum suppliers William Ellery and James Cahoon each sued Abigail once in the early 1750s for accounts that had grown with only partial cash payments in return. NPCCP, 1752 May term, #263; NPCCP, 1753 November term, #418.

42. Charleston CCP, 1807 0271a; 1807 0272a; 1814 0104a; 1814 0131a.

43. Charleston CCP, 1800 0555a; 1800 0556a.

44. Charleston County Inventories, Book G, pp. 251–53. Microfilm CH 8, SCDAH.

45. SCCCP, 1760, 051a 179a.

46. See David Knoke and James H. Kulkinski, "Network Analysis: Basic Con-

cepts," in Grahame Thompson et al., eds., *Markets, Hierarchies, and Networks: The Coordination of Social Life* (London: Sage, 1991), 177.

47. Amanda Vickery, "His and Hers: Gender, Consumption and Household Acounting in Eighteenth-Century England," *Past and Present*, supplement 1 (2006): 17.

48. Charleston CCP, 1799 0418a.

49. Margaretta Lovell, *Art in a Season of Revolution: Painters, Artisans, and Patrons in Early America* (Philadelphia: University of Pennsylvania Press, 2005), chapter 7.

50. See NPCCP and Newport Probate Records, vol. 2: 68–69 (1788), NCH.

51. Searing rented an unnamed female slave's work from Elizabeth Almy. In documents from her executor's lawsuit, Elizabeth Almy's purchases of linen, sugar, and tea were credited to Searing against John Almy's account, as were multiple cash loans made to Elizabeth and, largest of all, a payment to John Bours that Searing made on Elizabeth's behalf. NPCCP, 1770 November term, #7. For Searing's bread accounts, see NPCCP, 1768 November term, #293; NPCCP, 1774 May term, #31.

52. Petitions to the General Assembly, vol. 13, no. 127 (1769), RISA. Pinnegar was granted relief under the 1756 Act for the Relief of Insolvent Debtors.

53. Petitions to the General Assembly, vol. 13, no. 112 (1769), RISA; *Newport Mercury*, August 27, 1770.

54. Charleston CCP, 1810 0118a.

55. See Laurel Thatcher Ulrich, *A Midwife's Tale: The Life of Martha Ballard, Based on Her Diary, 1785–1812* (New York: Vintage Books, 1990), 86.

56. (*Charleston*) *City Gazette and Daily Advertiser*, May 16, 1800.

57. SCCCP, 1770, 087a 062a.

58. SCCCP, 1770, 089a 0274a. This was one of several of Hepzibah's old debts that James was brought to court with her to account for; his former wife Mary had also embroiled them in several suits, as did James on his own.

59. For the purposes of this discussion, administrators (appointed by the court) and executors (named in the will) will be treated as a single group.

60. Of the women involved in common pleas litigation in Charleston, the percentage who were appearing as administrators or executors was 68 percent in 1755, 55 percent in 1760, 33 percent in 1770, 48 percent in 1775, 33 percent in 1780, 53 percent in 1790, 49 percent in 1800, 33 percent in 1810, and 29 percent in 1820. Of the women involved in Common Pleas litigation in Newport, the percentage who were appearing as administrators or executors was 46 percent in 1750, 23 percent in 1760, 21 percent in 1770, 51 percent in 1780, 49 percent in 1790, 39 percent in 1800, 30 percent in 1810, and 27 percent in 1820. For a detailed discussion of these figures and the particulars of the cases, see Hartigan-O'Connor, "The Measure of the Market," 138–44.

61. NPCCP, 1750 May term, #219.

62. SCCCP, 1790, 165a 0739a.

63. SCCCP, 1770, 008a 0157a.

64. NPCCP, 1800 Special January term, #54; NPCCP, 1800 Special January term, #55.

65. Lisa Wilson argues that the appointment of co-executors was designed to lessen the burden on a bereaved spouse and was not an indication of mistrust in women's abilities. See Wilson, *Life After Death*, 48.

66. Marla Miller, *The Needle's Eye: Women and Work in the Age of Revolution* (Amherst: University of Massachusetts Press, 2006), 9–10. Miller notes that many of the joint account books she uncovered had been classified as detailing only the

work of men; she concludes that many "householder" account books actually record joint enterprises.

67. See Ellen Hartigan-O'Connor, "Abigail's Accounts: Economy and Affection in the Early Republic," *Journal of Women's History* 17 (Fall 2005): 35–58.

68. See Elaine Forman Crane, *Ebb Tide in New England: Women, Seaports, and Social Change, 1630–1800* (Boston: Northeastern University Press, 1998), 126–27.

69. NPCCP, 1770 November term, # 7.

70. Aaron Lopez, "Taylors and Spinners" book, 1769–1774 (# 767), NHS, pp. 6, 21, 35.

71. *Newport Mercury,* August 22, 1774. For "self-divorce," see Clare Lyons, *Sex Among the Rabble: An Intimate History of Gender and Power in the Age of Revolution, Philadelphia, 1730–1830* (Chapel Hill: University of North Carolina Press, 2006), chapter 1. Mary Beth Sievens's study of more than 1,500 "runaway wife" notices in early national New England revealed the economic tensions within the household that threatened traditional patriarchal authority. See "Female Consumerism and Household Authority in Earl National New England," *Early American Studies* 4 (Fall 2006): 353–71. Sarah Leavitt discusses runaway wife advertisements in Rhode Island in "'She Hath Left My Bed and Board': Runaway Wives in Rhode Island, 1790–1810," *Rhode Island History* 58, no. 3 (August 2000): 91–104.

72. Crane, *Ebb Tide in New England,* 127–29. See also Elaine F. Crane, "Skirting the Law: Women and the Legal System in Early Rhode Island," *Newport History* 67, part 4, no. 233 (Spring 1996): 173–84; and Serena Zabin, "Women's Trading Networks and Dangerous Economies in Eighteenth-Century New York City," *Early American Studies* 4 (Fall 2006): 298. The most detailed examination of the motivations for seeking feme sole trader status is Mary Roberts Parramore, "'For Her Sole and Separate Use': Feme Sole Trader Status in Early South Carolina" (master's thesis, University of South Carolina, 1991).

73. Lorri Glover, *All Our Relations: Blood Ties and Emotional Bonds Among the Early South Carolina Gentry* (Baltimore: Johns Hopkins University Press, 2000), chapter 4.

74. Michael Woods, "The Culture of Credit in Colonial Charleston," *South Carolina Historical Magazine* 99 (October 1998): 374–79.

75. Dayton, *Women Before the Bar,* 87, 92–93 (quotation p. 92); Carole Shammas, Marylynn Salmon, and Michel Dahlin, *Inheritance in America from Colonial Times to the Present* (New Brunswick, N.J.: Rutgers University Press, 1987), 58–61.

76. NPCCP, May term, 1750, #294; NPCCP Nov. term, 1750, #181; NPCCP November term, 1750, #201.

77. *Newport Mercury,* June 10, 1800.

78. Coclanis, *The Shadow of a Dream,* 104. For a discussion of transatlantic credit in colonial business, see Jacob M. Price, *Capital and Credit in British Overseas Trade: The View from the Chesapeake, 1700–1776* (Cambridge, Mass.: Harvard University Press, 1980). For a discussion of credit in one colonial city, see Wilbur C. Plummer, "Consumer Credit in Colonial Philadelphia," *Pennsylvania Magazine of History and Biography* 66, no. 4 (October 1942): 385–409. Patricia Cleary has identified the largest number of women shopkeepers and merchants—more than four hundred—in her study of late colonial New York, Boston, and Philadelphia. She discusses the citywide and international connections of several of these women in depth. See "'She Merchants' of Colonial America: Women and Commerce on the Eve of the Revolution" (Ph.D. diss., Northwestern University, 1989).

79. Jennifer J. Baker, *Securing the Commonwealth: Debt, Speculation, and Writing in the Making of America* (Baltimore: Johns Hopkins University Press, 2005), 138.

80. Bisset, quoted in Toby Ditz, "Shipwrecked; or, Masculinity Imperiled: Mercantile Representations of Failure and the Gendered Self in Eighteenth-Century Philadelphia," *Journal of American History* 81, no. 1 (June 1994): 67. Bruce H. Mann traces these shifting meanings of credit and their political consequences for the early republic in *Republic of Debtors: Bankruptcy in the Age of American Independence* (Cambridge, Mass.: Harvard University Press, 2002).

81. Ditz, "Shipwrecked," 51. For the relative importance of personal identity in market transactions, see Yoram Ben-Porath, "The F-Connection: Families, Friends, and Firms and the Organization of Exchange," *Population and Development Review* 6 (1980): 1–30.

82. Mary Beth Norton, *Founding Mothers and Fathers: Gendered Power and the Forming of American Society* (New York: Alfred A. Knopf, 1996), 231–32. For a discussion of how the changing meaning of "crédit" in seventeenth- and eighteenth-century France indicates a gradual shift from a personal to a material "frame of reference" for social and political relationships, see Jay M. Smith, "No More Language Games: Words, Beliefs, and the Political Culture of Early Modern France," *American Historical Review* (December 1997): 1413–40.

83. Laurel Thatcher Ulrich, *Goodwives: Image and Reality in the Lives of Women in Northern New England, 1650–1750* (1980; New York: Vintage Books, 1991), 34.

84. Muldrew, *The Economy of Obligation*, 315.

85. Gordon Wood cites Rhode Island's early bankruptcy protections as acknowledgment of a "modern" attitude toward debt in *The Radicalism of the American Revolution* (1991; New York: Vintage Books, 1993), 140–41.

86. Insolvent male petitioners in Rhode Island frequently cited the need to take on relatives' debts, as well as trading failures. Peter J. Coleman, *Debtors and Creditors in America: Insolvency, Imprisonment for Debt, and Bankruptcy, 1607–1900* (Madison: State Historical Society of Wisconsin, 1974), 97–98.

87. Finn, *The Character of Credit*, 3–4.

Chapter 4. Translating Money

1. The Newport Historical Society houses a range of tax lists from the late eighteenth and early nineteenth centuries. Two works that have analyzed these lists in some detail include Elaine Forman Crane, *A Dependent People: Newport, Rhode Island in the Revolutionary Era* (New York: Fordham University Press, 1985); and Lynne Withey, *Urban Growth in Colonial Rhode Island: Newport and Providence in the Eighteenth Century* (Albany: State University of New York Press, 1984). Withey's "Population Change, Economic Development, and the Revolution: Newport, Rhode Island, as a Case Study, 1760–1800" (Ph.D. diss., University of California at Berkeley, 1976) is exceptionally detailed and helpful in understanding the tax lists and the wealth and population patterns they reveal.

2. Alice Hanson Jones concluded that "women wealthholders held substantially lower amounts than men," but noted that the presence of women as wealthholders was "not inconsequential." See Jones, *Wealth of a Nation to Be: The American Colonies on the Eve of the Revolution* (New York: Columbia University Press, 1980), 198–99 and 214–16. The wealthiest women in Jones's sample were also from the Charleston area. There are no recent systematic treatments specifically of women in Charleston, but data from all early cities show relative female poverty.

3. Marylynn Salmon's *Women and the Law of Property in Early America* (Chapel

Hill: University of North Carolina Press, 1986) is the most comprehensive work on early American women's property rights. Lenore Davidoff and Catherine Hall discuss the issues of property holding and the female life cycle in England in *Family Fortunes: Men and Women of the English Middle Class* (Chicago: University of Chicago Press, 1987), chapter 6. Several of the articles in Renée Hirschon, ed., *Women and Property: Women as Property* (New York: St. Martin's Press, 1984), present helpful anthropological perspectives.

4. For two different assessments of the extensive literature on the economic and political issues surrounding the "transition to capitalism," see Michael Merrill, "Putting 'Capitalism' in Its Place: A Review of Recent Literature," *William and Mary Quarterly*, 3rd ser., 52, no. 2 (April 1995): 315–26; and Paul A. Gilje, "The Rise of Capitalism in the Early Republic," *Journal of the Early Republic* 16, no. 2 (Summer 1996): 159–81, and the essays included in the rest of the special issue. Edwin J. Perkins surveys the shift from public to private control of the economy in *American Public Finance and Financial Services, 1700–1815* (Columbus: Ohio State University Press, 1994).

5. Viviana A. Zelizer, *The Social Meaning of Money: Pin Money, Paychecks, Poor Relief, and Other Currencies* (Princeton, N.J.: Princeton University Press, 1997), 19.

6. Beverly Lemire, *The Business of Everyday Life: Gender, Practice, and Social Politics in England, c. 1600–1900* (New York: Manchester University Press, 2005), chapter 7.

7. Laurel Thatcher Ulrich, *A Midwife's Tale: The Life of Martha Ballard, Based on Her Diary, 1785–1812* (New York: Vintage Books, 1990), 88–90; Lemire, *The Business of Everyday Life*, 203.

8. My discussion draws from John J. McCusker, *Money and Exchange in Europe and America, 1600–1775: A Handbook* (Chapel Hill: University of North Carolina Press, 1978). For a Marxist perspective on the function of "cash" in the rural economy, see Michael Merrill, "Cash Is Good to Eat: Self-Sufficiency and Exchange in the Rural Economy of the United States," *Radical History Review* 4 (Winter 1977): 42–71.

9. The declaration, writ, and lists submitted into evidence vary in the details of the description of Rumreil's money, as well as the other goods taken. I have reproduced, in simplified form, the most complete of the lists. This list, written as evidence, included numbers for all of her lottery tickets. March 1762 term, Newport Superior Court, Record Book e, pp. 182–83 and evidence from case file.

10. SCCCP, Judgment Rolls, 041a 0189a, 1755.

11. South Carolina Inventories, vol. t, p. 598.

12. Jennifer J. Baker, *Securing the Commonwealth: Debt, Speculation, and Writing in the Making of America* (Baltimore: Johns Hopkins University Press, 2005), introduction. Edwin J. Perkins presents a useful narrative of early American money, concluding that paper money worked well in the colonial period in *American Public Finance and Financial Services*.

13. Petitions to the General Assembly, vol. 19, p. 63 (August 1782), RISA.

14. For colonial currencies and inflation, see McCusker, *Money and Exchange*, 135–37 and 220–21; Curtis P. Nettels, *The Emergence of a National Economy, 1775–1815* (New York: Harper & Row, 1962), chapter 2; and Anne Bezanson, *Prices and Inflation During the American Revolution: Pennsylvania, 1770–1790* (Philadelphia: University of Pennsylvania Press, 1951), discuss revolutionary-era inflation.

15. Petitions to the General Assembly, vol. 8, p. 56 (August 1752), RISA.

16. Petitions to the General Assembly, vol. 16, p. 73 (1776), RISA.

17. (*Charleston*) *City Gazette and Daily Advertiser*, January 12, 1791.

18. To aid him in this service, Robinson petitioned the General Assembly again for access to Barker's money. Petitions to the General Assembly, vol. 26, p. 85 (1792), RISA.

19. For an extensive and fascinating discussion of bank notes and the meanings of value in the nineteenth century, see Stephen Mihm, *A Nation of Counterfeiters: Capitalists, Con Men, and the Making of the United States* (Cambridge, Mass.: Harvard University Press, 2007).

20. Rhode Island followed the practice of Massachusetts by replacing the inflated paper currency known as "old tenor" with "lawful money" currency in 1763; £1 Lawful Money was equal to just over £23 Old Tenor, a rate that was reset six years later at £1 to more than £26. For exact details, with conversion rates expressed in new pence, see McCusker, *Money and Exchange*, 135–36.

21. The naming of specific currencies does not mean that people were using actual bills or coins printed in these denominations. Until later in the nineteenth century, "multiple media of exchange circulated, their local values expressed in terms of an abstract unit of account." Ronald Michener and Robert Wright, "State 'Currencies' and the Transition to the U.S. Dollar: Clarifying Some Conclusions," *American Economic Review* 95, no. 3 (June 2005): 685.

22. Patricia Cline Cohen, *A Calculating People: The Spread of Numeracy in Early America* (Chicago: University of Chicago Press, 1982), 126–29.

23. Example of five-shilling note located in the "paper money" file at SCHS, Gift of James Asimus, 1927. Eric Helleiner discusses the role of the images printed and embossed on currency in forging national identities in *The Making of National Money: Territorial Currencies in Historical Perspective* (Ithaca, N.Y.: Cornell University Press, 2003), 101–7.

24. *South Carolina Gazette*, June 29–July 6, 1765.

25. Comptroller General, Accounts Audited of Claims Growing out of the Revolution, file no. 5962, from claims growing out of the American Revolution, 0118 00325 00, SCDAH.

26. Gordon Wood, *The Radicalism of the American Revolution* (New York: Vintage Books, 1991), 141. See also Bruce Mann, *Neighbors and Strangers: Law and Community in Early Connecticut* (Chapel Hill: University of North Carolina Press, 1987), 33.

27. Robert Olwell, *Masters, Slaves, and Subjects: The Culture of Power in the South Carolina Low Country, 1740–1790* (Ithaca, N.Y.: Cornell University Press, 1998), 155–58.

28. Jabez Carpenter Ledger, 1755–72, p. 111, NHS.

29. Ibid., pp. 13, 136, 246, 258, 319, 351; 29, 142, 205, 270; 21, 103, 147.

30. See, for example, Account Book, Mrs. Ball to Ann Savage, John Ball, Sr., Papers, box 1, folder 9, Rare Book, Manuscript, and Special Collections Library, Duke University.

31. Ann Smart Martin, "Ribbons of Desire: Consumers in Early Virginia," in Amanda Vickery and John Styles, eds., *Gender, Taste and Material Culture in Britain and North America in the Long Eighteenth Century* (New Haven: Yale University Press, 2006) 179–200.

32. Paul Cross Papers, 1768–1803, SCL.

33. Henry Muckenfuss Daybook, 1810, SCL.

34. See, for example, Elizabeth Carpenter Record Book, 1741–1749, p. 111, NHS. This book records the transactions from Jabez Carpenter's business.

35. NPCCP, 1771, May term, #294.

36. Elaine Forman Crane, *Ebb Tide in New England: Women, Seaports, and Social Change, 1630–1800* (Boston: Northeastern University Press, 1998), 195.

37. June 5, 1802, letter from Jane Ball at Kensington to her son Isaac Ball in Charleston, Ball Family Papers, box 1, folder 22, SCL.

38. See discussion of this legal precedent and its overturning in 1846 in Cynthia Kennedy, *Braided Relations, Entwined Lives: The Women of Charleston's Urban Slave Society* (Bloomington: Indiana University Press, 2005), 152.

39. John Campbell writes about rural slaves that "possession of money itself encouraged slaves to leave the plantation surreptitiously at night to spend their earnings as they desired—and thereby assert their independence . . . money became synonymous with independence and control over their lives" in "As 'A Kind of Freeman'?: Slaves' Market-Related Activities in the South Carolina Up Country, 1800–1860," in Ira Berin and Philip D. Morgan, eds., *Cultivation and Culture: Labor and the Shaping of Slave Life in the Americas* (Charlottesville: University Press of Virginia, 1993), 248. Betty Wood makes similar observations about slaves in lowcountry Georgia in "'White Society' and the 'Informal' Slave Economies of Lowcountry Georgia, c. 1763–1830," *Slavery and Abolition* 11, no. 3 (December 1990): 313–17.

40. Charleston CCP, Judgment Rolls, 1820 0186a, 1820.

41. Petitions to the General Assembly, vol. 8, p. 99 (February 1753), RISA. For the financial difficulties of sailors' families, see Ruth Wallis Herndon, "The Domestic Cost of Seafaring: Town Leaders and Seamen's Families in Eighteenth-Century Rhode Island," in Margaret S. Creighton and Lisa Norling, eds., *Iron Men, Wooden Women: Gender and Seafaring in the Atlantic World, 1700–1920* (Baltimore: Johns Hopkins University Press, 1996), 55–69.

42. Cynthia Kierner, *Southern Women in Revolution, 1776–1800: Personal and Political Narratives* (Columbia: University of South Carolina Press, 1998), 203.

43. Margaret R. Hunt, *The Middling Sort: Commerce, Gender, and the Family in England, 1680–1780* (Berkeley: University of California Press, 1996), 89.

44. Carole Shammas, "Early American Women and Control over Capital," in Ronald Hoffman and Peter J. Albert, eds., *Women in the Age of the American Revolution* (Charlottesville: University Press of Virginia, 1989), 134–54.

45. Mary Roberts Parramore, "'For Her Sole and Separate Use': Feme Sole Trader Status in Early South Carolina" (master's thesis, University of South Carolina, 1991), 103.

46. Petitions to the General Assembly, vol. 28, p. 50 (June 1793), RISA.

47. Petitions to the General Assembly, vol. 39, p. 105 (June 1810), RISA.

48. Alice Hanson Jones's study of probate inventories in 1774 found that well-off widows had more wealth in financial assets than in real estate or livestock, although "not more often than they held slaves in the South." Jones, *Wealth of a Nation to Be*, 146.

49. South Carolina Inventories, vol. w, p. 411.

50. Petitions to the General Assembly, vol. 28, p. 145 (June 1794), and attached inventory (October 1794), RISA.

51. Walter Johnson, *Soul by Soul: Life Inside the Antebellum Slave Market* (Cambridge, Mass.: Harvard University Press, 1999), 25, 26.

52. South Carolina Secretary of State, Bills of Sale, 003x 00310 00, entered December 22, 1806; 004d 00272 00, entered July 16, 1811, SCDAH. Sarah Hawie was involved in several additional slave sales, including one more purchase from Susanna Cochran; see South Carolina Secretary of State, Bills of Sale, 003x 00311 00, entered December 22, 1806.

53. South Carolina Secretary of State, Bills of Sale, 004p 00243 00, entered July 30, 1818; 003x 00383 00, entered May 12, 1807; 004p 00330 00, entered November 5, 1818, SCDAH.

54. Melish, *Disowning Slavery*, 66–69, 101–2.

55. NPCCP, 1810 May term, #149.

56. 2 mo. 20, 1814, letter from Benjamin Hadwen to his sister [Ruth Williams], Williams Papers, New England Women and Their Families in the 18th and 19th Centuries: Personal Papers, Letters, and Diaries, series b: selections from the Newport Historical Society (Bethesda, Md.: LexisNexis Academic & Library Solutions, 2000), microfilm, reel 19 (hereafter Williams Papers). On female investors in the South Sea Bubble, see Ann M. Carlos and Larry Neal, "Women Investors in Early Capital Markets, 1720–1725," *Financial History Review* 11, no. 2 (2004): 197–224.

57. Cynthia A. Kierner, *Beyond the Household: Women's Place in the Early South, 1700–1835* (Ithaca, N.Y.: Cornell University Press, 1998), 191–92; Barbara L. Bellows, *Benevolence Among Slaveholders: Assisting the Poor in Charleston, 1670–1860* (Baton Rouge: Louisiana State University Press, 1993).

58. Sheryllynne Haggerty, *The British-Atlantic Trading Community, 1760–1810: Men, Women, and the Distribution of Goods* (Boston: Brill, 2006), 161.

59. 4 mo. 9, 1818, letter from Abigail Robinson to her sister, [Mary Robinson Morton], Robinson Family Papers, New England Women and Their Families in the 18th and 19th Centuries: Personal Papers, Letters, and Diaries, series b: selections from the Newport Historical Society (Bethesda, Md.: LexisNexis Academic & Library Solutions, 2000), microfilm, reel 15 (hereafter Robinson Papers).

60. African Union Society Minutes, 1790–1797, Union Congregational Church Records, NHS.

61. Mrs. [Ann] Taylor, *Practical Hints to Young Females, on the Duties of A Wife, Mother, and Mistress of a Family* (Boston: Wells and Lilly, 1816), 21–22, 23.

62. Mrs. [Hester] Chapone, *Letters on the Improvement of the Mind, Addressed to a Young Lady* (Hagers-Town, Md.: printed by William D. Bell for Gabriel Nourse, 1815), 2:159.

63. Cohen, *A Calculating People*, chapter 4.

64. Taylor, *Practical Hints*, 153. See also "A Gentleman in this City," *Advice to the Fair Sex; in a series of letters on Various Subjects: Chiefly Describing the Graceful Virtues* . . . (Philadelphia: Robert Corcoran, 1803), 90.

65. Mrs. [Ann] Taylor, *The Present of a Mistress to a Young Servant; Consisting of Friendly Advice and Real Histories* (Philadelphia: Mathew Carey; Boston: Wells and Lilly, 1816), 83.

66. Ibid., 68.

67. Ibid., 70.

68. June 3, 1751, Protestant Episcopal Church, St. Philips, Charleston, WPA records of Registers and Minutes, Minutes (Vestry), 1732–1755, [original p. 202, typescript 162], SCL.

69. August 20, 1751, Protestant Episcopal Church, St. Philips, Charleston, WPA records of Registers and Minutes, Minutes (Vestry), 1732–1755, [original p. 203, typescript 162], SCL. On "earmarking," see Zelizer, *The Social Meaning of Money*, chapter 4.

70. Simon Newman, *Embodied History: The Lives of the Poor in Early Philadelphia* (Philadelphia: University of Pennsylvania Press, 2003), chapter 1.

71. April 5, 1812, letter from M.I. Manigault to her mother Mrs. A. Izard, Manigault Family Papers, box 4, folder 72, SCL. In Manigault's opinion, the actions

of her sister-in-law, "one of the strictest economists that ever were . . . amount but to little" other than emotional benefits.

72. April 12, 1807, letter from Alice Izard to Henry Izard, Izard Family Papers, box 2, folder 26, SCL.

73. Cara Anzilotti, "Autonomy and the Female Planter in Colonial South Carolina," *Journal of Southern History* 63, no. 2 (May 1997): 246.

74. Judith Ridner, "'To Have a Sufficient Maintenance': Women and the Economics of Freedom in Frontier Pennsylvania, 1750–1800," in Larry Eldridge, ed., *Women and Freedom in Early America* (New York: New York University Press, 1997), 176.

75. Petitions to the General Assembly, vol. 17, p. 76 (August 20, 1779), RISA.

76. Kierner, *Southern Women in Revolution,* 232.

77. Linda K. Kerber, "The Paradox of Women's Citizenship in the Early Republic: The Case of Martin vs. Massachusetts, 1805," in Kerber *Toward an Intellectual History of Women: Essays* (Chapel Hill: University of North Carolina Press, 1997), 276; Crane, *A Dependent People,* 158. On female citizenship during the Revolution, see also Linda Kerber, *No Constitutional Right to Be Ladies: Women and the Obligations of Citizenship* (New York: Hill and Wang, 1998), chapter 1.

78. Mary Beth Norton, "Eighteenth-Century American Women in Peace and War: The Case of the Loyalists," *William and Mary Quarterly,* 3rd ser., 33, no. 3 (July 1976): 386–409.

79. William Ellery Account Book, 1780–1805, Ellery Family Papers, Mss 407, p. 19, RIHS.

80. December 8 [1784 or 1785] letter from Catherine Read to Elizabeth Ludlow, Read Family Papers, folder 1, SCL.

81. "Petition of Sundry Inhabitants of Charlestown," Journal of the Commons House of Assembly, February 5, 1747, 154–55, quoted in Robert Olwell, "'Loose, Idle, and Disorderly': Slave Women in the Eighteenth-Century Charleston Marketplace," in David Barry Gaspar and Darlene Clark Hine, eds., *More than Chattel: Black Women and Slavery in the Americas* (Bloomington: Indiana University Press, 1996), 101.

82. December 1, 1806, entry, Town Council Minute Book, 1803–1807, # 2041, NHS.

83. Taylor, *Practical Hints,* 170, 174. Nathan O. Hatch notes that a different kind of "economy"—one characterized by market competition among denominations for believers—became the prevailing culture of American Protestantism. Hatch, *The Democratization of American Christianity* (New Haven: Yale University Press, 1989), chapter 5.

84. T. H. Breen, "Narrative of Commercial Life: Consumption, Ideology, and Community in the Eve of the American Revolution," *William and Mary Quarterly,* 3rd ser., 50, no. 3 (July 1993): 472. Phyllis Whitman Hunter traces an emerging eighteenth-century commercial culture "narrative" in Boston in *Purchasing Identity in the Atlantic World: Massachusetts Merchants, 1670–1780* (Ithaca, N.Y.: Cornell University Press, 2001).

85. 9 mo. 13, 1787, letter from Mary Robinson to [Elizabeth Foulke, in Philadelphia], Robinson Papers, reel 17.

86. October 5, 1808, letter from [Ann Simons] to Mary [Singleton], Singleton Family Papers, #668, Southern Historical Collection, University of North Carolina Library.

87. 1 mo. 16, 1818, letter from Abigail Robinson to [Mary Robinson Morton], Robinson Papers, reel 15. Barbara Clark Smith argues that this familiarity with prices gave free women a prominent economic and political role in Revolution-

ary protest movements in "Food Rioters and the American Revolution," *William and Mary Quarterly*, 3rd ser., 51, no. 1 (January 1994).

88. 3 mo. 23, 1813, letter from [E Earl] to Obadiah and Ruth Williams, Williams Papers, reel 19, #124.

89. March 20, 1806, letter from Joseph Manigault to Gabriel Manigault, Manigault Family Papers, box 3, folder 46, SCL.

90. April 22, 1812, letter from J. Vaughan to Mrs. M. I. Manigault, Manigault Family Papers, box 4, folder 72, SCL.

91. November 23, 1776, letter from Ly[dia] Simons to her Brother John Ball at Kensington, Ball Family Papers, 11/516/3a, SCHS.

92. S. Max Edelson, "The Characters of Commodities: The Reputations of South Carolina Rice and Indigo in the Atlantic World," in Peter Coclanis, ed., *The Atlantic Economy During the Seventeenth and Eighteenth Centuries: Organization, Operation, Practice, and Personnel* (Columbia: University of South Carolina Press, 2005), 344–48.

93. See comments of Sarah Josepha Hale, quoted in Nancy Cott, *The Bonds of Womanhood: "Woman's Sphere" in New England, 1780–1835* (New Haven: Yale University Press, 1977), 68.

94. Bellows, *Benevolence Among Slaveholders*, 38.

95. Jeanne Boydston, "The Woman Who Wasn't There: Women's Market Labor and the Transition to Capitalism in the United States," *Journal of the Early Republic* 16, no. 2 (Summer 1996): 199. An extensive literature explores the concept of separate male and female "spheres" of life in the late eighteenth and nineteenth centuries. See Linda Kerber's discussion of this historiography in "Separate Spheres, Female Worlds, Woman's Place: The Rhetoric of Women's History," *Journal of American History* 75, no. 1 (June 1988): 9–39.

96. For southern versions of "domesticity," see Kierner, *Beyond the Household*, chapter 5.

Chapter 5. Shopping Networks and Consumption as Collaboration

1. Elise Pinckney, ed., "Letters of Eliza Lucas Pinckney, 1768–1782," *SCHM* 76, no. 3 (July 1975): 151.

2. T. H. Breen, *The Marketplace of Revolution: How Consumer Politics Shaped American Independence* (New York: Oxford University Press, 2004), 151. See Richard L. Bushman, "Shopping and Advertising in Colonial America," in Cary Carson, Ronald Hoffman, and Peter J. Albert, eds., *Of Consuming Interests: The Style of Life in the Eighteenth Century* (Charlottesville: University Press of Virginia, 1994), 233–51; and T. H. Breen, "An Empire of Goods: The Anglicization of Colonial America, 1690–1776," *Journal of British Studies* 25 (October 1986): 467–99. The historical work on eighteenth- and nineteenth-century shopping in Britain, which does not emphasize independence, is extensive and useful. See, for example, Helen Berry, "Polite Consumption: Shopping in Eighteenth-Century England," *Transactions of the Royal Historical Society* 12 (2002): 375–94; Elizabeth Kowaleski-Wallace, *Consuming Subjects: Women, Shopping, and Business in the Eighteenth Century* (New York: Columbia University Press, 1997); Alison Adburgham, *Shops and Shopping, 1800–1914: Where, and in What Manner the Well-Dressed Englishwoman Bought Her Clothes* (London: George Allen and Unwin Ltd., 1964); Dorothy Davis, *A History of Shopping* (London: Routledge & Kegan Paul, 1966); Tammy Whitlock, *Crime, Gender, and Consumer Culture in Nineteenth-Century England* (Aldershot: Ashgate,

2005). Beyond those works specifically devoted to shopping, the growing literature on consumption is central to an understanding of female consumption patterns, beginning with the classic works: Neil McKendrick, John Brewer, and J. H. Plumb, *The Birth of a Consumer Society: The Commercialization of Eighteenth-Century England* (Bloomington: Indiana University Press, 1982); John Brewer and Roy Porter, eds., *Consumption and the World of Goods* (London: Routledge, 1993); Carson et al., *Of Consuming Interests*; Carole Shammas, *The Pre-Industrial Consumer in England and America* (Oxford: Clarendon, 1990); Lorna Weatherill, *Consumer Behavior and Material Culture in Britain, 1660–1760* (London: Routledge, 1988). Newer work on Britain and America includes Maxine Berg, *Luxury and Pleasure in Eighteenth-Century Britain* (New York: Oxford University Press, 2005); Paul G. E. Clemens, "The Consumer Culture of the Middle Atlantic, 1760–1820," *William and Mary Quarterly*, 3rd ser., 62, no. 4 (October 2005): 577–624.

3. *Newport Mercury*, July 2, 1785. T. H. Breen discusses the attacks on "the Jezebels of the consumer revolution" in chapter 5 of *The Marketplace of Revolution*, and concludes that shopping was a source of "a growing sense of empowerment" for American women; see p. 182.

4. Elizabeth A. Perkins, "The Consumer Frontier: Household Consumption in Early Kentucky," *Journal of American History* 78, no. 2 (September 1991): 495–96. See also Allan Kulikoff, *Tobacco and Slaves: The Development of Southern Cultures in the Chesapeake, 1680–1800* (Chapel Hill: University of North Carolina Press, 1986), 225–26.

5. Kowaleski-Wallace, *Consuming Subjects*, 91–92.

6. Weatherill, *Consumer Behavior*, chapter 6; Amanda Vickery, *The Gentleman's Daughter: Women's Lives in Georgian England* (New Haven: Yale University Press, 1998), 168.

7. For some recent examples of scholarship on intermediaries, see Sheryllynne Haggerty, *The British-Atlantic Trading Community, 1760–1810: Men, Women, and the Distribution of Goods* (London: Brill, 2006); and Wendy Woloson, "In Hock: Pawning in Early America," *Journal of the Early Republic* 27, no. 1 (Spring 2007): 35–81.

8. Three essays in John Styles and Amanda Vickery, eds., *Gender, Taste, and Material Culture in Britain and North America, 1700–1830* (New Haven: Yale University Press, 2006), discuss proxy shopping in different contexts: Ellen Hartigan-O'Connor, "Collaborative Consumption and the Politics of Choice in Early American Port Cities," 125–50; Ann Smart Martin, "Ribbons of Desire: Gendered Stories in the World of Goods," 179–200; and Claire Walsh, "Shops, Shopping, and the Art of Decision Making," 151–87.

9. Textile metaphors have captured many aspects of trading relationships. Laurel Ulrich used the metaphor of "checkered cloth" to describe life on the Maine frontier of the early republic in order to capture the places of intersection and those of "harmonious separation" between men's and women's lives. Ulrich, *A Midwife's Tale: The Life of Martha Ballard, Based on Her Diary, 1785–1812* (New York: Vintage Books, 1990), 84. T. H. Breen recounts Benjamin Franklin describing the British empire being held together with "thread" in Breen, *Marketplace of Revolution*, 196.

10. Yoram Ben-Porath argues that identity is important in "transactions in which, because of imperfect information, there is uncertainty about the quality of the object or the terms of the transaction." See "The F-Connection: Families, Friends, and Firms and the Organization of Exchange," *Population and Development Review* 6 (1980): 7.

11. See Naomi Lamoreaux, *Insider Lending: Banks, Personal Connections, and Eco-*

nomic Development in Industrial New England (Cambridge: Cambridge University Press, 1996).

12. Jabez Carpenter Ledger, 1755–72, p. 111, NHS.

13. 10 mo. 22, 1794, letter from Mary Robinson Morton to Sarah Robinson, Robinson Papers, New England Women and Their Families in the 18th and 19th Centuries: Personal Papers, Letters, and Diaries, series b: selections from the Newport Historical Society (Bethesda, Md.: LexisNexis Academic & Library Solutions, 2000), microfilm, reel 14 (hereafter Robinson Papers).

14. Royal Tyler, *The Contrast: A Comedy in Five Acts* (Philadelphia: Thomas Wignell), 8.

15. For the seventeenth century, see Darett Rutman and Anita Rutman, *A Place in Time: Middlesex County, Virginia, 1650–1750* (New York: W. W. Norton, 1984); and Lorena S. Walsh, "Community Networks in the Early Chesapeake," in Lois Green Carr, Philip Morgan, and Jean B. Russo, *Colonial Chesapeake Society* (Chapel Hill: University of North Carolina Press, 1988), 200–241.

16. 11 mo. 17, 1809, letter from Mary Robinson Morton to Abigail Robinson, Robinson Papers, reel 14.

17. December 20, 1770, letter to Messrs. Greenwood & Higginson, Leger & Greenwood Letterbook, 1770–1775, 1788, p. 2, William L. Clements Library, Ann Arbor, Michigan.

18. August 26, 1802, letter from M. Hering to M. Middleton, Hering Family Papers, 24/63/2, SCHS.

19. July 26, 1801, letter from Margaret Manigault in New York to Mrs. Izard in Charleston, Manigault Family Papers, Box 2, folder 31, SCL.

20. 3 mo. 12, 1799, letter from Abigail Robinson to Mary Robinson Morton, Robinson Papers, reel 2.

21. Toby L. Ditz, "Formative Ventures: Eighteenth-Century Commercial Letters and the Articulation of Experience," 59–78, and Ylva Hasselberg, "Letters, Social Networks, and the Embedded Economy in Sweden: Some Remarks on the Swedish Bourgeoisie, 1800–1850," 95–107, in Rebecca Earle, ed., *Epistolary Selves: Letters and Letter-writers, 1600–1945* (Brookfield, Vt.: Ashgate, 1999).

22. 11 mo. 18, 1801, letter from Abigail Robinson to her sister [Mary Robinson Morton], Robinson Papers, reel 15.

23. Consumer networks by definition had overlapping business and personal purposes. Morton's friends searching for cotton-wick candles contacted her not only because she had a helpful sister in Newport but also because her father had a candle-making business. Her subsequent note that "many others of our acquaintance here & in New York" wanted these particular candles was a communication to her sister about consumer desires and a commercial tip for her father. 12 mo. 10, 1795, letter from Mary Robinson Morton to Thomas and Sarah Robinson, Robinson Papers, reel 1. For a detailed discussion of commercial networks and their role in spreading information and reducing costs, see Haggerty, *The British-Atlantic Trading Community*, chapter 4.

24. David Hancock, "'A Revolution in the Trade: Wine Distribution and the Development of the Infrastructure of the Atlantic Market Economy, 1703–1807," in John J. McCusker and Kenneth Morgan, eds., *The Early Modern Atlantic Economy* (New York: Cambridge University Press, 2000), 144. Kenneth Morgan found the same kinds of comments about cloth in the letters of dry goods retailers. See his article in the same collection, "Business Networks in the British Export Trade to North America, 1750–1800," 36–62.

25. Bruce Mann, *Republic of Debtors: Bankruptcy in the Age of American Independence* (New York: Cambridge University Press, 2002), chapter 4.

26. March 28, 1805, letter from Alice Izard to Margaret Manigault, Manigault Family Papers, box 3, folder 43, SCL.

27. Jabez Carpenter Ledger, 1775–1772, p. 72, NHS.

28. Jabez Carpenter Ledger, 1755–1772, pp. 268, 155, NHS.

29. John Styles, "Custom or Consumption? Plebeian Fashion in Eighteenth-Century England," in Maxine Berg and Elizabeth Eger, eds., *Luxury in the Eighteenth Century: Debates, Desires and Delectable Goods* (London: Palgrave, 2003), 103–15. NPCCP, 1768 November term, #281; NPCCP, 1763 November term, #193.

30. Margot Finn, "Women, Consumption, and Coverture in England, c. 1760–1860," *Historical Journal* 39, no. 3 (September 1996): 709. See also Craig Muldrew, "'A Mutual Assent of her Mind'? Women, Debt Litigation, and Contract in Early Modern England," *History Workshop Journal*, no. 55 (2003): 47–71.

31. Mary Beth Sievens highlights the "overconsumption" charges in "runaway wife" advertisements. See "Female Consumerism and Household Authority in Earl National New England," *Early American Studies* 4 (Fall 2006): 353–71.

32. NPCCP, 1768 November term, #281.

33. NPCCP, 1763 November term, #193.

34. April 25, 1809, letter from Ann Simons to Mary Singleton, Singleton Family Papers, #668, box 1, folder 4, Southern Historical Collection, Wilson Library, University of North Carolina.

35. Ibid.

36. January 21, 1797, letter from Mary Pinckney to Mrs. Manigault, Manigault Family Papers, box 1, folder 17, SCL.

37. Fellow Charlestonian "Mr. Middleton, who is a great purchaser" had discovered the secret bargains of night auctions, and done better. February 13, 1797, letter from M. Pinckney to Mrs. G. Manigault, Manigault Family Papers, box 1, folder 22, SCL.

38. Ibid.

39. December 17, 1810, letter from J. E. Poyas to Eliza Catherine Ball, Ball Family Papers, box 2, folder 30, SCL.

40. 2 mo. 8, 1815, letter from Ann Robinson to Mary Robinson Morton, Robinson Papers, reel 15.

41. Jeanne Boydston, *Home and Work: Housework, Wages, and the Ideology of Labor in the Early Republic* (New York: Oxford University Press, 1990), 20, 28–29 and chapter 1, passim. In cities, women's housework was often translated into cash values; see my earlier discussion of the Atlantic service economy in Chapter 2.

42. September 16, [1790?], letter from C. R. to Mrs. Charles Ludlow, Read Family Papers, box 1, folder 2, SCL.

43. December 20, 1798, letter from John Ball, Sr. to John Ball, Jr., Ball Family Papers, 11/516/11, SCHS; March 19, 1779, letter from John Ball Sr. to his son John Ball Jr., Ball Family Papers, 11/516/11a, SCHS. Ball wanted his son to display sufficient "liberality" to maintain his elite status; see Rhys Isaac, *The Transformation of Virginia, 1740–1790* (New York: W. W. Norton, 1988), 90, 108, 131–33.

44. For discussions of Newport poor relief, see Lynne Withey, *Urban Growth in Colonial Rhode Island: Newport and Providence in the Eighteenth Century* (Albany: State University of New York Press, 1984), 56–71; Elaine Forman Crane, *A Dependent People: Newport, Rhode Island in the Revolutionary Era* (New York: Fordham

University Press, 1992), 63–68; Carl Bridenbaugh, *Cities in Revolt: Urban Life in America, 1743–1776* (New York: Oxford University Press, 1955), 124–26, 323–24; for Charleston, see Bridenbaugh, *Cities in Revolt,* 123–26, 322–23; Stephen Edward Wiberly, Jr., "Four Cities: Public Poor Relief in Urban America" (Ph.D. diss., Yale University, 1975); Barbara Ulmer, "Benevolence in Colonial Charleston," *Proceedings of the South Carolina Historical Association, 1980* (Aiken: University of South Carolina, 1980): 1–12; Walter Fraser, Jr., "Controlling the Poor in Colonial Charles Town," *Proceedings of the South Carolina Historical Association, 1980,* 13–30; Barbara L. Bellows, *Benevolence Among Slaveholders: Assisting the Poor in Charleston, 1670–1860* (Baton Rouge: Louisiana State University Press, 1993). For an extensive discussion of poor relief in New England, see Ruth Wallis Herndon, *Unwelcome Americans: Living on the Margin in Early New England* (Philadelphia: University of Pennsylvania Press, 2001).

45. February 4, 1788, Town Council Notes, 1784–1794, # 2013, NHS. Jeanne Boydston pointed out that shopping information could help working-class women in the nineteenth century save money in her classic article "To Earn Her Daily Bread: Housework and Antebellum Working-Class Subsistence," *Radical History Review* 35 (May 1986): 7–25.

46. Wiberly, "Four Cities," 157–58.

47. Jabez Carpenter Ledger, 1755–72, pp. 29, 142, 205, 270. For additional extended examples, see Aaron Lopez, "Taylors and Spinners" book, 1769–1774 (# 767), NHS.

48. Account Book, Mrs. Ball to Ann Savage, John Ball Sr., Papers, box 1, folder 9, Rare Book, Manuscript, and Special Collections Library, Duke University.

49. Edward Ball, *Slaves in the Family* (New York: Ballantine Books, 1999), 295–96. The Ball family relationships soured over financial battles waged for Caroline's husband's estate.

50. Laurel Thatcher Ulrich has written extensively about "changing works." See *A Midwife's Tale,* chapter 2, and *The Age of Homespun: Objects and Stories in the Creation of an American Myth* (New York: Alfred A. Knopf, 2001), 218–21, and chapter 8, passim.

51. Christine Stansell, *City of Women: Sex and Class in New York, 1789–1860* (1982; Urbana: University of Illinois Press, 1987), 55–62.

52. October 8, 1812, letter from A. I. Deas to Margaret Manigault, Manigault Family Papers, box 4, folder 75, SCL.

53. James Murray, quoted in Patricia Cleary, *Elizabeth Murray: A Woman's Pursuit of Independence in Eighteenth-Century America* (Amherst: University of Massachusetts Press, 2000), 93. For women in other cities who found similar pleasure and entertainment in leisurely shopping and visiting, see Elizabeth Drinker's comments in her October 20, 1759, and January 26, 1760, entries in Elaine Forman Crane, ed., *The Diary of Elizabeth Drinker* (Boston: Northeastern University Press, 1991), 1:36, 45. Esther Edwards Burr described shopping for butter, apples, and other food items in the course of afternoons of visiting but not afternoons of shopping. She obtained clothing, furniture, and manufactured goods on trips to New York City or through the efforts of her friend in Boston. See Carol Karlsen and Laurie Crumpacker, eds., *The Journal of Esther Edwards Burr, 1754–1757* (New Haven: Yale University Press, 1984), 25–26, 155, 170, 196–97.

54. November 17, [1812], letter from C[atherine] R[ead] to Mrs. Charles Ludlow, Read Family Papers, folder 5, SCL.

55. The family generated four accounts, one for each woman and an account

that executors (including Catherine) charged to the deceased Benjamin Simons's account. Charleston CCP, Judgment Rolls, 1800 0556a, 1800; Charleston CCP, Judgment Rolls, 1800 0555a, 1800.

56. 4 mo. 3, 1806, letter from MR [Mary Rotch] to Ruth Hadwin, Williams Family Papers, New England Women and Their Families in the 18th and 19th Centuries: Personal Papers, Letters, and Diaries, series b: selections from the Newport Historical Society (Bethesda, Md.: LexisNexis Academic & Library Solutions, 2000), microfilm, reel 19, item #44.

57. 2 mo. 8, 1820, letter from Mary Robinson Morton to Abigail Robinson, Robinson Papers, reel 14; 11 mo. 17, 1809 letter from Mary Robinson Morton to Abigail Robinson, Robinson Papers, reel 14.

58. October 3, 1787, letter from Ann Kinloch to Cleland Kinloch, Cheves-Middleton Papers, 12/160/3, SCHS.

59. Mrs. [Hester] Chapone, *Letters on the Improvement of the Mind, Addressed to a Young Lady* (Hagers-Town, Md.: William D. Bell for Gabriel Nourse, 1815), 2: 160–61. Her collected works were available for sale in Newport; see *Newport Mercury*, November 3, 1810. Charlestonian Eliza Pinckney also owned an edition of the *Letters*.

60. William Kenrick, *The Whole Duty of Woman: or, an unfallible Guide to the Fair Sex* (London, 1737), 644. This advice book had many printings in America in the late eighteenth and early nineteenth centuries.

61. February 18, 1805, letter from Alice Izard to Mrs. Manigault, Manigault Family Papers, box 2, folder 42, SCL.

62. Philip Morgan emphasizes the "active and reciprocal" economic transactions embodied in slaves' errand running and message taking, which allowed them personal discretion and a form of power relative to whites. Morgan, *Slave Counterpoint: Black Culture in the Eighteenth-Century Chesapeake and Lowcountry* (Chapel Hill: University of North Carolina Press, 1998), 318–26.

63. NPCCP, 1763 November term, #193.

64. August 19, 1803, letter from Jane Ball to Isaac Ball, Ball Family Papers, box 1, folder 24, SCL. *The Royal Gazette*, March 24–28, 1781.

65. Joan Cashin, *A Family Venture: Men and Women on the Southern Frontier* (New York: Oxford University Press, 1991), 89.

66. Barbara Clark Smith, "Food Rioters and the American Revolution," *William and Mary Quarterly*, 3rd ser., 51, no. 1 (January 1994): 28. Historians have debated the role of food markets and their relationship to the growth of capitalism in eighteenth century Britain and America; some discuss women's roles in these economic transformations. See, for example, E. P. Thompson, *Customs in Common: Studies in Traditional Popular Culture* (New York: The New Press, 1993); Allan Kulikoff, *The Agrarian Origins of American Capitalism* (Charlottesville: University of Virginia Press, 1992); John Bohstedt, "The Myth of the Feminine Food Riot: Women as Proto-Citizens in English Community Politics, 1790–1810," in Harriet Applewhite and Darline Levy, eds., *Women and Politics in the Age of the Democratic Revolution* (Ann Arbor: University of Michigan Press, 1990), 21–59; Gary Nash, *The Urban Crucible: Social Change, Political Consciousness, and the Origins of the American Revolution* (Cambridge, Mass.: Harvard University Press, 1979). For the transition of marketplace to market process, see Jean-Christophe Agnew, *Worlds Apart: The Market and the Theater in Anglo-American Thought, 1550–1750* (Cambridge: Cambridge University Press, 1986).

67. For customary and laissez-faire market practices in England, see Thompson, *Customs in Common*, chapters 4 and 5. Daniel Vickers argues that in colonial New

England there were far fewer regulations on labor and commodity markets than in England. Regulators believed that "the problem lay not in the principle of the labor market as a whole, but in the occasional machinations of sinful individuals." Vickers, *Farmers and Fishermen: Two Centuries of Work in Essex County, Massachusetts, 1630–1850* (Chapel Hill: University of North Carolina Press, 1994), 27–28.

68. *South Carolina Gazette*, September 24, 1772.

69. Robert Olwell, *Masters, Slaves, and Subjects: The Culture of Power in the South Carolina Low Country, 1740–1790* (Ithaca, N.Y.: Cornell University Press, 1998), 173.

70. *South Carolina Gazette*, September 24, 1772.

71. (*Charleston*) *City Gazette and Daily Advertiser*, July 11, 1809. For slaves' trading networks, see Ira Berlin, *Many Thousands Gone: The First Two Centuries of Slavery in North America* (Cambridge, Mass.: Harvard University Press, 1998), 312; Philip Morgan, "Black Life in Eighteenth-Century Charleston," *Perspectives in American History*, n.s. 1 (1984): 194–95.

72. Quoted in Bridenbaugh, *Cities in Revolt*, 280. For markets as "subsidiary institutions," see Sydney James, *The Colonial Metamorphoses in Rhode Island: A Study of Institutions in Change* (Hanover, N.H.: University Press of New England, 2000), 198–99. Officials in several cities were also willing to abate or wave poor women's tax payments. See Elaine Forman Crane, *Ebb Tide in New England: Women, Seaports, and Social Change, 1630–1800* (Boston: Northeastern University Press, 1998), 119; and Karin Wulf, *Not All Wives: Women of Colonial Philadelphia* (Ithaca, N.Y.: Cornell University Press, 2000), 202–4.

73. Middleton Account Book for Newport, R.I. 1795–1796 (12/177/1), Middleton Family Papers, SCHS.

74. Kowaleski-Wallace, *Consuming Subjects*, 81–82.

75. Ibid., 87. This is a reversal of portrayals of shopping in France from the seventeenth through the late nineteenth centuries, in which the shopper is typically a man, coming to flirt and potentially sample the "wares" of the female shopkeeper. See Jennifer Jones, "*Coquettes* and *Grizettes*: Women Buying and Selling in Ancien Régime Paris" in Victoria de Grazia and Ellen Furlough, eds., *The Sex of Things: Gender and Consumption in Historical Perspective* (Berkeley: University of California Press, 1996), 31–32.

76. Quoted in Kowaleski-Wallace, *Consuming Subjects*, 88.

77. Carole Shammas found that female customers of dry goods merchants in Philadelphia prior to the Revolution constituted less than 5 percent of the business. Her findings correspond with those of Elaine Forman Crane, who found women's names scarce among New England account books that she surveyed. Carole Shammas, "The Female Social Structure of Philadelphia in 1775," *Pennsylvania Magazine of History and Biography* 107, no. 1 (January 1983): 75–76; Crane, *Ebb Tide*, 131–32. Both agree that the numbers had declined from earlier in the century, when 15 percent of a typical merchant's customers were women.

78. Patricia Cleary, "'Who Shall Say We Have Not Equal Abilitys with the Men when Girls of 18 Years of Age Discover Such Great Capacitys?': Women of Commerce in Boston, 1750–1776," in Conrad Edick Wright and Katheryn P. Viens, eds., *Entrepreneurs: The Boston Business Community, 1700–1850* (Boston: Massachusetts Historical Society, 1997), 49–50; Shammas, *The Pre-Industrial Consumer*, 278, 283–85; Thomas M. Doerflinger, *A Vigorous Spirit of Enterprise: Merchants and Economic Development in Revolutionary Philadelphia* (Chapel Hill: University of North Carolina Press, 1986), chapter 2. Well-to-do women who placed custom commissions and female family members were also typical customers of merchants.

79. (Charleston) *City Gazette*, May 30, 1791.

80. *Newport Mercury*, May 2–May 9, 1768.

81. Daniel Defoe, *The Complete English Tradesman*, 4th ed. (London, 1737; reprint Manila: Historical Conservation Society, 1989), 42.

82. *South Carolina Gazette*, February 15, 1770.

83. *Newport Mercury*, May 4, 1805.

84. Richard Bushman argues that the complex relationship between buyer and seller hinged on this balance—shopkeepers tutored their customers, but through complaisance and flattery. In his or her manner and promises, the shopkeeper offered to bring the customer into the circle of gentility. Bushman, "Shopping and Advertising," 249–51.

85. Journal of Sarah Rodman, 9 mo. 5, 1793, Robinson Papers, reel 5, frame 883. This is a copy of her journal, by her sister "CR" (Charity Rodman), for another relative. Charity Rodman's note indicates that Sarah died while in New York, of the fever.

86. Thanks to Lisa Norling for the observation and the phrase.

87. Charles Fraser, *Reminiscences of Charleston* (Charleston: John Russell, 1854), 13; Cleary, *Elizabeth Murray*, 46–47; January 21, 1797, letter from Mary Pinckney to Mrs. Manigault, Manigault Family Papers, box 1, folder 17, SCL. On bargaining in eighteenth- and nineteenth-century English and French stores, see Davis, *A History of Shopping*, 182–83; Adburgham, *Shops and Shopping*, 20, 49, 138, 140–42. Bargaining was apparently common in Parisian shops longer than in English ones.

88. Cleary, *Elizabeth Murray*, 46–47.

89. Samuel Vinson Ledger Book, 1797–1813, # 514, NHS. The cost of a coffin ranged from nine shillings for a child's coffin to £3 for a "cherry tree coffin"; £1.10 was the most commonly paid price.

90. In spite of gradual emancipation laws, some slaveowners tried to maintain relationships of mutual obligation with slaves and former slaves, which served to "blur the boundaries between slave and free." See Joanne Pope Melish, *Disowning Slavery: Gradual Emancipation and "Race" in New England, 1780–1860* (Ithaca, N.Y.: Cornell University Press, 1998), 99.

91. Thomas M. Doerflinger calls the vendues "discount stores" in *A Vigorous Spirit of Enterprise*, 171. For the large number of vendue masters, see Eleazer Elizer, *A Directory for 1803* (Charleston: W. P. Young, 1803). T. H. Breen speculates that auctions may have played a greater role in distributing imported goods than shops; see *The Marketplace of Revolution*, 140.

92. November 28, 1792, letter from Mrs. Manigault to G. Manigault, Manigault Family Papers, box 1, folder 17; November 30, 1792, letter from Mrs. Manigault to G. Manigault, Manigault Family Papers, box 1, folder 17, SCL.

93. July 21, 1809, letter from Henry Izard to Mrs. Manigault, Ralph Izard Family Papers, box 2, folder 34, SCL.

94. For Newport auctions, see, for example, *Newport Mercury or, the Weekly Advertiser*, October 17, 1758. Elaine Forman Crane, *A Dependent People: Newport, Rhode Island, in the Revolutionary Era* (New York: Fordham University Press, 1992), 21, 51. For Charleston, see Walter J. Fraser Jr., *Charleston! Charleston!: The History of a Southern City* (Columbia: University of South Carolina Press, 1989), 188; Olwell, *Masters, Slaves, and Subjects*, 167–68; Daniel C. Littlefield, "Charleston and Internal Slave Redistribution," *SCHM* 87, no. 2 (April 1986): 94–98.

95. *Newport Mercury or, the Weekly Advertiser*, October 17, 1758. For a discussion of the ways slave traders constructed human beings as commodities, see Edward

E. Baptist, "'Cuffy,' 'Fancy Maids,' and 'One-Eyed Men': Rape, Commodification, and the Domestic Slave Trade in the United States," *American Historical Review* 106, no. 5 (December 2001): 1631–36; and Walter Johnson, *Soul by Soul: Life Inside the Antebellum Slave Market* (Cambridge, Mass.: Harvard University Press, 1999), chapters 1 and 4.

96. Henry Laurens, quoted in Morgan, *Slave Counterpoint*, 76.

97. Laurens quoted in ibid., 67; Bartram quoted in ibid., 66. For additional discussion of whites' language concerning Africans of specific geographic origin, see Michael Mullin, *Africa in America: Slave Acculturation and Resistance in the American South and the British Caribbean, 1736–1831* (Urbana: University of Illinois Press, 1992), chapter 1; and Berlin, *Many Thousands Gone*, 144–45.

98. Johnson, *Soul by Soul*, chapter 6. Robert Olwell notes that there are few descriptions of the slave auctions at all in the eighteenth and early nineteenth centuries in *Masters, Slaves, and Subjects*, 167. Female abolitionists later in the nineteenth century did attend these auctions. Harriet Martineau described witnessing a Charleston auction of enslaved women and children in *Retrospect of Western Travel* (London: Saunders and Otley, 1838), 1:234–36. For an example of an eighteenth-century white woman making purchases at the Charleston slave auctions, see Cara Anzilotti, "Autonomy and the Female Planter in Colonial South Carolina," *Journal of Southern History* 62, no. 2 (May 1997): 254–55.

99. Melish describes this process in *Disowning Slavery*, chapters 2 and 3. For Newporters in the postwar slave trade, see Withey, *Urban Growth in Colonial Rhode Island*, 97.

100. Walter Edgar, *South Carolina: A History* (Columbia: University of South Carolina Press, 1998), 67; Fraser, *Charleston! Charleston!* 185–89; Morgan, *Slave Counterpoint*, 62.

101. For a detailed study of the "production" of independence in South Carolina, see Stephanie McCurry, *Masters of Small Worlds: Yeoman Households, Gender Relations, and the Political Culture of the Antebellum South Carolina Low Country* (New York: Oxford University Press, 1995), chapter 2.

102. Vickery, *The Gentleman's Daughter*, 183.

Chapter 6. Women, Commerce, and the Republic of Goods

1. Paul G. E. Clemens uses the term "first consumer economy" to describe the period between 1760 and 1820, when a modest range of consumer goods became "ordinary" in the lives of Americans in the mid-Atlantic in "The Consumer Culture of the Middle Atlantic, 1760–1820," *William and Mary Quarterly*, 3rd ser., 62, no. 4 (October 2005): 578. T. H. Breen's influential *The Marketplace of Revolution: How Consumer Politics Shaped American Independence* (New York: Oxford University Press, 2004) traces the success of patriots' use of a politicized consumer culture to unify British North American colonists. My thanks to Linzy Brekke for the phrase "consumer citizenship."

2. *Newport Mercury*, September 4, 1775.

3. David Waldstreicher argues that, in fact, "style was substance, and rhetoric was action." "Federalism, the Styles of Politics, and the Politics of Style," in Doron Ben-Atar and Barbara B. Oberg, eds., *Federalists Reconsidered* (Charlottesville: University Press of Virginia, 1998), 100.

4. William Tennent, "To the Ladies of South Carolina," in Newton B. Jones,

ed., "Writings of the Reverend William Tennent, 1740–1777," *SCHM* 61, no. 3 (July 1960): 136–37.

5. (*Charleston*) *City Gazette and Daily Advertiser,* January 20, 1809.

6. Rosemary Zagarri, *Revolutionary Backlash: Women and Politics in the Early American Republic* (Philadelphia: University of Pennsylvania Press, 2007); Susan Branson, *These Fiery Frenchified Dames: Women and Political Culture in Early National Philadelphia* (Philadelphia: University of Pennsylvania Press, 2001); Catherine Allgor, *Parlor Politics: In Which the Ladies of Washington Help Build a City and a Government* (Charlottesville: University of Virginia Press, 2002).

7. Joan Gunderson, "Independence, Citizenship, and the American Revolution," *Signs* 13 (1987): 59–77; Susan Juster, *Disorderly Women: Sexual Politics and Evangelicalism in Revolutionary New England* (Ithaca, N.Y.: Cornell University Press, 1994); Elaine Forman Crane, "Dependence in the Era of Independence: The Role of Women in a Republican Society," in Jack P. Greene, ed., *The American Revolution: Its Character and Limits* (New York: New York University Press, 1987): 253–75; Carroll Smith-Rosenberg, "Dis-Covering the Subject of the 'Great Constitutional Discussion,' 1786–1789," *Journal of American History* 79, no. 3 (December 1992): 841–73; Jeanne Boydston, "The Woman Who Wasn't There: Women's Market Labor in the Transition to Capitalism in the United States," *Journal of the Early Republic* 16, no. 2 (Summer 1996): 183–206.

8. Laurel Thatcher Ulrich, *The Age of Homespun: Objects and Stories in the Creation of an American Myth* (New York: Alfred A. Knopf, 2001), 143.

9. Laurel Thatcher Ulrich, "Hannah Barnard's Cupboard: Female Property and Identity in Eighteenth-Century New England," in Ronald Hoffman, Mechal Sobel, and Frederika J. Teute, eds., *Through a Glass Darkly: Reflections on Personal Identity in Early America* (Chapel Hill: University of North Carolina Press, 1997), 257. Some women did inherit real property. Wealthy Charleston heiresses, for example, inherited productive land with slaves to work it.

10. Mary Beth Norton, "Eighteenth-Century American Women in Peace and War: The Case of the Loyalists," *William and Mary Quarterly,* 3rd ser., 33, no. 3 (July 1976): 396.

11. Quoted in Philip D. Morgan, *Slave Counterpoint: Black Culture in the Eighteenth-Century Chesapeake and Lowcountry* (Chapel Hill: University of North Carolina Press, 1998), 375.

12. J. G. A. Pocock makes a similar point about "modes of consciousness suited to a world of moving objects," in *Virtue, Commerce, and History: Essays on Political Thought and History, Chiefly in the Eighteenth Century* (Cambridge: Cambridge University Press, 1985), 108–9.

13. May 2, 1812, letter from M. I. Manigault to Mrs. Izard, Manigault Family Papers, box 4, folder 72, SCL.

14. Aaron Lopez, "Taylors and Spinners" account book, 1769–1774, #767, NHS.

15. Ulrich, *The Age of Homespun,* 191–206. Scholars have debated the extent of early American production for the market, and to what degree participation in markets implicated farmers, especially, in capitalist relations. The early articles in this debate, including Michael Merrill, "Cash Is Good to Eat: Self-Sufficiency and Exchange in the Rural Economy of the United States," *Radical History Review* 4 (Winter 1977): 42–71; James A. Henretta, "Families and Farms: Mentalité in Pre-Industrial America," *William and Mary Quarterly,* 3rd ser., 35, no. 1 (January 1978): 3–32; Bettye Hobbs Pruitt, "Self-Sufficiency and the Agricultural Economy of Eighteenth–Century Massachusetts," *William and Mary Quarterly,* 3rd ser., 41 (1984): 333–64; Winifred B. Rothenberg, "The Market and Massachusetts Farm-

ers, 1750–1855," *Journal of Economic History* 41, no. 2 (June 1981): 283–314, were followed by a vast literature. For a summary of the recent scholarly trends, see Paul A. Gilje, "The Rise of Capitalism in the Early Republic," *Journal of the Early Republic* 16, no. 2 (Summer 1996): 159–81.

16. Newport Supreme Court Record Book, September term 1775, vol. f, pp. 121–22, Rhode Island Judicial Archives. Susan Branson discusses female crime networks in "Beyond Respectability: The Female World of Love and Crime in Late Eighteenth and Early Nineteenth Century Philadelphia," in *Studies in Eighteenth-Century Culture*, ed. Sydny Conger and Julie Hayes (Baltimore: Johns Hopkins University Press, 1996), 25:245–64. More than half of the women accused of crime in Philadelphia in the 1780s were accused of theft.

17. Serena Zabin notes that through theft and resale of clothing, alcohol, and other consumer goods, poor women and men helped extend material culture. Serena Zabin, "Places of Exchange: New York City, 1700–1763" (Ph.D. diss., Rutgers, The State University of New Jersey, 2000), 141–73.

18. NPCCP, 1810 May term, #149.

19. For example, NPCCP, 1750 May term, #209. Pewter spoons were also taken as bail for women. For example, Abigail Stoneman's daughter offered the sheriff a spoon when her mother was summoned in 1770. See Newport Supreme Court Record Book, September term 1770, vol. e, unnumbered, Rhode Island Judicial Archives.

20. *The Autobiography of Benjamin Franklin*, introduction and notes by R. Jackson Wilson (New York: The Modern Library, 1981), 101.

21. July 26, 1808, letter from Alice Izard to Henry Izard, Ralph Izard Family Papers, box 2, folder 31, SCL.

22. Christine Stansell, *City of Women: Sex and Class in New York, 1789–1860* (Urbana: University of Chicago Press, 1982), 51. A servant who received cast-off clothing from her mistress did not necessarily see herself as taking on her mistress's social status when she put on her shift. Clothing was valuable in itself. See Amanda Vickery, *The Gentleman's Daughter: Women's Lives in Georgian England* (New Haven: Yale University Press, 1998), 184.

23. *Newport Mercury*, December 10, 1799; *Gazette of the State of South-Carolina*, November 18, 1784, reprinted in Lathan A. Windley, comp., *Runaway Slave Advertisements: A Documentary History from the 1730s to 1790* (Westport, Conn.: Greenwood Press, 1983), 386.

24. *South-Carolina and American General Gazette*, February 12–20, 1772, reprinted in Windley, *Runaway Slave Advertisements*, 444.

25. March 7, 1808, letter from Anne Hart to Anne Wilson; March 8, 1808, letter from Anne Hart to Sally G. S. Clark, Oliver Hart papers, box 1, folder 6, SCL.

26. 1 mo. 27, 1818, letter from Abigail Robinson to her sister, [Mary Robinson Morton], Robinson Family Papers, New England Women and Their Families in the Eighteenth and Nineteenth Centuries: Personal Papers, Letters, and Diaries, series b: selections from the Newport Historical Society (Bethesda, Md.: LexisNexis Academic and Library Solutions, 2000), reel 15 (hereafter Robinson Papers).

27. May 14, 1785, letter from Anne Hart to Oliver Hart, Oliver Hart papers, box 1, folder 4, SCL.

28. *SCHM* 58, no. 1 (January 1957): 27.

29. August 1758 letter from Eliza Pinckney to Mr. Gerrard, in *The Letterbook of Eliza Lucas Pinckney, 1739–1762*, ed. Elise Pinckney (Columbia: University of South Carolina Press, 1972), 97.

30. May 4, 1809, letter from Alice Izard to Henry Izard, Ralph Izard Family Papers, box 2, folder 33, SCL.

31. *The (Charleston) Investigator*, September 3, 1812.

32. G. J. Barker-Benfield, *The Culture of Sensibility: Sex and Society in Eighteenth-Century Britain* (Chicago: University of Chicago Press, 1992), xxvi. See also Susan M. Stabile, *Memory's Daughters: The Material Culture of Remembrance in Eighteenth-Century America* (Ithaca, N.Y.: Cornell University Press, 2004). Historian Amanda Vickery cautions that "sentimental materialism, along with mahogany furniture, may have been a luxury many women simply could not afford." Vickery, *The Gentleman's Daughter*, 193.

33. June 30 [1791] letter from Catherine Read to Charles Ludlow, Read Family Papers, box 2, folder 3, SCL.

34. November 30, 1786, letter from Sophia Penn to Mrs. Manigault, Manigault Family Papers, box 1, folder 14, SCL.

35. Jack L. Cross, ed., "Letters of Thomas Pinckney, 1775–1780," *SCHM* 58, no. 1 (January 1957): 29.

36. Barker-Benfield, *The Culture of Sensibility*, 175. Barker-Benfield notes that fashion was a powerful language in private, as well as public interactions.

37. *(Charleston) Columbian Herald*, January 4, 1785.

38. Kate Haluman, "Fashion and the Culture Wars of Revolutionary Philadelphia," *William and Mary Quarterly*, 3rd ser., 62, no. 4 (October 2005): 641.

39. *Newport Mercury*, March 12, 1770.

40. 4 mo. 20, 1804, letter from H. E. [Hetty Earl] to her cousin [Mary Robinson Morton], Robinson Papers, reel 15.

41. February 3, 1814, letter from C[atherine] R[ead] to Mrs. Charles Ludlow, Read Family Papers, box 1, folder 6, SCL.

42. Shields uses the term "sensus communis" to convey the "common sense" of themselves that these women shared and spread to rural women in the eighteenth century; David S. Shields, *Civil Tongues and Polite Letters in British America* (Chapel Hill: University of North Carolina Press, 1997), 111.

43. October 2, 1802, letter from Alice Izard to Mrs. Manigault, Manigault Family Papers, box 2, folder 38, SCL.

44. Shields, *Civil Tongues*, 110–11; Cynthia Kierner, *Beyond the Household: Women's Place in the Early South, 1700–1835* (Ithaca, N.Y.: Cornell University Press, 1998), 43–46; Richard Bushman, *The Refinement of America: Persons, Houses, Cities* (New York: Vintage Books, 1992), 406.

45. Paul G. E. Clemens points out the differences between the "more or less undifferentiated mass culture that cut across class and urban-rural divides" of the late nineteenth century and the first consumer economy of the late eighteenth. See Clemens, "Consumer Culture," 580.

46. October 3, 1787, letter from Ann Kinloch to Cleland Kinloch, Cheves-Middleton papers, 12/160/3, SCHS.

47. December 13, 1796, letter from M. Pinckney to Mrs. G. Manigault, Manigault Family Papers, box 1, folder 22, SCL.

48. Hannah Rodman Journal, 1783–1787; entry for 12 mo. 30, 1787, Robinson Papers, reel 8.

49. Hannah Rodman Fisher Journal, 1792–1793; entry for 7 mo. 3, 1793, Robinson Papers, reel 8.

50. 2 mo. 27, 1799, letter from A. Robinson in Newport to her sister [Mary Morton], Robinson Papers, reel 2.

51. For the clothing of urban slaves, see Ira Berlin, *Many Thousands Gone: The*

First Two Centuries of Slavery in North America (Cambridge, Mass.: Harvard University Press, 1998), 137–38, 160. Linda Baumgarten, "'Clothes for the People': Slave Clothing in Early Virginia," *Journal of Early Southern Decorative Arts* (November 1988): 43, emphasizes the homogeneity of slave clothing.

52. (*Charleston*) *City Gazette and Commercial Daily Advertiser*, March 30, 1815.

53. *State Gazette of South Carolina*, February 11, 1788, reprinted in Windley, *Runaway Slave Advertisements*, 406.

54. (*Charleston*) *City Gazette and Commercial Daily Advertiser*, July 10, 1815.

55. *South-Carolina and American General Gazette*, November 4, 1780, reprinted in Windley, *Runaway Slave Advertisements*, 571–72. See also Linda Baumgarten, *What Clothes Reveal: The Language of Clothing in Colonial and Federal America* (Williamsburg: The Colonial Williamsburg Foundation, 2002), 136–38; Philip Morgan, *Slave Counterpoint*, 126–33 and 598–99. On slaves and the display of goods, see Dylan C. Penningroth, *The Claims of Kinfolk: African American Property and Community in the Nineteenth-Century South* (Chapel Hill: University of North Carolina Press, 2003), 107.

56. John Bennett, *Letters to a Young Lady on a Variety of Useful and Interesting Subjects . . .* (Worcester, Mass.: Thomas & Andrews, 1798), 144.

57. [Ann] Taylor, *Practical Hints to Young Females, on the Duties of a Wife, a Mother, and a Mistress of a Family* (Boston: Wells and Lilly, 1816), 28. This volume was still available in Newport in 1820; see *Newport Mercury*, July 15, 1820.

58. Ships loaded with British manufactures that were turned away in Charleston reportedly landed in Newport, "where they imagined they should not meet with the *least Discouragement* in the Sale!!!" *Newport Mercury*, August 21, 1769. On nonimportation debates, see Elaine Forman Crane, *A Dependent People: Newport, Rhode Island in the Revolutionary Era* (New York: Fordham University Press, 1992), 117–19; Pauline Maier, *From Resistance to Revolution: Colonial Radicals and the Development of American Opposition to Britain, 1765–1776* (New York: Knopf, 1972), 115; Richard Walsh, *Charleston's Sons of Liberty: A Study of the Artisans, 1763–1789* (Columbia: University of South Carolina Press, 1959), chapter 2; and David S. Lovejoy, *Rhode Island Politics and the American Revolution, 1760–1776* (Providence: Brown University Press, 1958), chapter 7.

59. *Newport Mercury*, May 15, 1769; *Newport Mercury*, March 14–21, 1768; *Newport Mercury*, May 29, 1769.

60. *South Carolina Gazette*, October 5, 1769. This was reprinted in the *Newport Mercury*.

61. *South Carolina Gazette*, June 22, 1769. See Cynthia Kierner, *Beyond the Household*, 75–77.

62. *Newport Mercury*, May 20, 1771; *South Carolina Gazette*, August 2, 1770. Newport had a corresponding plantation region in South Kingston, where enslaved women worked in large numbers as dairymaids and where enslaved female spinners may have been especially common. But they do not seem to have been publicly invisible the way that Charleston-area plantation spinners were.

63. *South Carolina Gazette*, June 1, 1769; Walsh, *Charleston's Sons of Liberty*, 49.

64. January 8, 1795, letter from A[lice] Izard to Ralph Izard, Ralph Izard Papers, box 1, folder 16, SCL. Izard also investigated the possibilities of raising silkworms on her plantation. She noted to her husband that "As you come through No. Carolina you will find many People employed in weaving, & if you could engage a good plain Weaver to live with us for a year I think we might find it advantageous; but it is impossible to succeed in things of this kind without having a Person who really understands the business to superintend it." Mary Beth Norton

notes that although southern colonies like Virginia were slower to take up the charge of increasing home manufactures, eventually slave owners shifted female slaves' work duties to encompass less planting work and more cloth making. See Norton, *Liberty's Daughters: The Revolutionary Experience of American Women, 1750–1800* (1980; Ithaca, N.Y.: Cornell University Press, 1996), 164–65. The timetable for this transition is not clear. See also Kierner, *Beyond the Household*, 15, 18.

65. Cynthia Kierner, *Southern Women in Revolution, 1776–1800: Personal and Political Narratives* (Columbia: University of South Carolina Press, 1998), 70–71. Some had called attention to the problem of ready-made clothing in 1785, when at a meeting of citizens at the City Exchange, a Dr. Budd had argued that although domestic ready-made clothing was superior, "we were eager to buy every thing imported, and thus we threw a particular benefit into the hands of foreigners, whilst our own work women were in a state of inactive penury." *Charleston Evening Gazette*, August 15, 1785.

66. Kierner, *Beyond the Household*, 78.

67. For Britain, see Kowaleski-Wallace, *Consuming Subjects*, part 1; for America, see Shields, *Civil Tongues*, chapters 3 and 4; and Kathleen Brown, *Good Wives, Nasty Wenches, and Anxious Patriarchs: Gender, Race, and Power in Colonial Virginia* (Chapel Hill: University of North Carolina Press, 1996), chapter 9.

68. David Kuchta, "The Making of the Self-Made Man: Class, Clothing, and English Masculinity, 1688–1832," in Victoria de Grazia and Ellen Furlough, eds., *The Sex of Things: Gender and Consumption in Historical Perspective* (Berkeley: University of California Press, 1996), 65, 66. For the link of luxury and effeminacy, see Barker-Benfield, *The Culture of Sensibility*, 104–5. For the reuse of clothing, see Baumgarten, *What Clothes Reveal*, chapter 6.

69. Linzy Brekke discusses the new "fashion orthodoxy" of the early republic and its implications for male political leaders in " 'To Make a Figure:' Clothing and the Politics of Male Identity in Eighteenth Century America," in Amanda Vickery and John Styles, eds., *Gender, Taste, and Material Culture in Britain and North America, 1700–1830* (New Haven: Yale University Press, 2006): 225–46.

70. *Pennsylvania Magazine or American Monthly Museum* (September 1775), 407–8.

71. *South Carolina Gazette*, June 7, 1770. Anne was accused of selling goods from her partnership with her son, Benjamin, who apparently told the committee formed to enforce the resolutions that the goods had been "opened and *disposed of . . .* by his Mother, *Ann Mathewes* (who is *also* a Subscriber to the Resolutions) during his Absence in the Country." For milliners' losses, see Kierner, *Beyond the Household*, 77–78.

72. See T. H. Breen, "Narrative of Commercial Life: Consumption, Ideology, and Community on the Eve of the American Revolution," *William and Mary Quarterly*, 3rd ser., 50, no. 3 (July 1993): 490.

73. 10 mo. 8, 17[85?], letter from Mary Robinson to her friend [Elizabeth Foulke, in Philadelphia?], Robinson Papers, reel 17.

74. December 1, 1811, Letter from A. Izard to Mrs. Manigault, Manigault Family Papers, box 4, folder 68, SCL.

75. April 2, 1809, letter from M. I. Manigault to Mrs. Pinckney, Manigault Family Papers, box 3, folder 57, SCL.

76. Laurel Thatcher Ulrich, "Wheels, Looms, and the Gender Division of Labor in Eighteenth-Century New England," *William and Mary Quarterly*, 3rd ser., 55, no. 1 (January 1998): 20.

77. *City Gazette and Daily Advertiser*, July 28, 1808.

78. *Newport Mercury,* July 9, 1808; originally printed in the *National Intelligencer.*

79. 1812 or c. 1813 [according to index] letter from Newport [from Mary Rotch to Ruth Hadwin Williams of Butternutts], Williams Papers, reel 19, frame 649, #110.

80. *City Gazette and Daily Advertiser,* July 8, 1807.

81. Private actions were a different matter; women's letters indicate that even women from wealthy Charleston families like Elizabeth Izard determined that "in such hard times as these it [is] necessary for us to endeavour to make our own clothes at home." Quoted in Kierner, *Beyond the Household,* 135.

82. *Newport Mercury,* May 7, 1808.

83. Rosemary Zagarri traces the rise and fall of "female politicians" in the shifting political culture of the revolutionary era in *Revolutionary Backlash.* Other historians who have discussed the many ways in which the revolutionary tradition was de-radicalized in the years of the early republic include Alfred Young, *The Shoemaker and the Tea Party: Memory and the American Revolution* (Boston: Beacon Press, 1999); and Paul A. Gilje, *The Road to Mobocracy: Popular Disorder in New York City, 1763–1834* (Chapel Hill: University of North Carolina Press, 1987).

84. Charlotte Sussman, *Consuming Anxieties: Consumer Protest, Gender, and British Slavery, 1713–1833* (Stanford, Calif.: Stanford University Press, 2000), 42.

85. Dror Wahrman, "The English Problem of Identity in the American Revolution," *American Historical Review* 106, no. 4 (2001): 1258.

86. *The Lady's Pocket Library . . . ,* third American edition (Chambersburg: Printed by Dover & Harper for Mathew Carey, Philadelphia, 1797), 6. This book was still advertised in Newport almost a decade later; see *Newport Mercury,* November 2, 1805.

87. For a formulation of the "best" versus "common" classification of material object in Georgian England, see Vickery, *The Gentleman's Daughter,* 184–85. More made a similar comparison between women and paintings to suggest the dangerous possibilities of women being "picked up in a public place" by men interested in acquiring them the way they acquire paintings. See discussion in John Brewer, "'The Most Polite Age and the Most Vicious': Attitudes Toward Culture as a Commodity, 1660–1800," in Ann Bermingham and John Brewer, eds., *The Consumption of Culture, 1600–1800: Image, Object, Text* (New York: Routledge, 1995), 356.

88. (*Charleston*) *City Gazette and Commercial Daily Advertiser,* November 20, 1816.

89. March 8, 1801, from Oliver Hering to Mary Middleton; June 19, 1801, from Oliver Hering to Mary Middleton, Hering Family Papers, 24/63/13, SCHS.

90. *City Gazette and Commercial Daily Advertiser,* September 19, 1816.

91. Letter [undated] from Abraham Greenwood in Charleston to Betsey [Greenwood], Leger and Greenwood letterbook, p. 215, William Clements Library, Ann Arbor, Michigan. Surrounded by letters written in 1788; this letter seems to have been written after the Revolution around the same time.

92. Phyllis Whitman Hunter explores the ways that this commercial cultural narrative replaced a religious narrative in *Purchasing Identity in the Atlantic World: Massachusetts Merchants, 1670–1780* (Ithaca, N.Y.: Cornell University Press, 2001), chapter 3. See also T. H. Breen, "Narrative of Commercial Life," 471–501.

93. Charleston CCP, Judgment Rolls, 1810 term, #109a 00. Only after Sally's actual owner, Mary Stone, signed a bond and went to court to release Sally from the workhouse were the details of Sally's status resolved.

94. February 22, 1807, letter from Alice Izard to Henry Izard, Ralph Izard Papers, box 2, folder 25, SCL.

95. Recorded May 6, 1799, Charleston bills of sale, microfilm, 003n 00041, SCDAH.

96. Charleston CCP, 1800 term #065a 00.

97. Newport Supreme Court Record Book, September term 1772, vol. f, pp. 33–34, Rhode Island Judicial Archives.

98. Melish, *Disowning Slavery*, 92–93; Gary Nash, "Forging Freedom: The Emancipation Experience in the Northern Seaport Cities, 1775–1820," in Ira Berlin and Ronald Hoffman, eds., *Slavery and Freedom in the Age of the American Revolution* (Urbana: University of Illinois Press, 1983), 31–32.

99. Carroll Smith-Rosenberg, "Dis-Covering the Subject of the 'Great Constitutional Discussion,' 1786–1789," *Journal of American History* 79 (December 1992): 843.

100. Ulrich, *The Age of Homespun*, 130.

101. Morgan, *Slave Counterpoint*, 598.

102. Leora Auslander, "The Gendering of Consumer Practices in Nineteenth-Century France," in Grazia and Furlough, *The Sex of Things*, 80.

Conclusion

1. Thomas Jefferson to George Washington, March 15, 1784, quoted in J. E. Crowley, *This Sheba, Self: The Conceptualization of Economic Life in Eighteenth-Century America* (Baltimore: Johns Hopkins University Press, 1974), 147.

2. See Lori Merish, *Sentimental Materialism: Gender, Commodity Culture, and Nineteenth-Century American Literature* (Durham, N.C.: Duke University Press, 2000), 36.

3. Adam Smith, *Theory of Moral Sentiments*, reprinted in Robert L. Heilbroner, ed., *The Essential Adam Smith* (New York: Norton, 1986), 87.

4. Toby Ditz, "Shipwrecked; or Masculinity Imperiled: Mercantile Representations of Failure and the Gendered Self in Eighteenth-Century Philadelphia," *Journal of American History* 81, no. 1 (June 1994): 72.

5. Lord Kames, *Sketches of the History of Man*, quoted in Merish, *Sentimental Materialism*, 40.

6. Enos Hitchcock, *Memoirs of the Bloomsgrove Family*, quoted in Merish, *Sentimental Materialism*, 67.

7. Linda Kerber's classic article reviewed the development of this historiography: "Separate Spheres, Female Worlds, Woman's Place: The Rhetoric of Women's History," *Journal of American History* 75, no. 1 (June 1988): 9–39. For two helpful assessments of the relative "utility" of domesticity discourse for late eighteenth- and early nineteenth-century Americans, see Lisa Norling, *Captain Ahab Had a Wife: New England Women and the Whalefishery, 1720–1870* (Chapel Hill: University of North Carolina Press, 2000); and Joan C. Williams, "Domesticity as the Dangerous Supplement of Liberalism," *Journal of Women's History* 2, no. 3 (Winter 1991): 69–88.

8. The supple discourse of domesticity also gave middle-class women license for ever-more public involvement in the lives of their communities, especially on issues concerning enslaved and poor women. See, for example, the classic Christine Stansell, *City of Women: Sex and Class in New York, 1789–1860* (1982; Urbana: University of Illinois Press, 1986). Bruce Dorsey's recent work on urban reform brings a close analysis of ideas about masculinity to the topic in *Reforming Men and Women: Gender in the Antebellum City* (Ithaca, N.Y.: Cornell University Press, 2002).

9. Deborah Valenze, *The Social Life of Money in the English Past* (New York: Cambridge University Press, 2006), 268–78, argues for a "diminished sense of the embeddedness of money" in late eighteenth- and early nineteenth-century British thought.

10. Jeanne Boydston, "The Woman Who Wasn't There: Women's Market Labor and the Transition to Capitalism in the United States," *Journal of the Early Republic* 16 (Summer 1996): 186.

11. Beverly Lemire develops this point in the context of the secondhand clothing trade in England between 1600 and 1850. See *The Business of Everyday Life: Gender, Practice and Social Politics in England, c. 1600–1900* (New York: Manchester University Press, 2005), chapter 4.

12. The importance of shopping in women's daily lives continued to grow into the nineteenth century. See Jeanne Boydston, *Home and Work: Housework, Wages, and the Ideology of Labor in the Early Republic* (New York: Oxford University Press, 1990), 102–3, 124–25.

13. April 20, 1804, letter from H. E. [Hetty Earl] in Newport to her cousin, [Mary Robinson Morton, in Philadelphia], Robinson Papers, New England Women and Their Families in the 18th and 19th Centuries: Personal Papers, Letters, and Diaries, series b: selections from the Newport Historical Society (Bethesda, Md.: LexisNexis Academic and Library Solutions, 2000), microfilm, reel 15.

14. Naomi Lamoreaux, *Insider Lending: Banks, Personal Connections, and Economic Development in Industrial New England* (1994; New York: Cambridge University Press, 1996).

15. Pamela Walker Laird, *Pull: Networking and Success Since Benjamin Franklin* (Cambridge, Mass.: Harvard University Press, 2006).

16. Jennifer L. Morgan, *Laboring Women: Reproduction and Gender in New World Slavery* (Philadelphia: University of Pennsylvania Press, 2004); Susan Branson, *These Fiery Frenchified Dames: Women and Political Culture in Early National Philadelphia* (Philadelphia: University of Pennsylvania Press, 2001); Catherine Allgor, *Parlor Politics: In Which the Ladies of Washington Help Build a City and a Government* (Charlottesville: University Press of Virginia, 2000).

17. Douglas Egerton, *He Shall Go Out Free: The Lives of Denmark Vesey*, rev. ed. (Lanham, Md.: Rowman and Littlefield, 2004), 205.

18. Susan Porter Benson, *Counter Cultures: Saleswomen, Managers, and Customers in American Department Stores, 1890–1940* (Urbana: University of Illinois Press, 1986); Elaine S. Abelson, *When Ladies Go A-Thieving: Middle-Class Shoplifters in the Victorian Department Store* (New York: Oxford University Press, 1989); William Leach, *Land of Desire: Merchants, Power, and the Rise of a New American Culture* (New York: Vintage Books, 1994). Walter Friedman examines the history of traveling salesmen, a different kind of institution, in *Birth of a Salesman: The Transformation of Selling in America* (Cambridge, Mass.: Harvard University Press, 2004).

Index

Acknowledgments

The ties that helped me to write this book have proven to be just as wide ranging and indispensable as the ties that buy at its focus. I have tallied up considerable debts in my intellectual and personal account books along the way. From the beginning, Susan Juster read draft after draft with an encouraging and critical eye, always pushing me to draw my ideas more broadly and think more expansively. Through her own example, she also set a standard as scholar and mentor that I admire all the more as I try to live up to it. David Hancock's initial skepticism made me sharpen by arguments, and his ongoing interest, support, and enthusiasm sustained me through many revisions. Carol Karlsen and Susan Scott Parrish were also there at the beginning, thinking of ways to make an ambitious project even more so.

As the project developed, I was fortunate to have the advice and suggestions of colleagues who read chapters (sometimes more than once). For their time and ideas, I thank Angel Kwollek-Folland, Michelle Mc-Donald, Linzy Brekke, Cathy Matson, Alan Taylor, Caroline Winterer, Dee Andrews, Caroline Cox, Eva Sheppard-Wolf, and Lynne Withey. Jack Bernhart, Pat Don, Glen Gendzel, Libra Hilde, Patricia Hill, Jeff Hummel, Mary Pickering, Rick Propas, Jonathan Roth and my other wonderful colleagues at San Jose State University read, advised, and provided excellent models of scholarship and teaching. I am grateful as well to my new colleagues at University of California, Davis, who have been instantly generous with advice and encouragement as the project moved through its final stages.

I have been fortunate to enjoy many conversations about women and commerce with scholars who had a lot to teach me. For their enthusiasm and generosity, I thank Ann Boylan, Joyce Botelho, Trevor Burnard, Tracey Deutsch, Sally Hadden, Sheryllynne Haggerty, Brian Luskey, Ann Smart Martin, Lisa Norling, Seth Rockman, Carole Shammas, Holly Snyder, Edith Sparks, John Styles, Lisa Tetrault, Claire Walsh, Jocelyn A. Wills, Wendy Woloson, and Serena Zabin. Many thanks to others who taught me the pleasures of collegiality and made me a far less lonely scholar: Barbara Berglund, Chloe Burke, Judy Daubenmier, Elana Gordis Earleywine, Christina Fuhrmann, Karen Hajra, Neel Hajra, Maria Elena Lara Kim, Anna Lawrence, Amy Locke, Michelle McDonald, Brian Mickey, Bob Mory, Andrew Needham, Kristin Olbertson, Pat Palmieri, Alyssa Picard, Julie Goldsmith Reiser, Bruce Willoughby, and Meredith Woocher.

I have had the pleasure of working at archives and libraries where I received invaluable assistance. I owe many thanks to the archivists and librarians at the Library Company of Philadelphia; Newport Historical Society; Rhode Island Historical Society; Rhode Island Judicial Archives; Rhode Island State Archives; South Carolina Department of Archives and History; South Carolina Historical Society; South Carolina Library; Rare Book, Manuscript, and Special Collections Library at Duke University; Southern Historical Collection at the University of North Carolina; and the William L. Clements Library. Charles Lesser and Steve Grimes were especially generous with their time and advice. Bryan Skib at the Harlan Hatcher Graduate Library of the University of Michigan was always willing to do battle for me in my quest to obtain obscure microfilm reels.

Financial support was critical for enabling me to conduct research in two such fascinating but expensive cities, as well as for providing time to write. The Department of History and the Rackham Graduate School at the University of Michigan, the Andrew W. Mellon Foundation, the National Society of Colonial Dames, the John Nicholas Brown Center, San Jose State University, the San Jose State College of Social Science, and the Sybil Weir/John Galm Endowment provided much-needed funds and encouragement of a material kind. Sheila Williams and Lorna Altstetter in the department of history at Michigan, as well as Diana Baker at San Jose State, reminded me to apply for money and helped me navigate various bureaucracies with kindness.

Portions of this book appeared in earlier form in Ellen Hartigan-O'Connor, "'She Said She Did not Know Money': Urban Women and Atlantic Markets in the Revolutionary Era," *Early American Studies* 4, no. 2 (2006): 291–321; in Ellen Hartigan-O'Connor, "Collaborative Consumption and the Politics of Choice in Early American Port Cities," in Amanda Vickery and John Styles, eds., *Gender, Taste and Material Culture in Britain and North America, 1700–1830* (New Haven: Yale University Press, 2006); and Ellen Hartigan-O'Connor, "Abigail's Accounts: Economy and Affection in the Early Republic," *Journal of Women's History* 17, no. 3 (Fall 2005): 35–58. I thank the original publishers for permission to reprint the revised work.

At the University of Pennsylvania Press, Susan Branson, Lisa Norling, Dan Richter, and Bob Lockhart all gave the manuscript a careful read-

ing and offered helpful suggestions to make it stronger. Equally important, their belief in the project was a great encouragement to improve it
further. Noreen O'Connor-Abel managed the copyediting with patience
and care.

My parents, Margaret and John O'Connor, and my sister, Megan
O'Connor, have inspired and supported me in countless ways—
recommending historical novels, driving me to archives, championing
the life of a scholar, touring around living history museums, cooking
extra meals, and entertaining restless children. The Hartigan family
taught me how to shop and much more. For all the love and help of family, I am truly grateful.

My longest and most detailed account is with my husband, Dennis.
Critical reader, unflagging supporter, and true love, he has made the
completion of this book possible. Together with our wonderful sons,
Eamon and Finn, he makes the rest a delight.